2

W9-DCB-548

NATIONAL INCOME
AND THE
PRICE LEVEL

A Study in Macroeconomic Theory

NATIONAL INCOME
AND THE
PRICE LEVEL

A Study in Macroeconomic Theory

Second Edition

MARTIN J. BAILEY
Associate Dean,
Graduate School of Management
University of Rochester

McGRAW-HILL BOOK COMPANY

New York   St. Louis   San Francisco   Düsseldorf   Johannesburg
Kuala Lumpur   London   Mexico   Montreal   New Delhi
Panama   Rio de Janeiro   Singapore   Sydney   Toronto

NATIONAL INCOME AND THE PRICE LEVEL:
A Study in Macroeconomic Theory

Copyright © 1962, 1971 by McGraw-Hill, Inc. All rights reserved.
Printed in the United States of America. No part of this
publication may be reproduced, stored in a retrieval system,
or transmitted, in any form or by any means, electronic,
mechanical, photocopying, recording, or otherwise, without
the prior written permission of the publisher.

Library of Congress Catalog Card Number 73-126744
ISBN 07-003221-1

. 4 5 6 7 8 9 0 M A M M 7 9 8 7 6 5 4 3 2

This book was set in Modern by The Maple Press Company, and printed on
permanent paper and bound by The Maple Press Company. The designer was
Jack Ellis; the drawings were done by John Cordes, J. & R. Technical Services,
Inc. The editors were Jack Crutchfield and Sally Mobley. Annette Wentz
supervised production.

PREFACE

The purpose of this work is to provide a clear and concise presentation of the theory of national income determination, within a framework of equilibrium analysis, and of some of the problems of theory and policy directly related thereto. As both a student and teacher, I have been dissatisfied with the need to search in many scattered sources for critical analyses of the interesting and sometimes controversial issues in this field: the key interpretive articles of Hicks and Lange, the searching ones of Modigliani, Patinkin, and Metzler, the post-1935 works of Keynes and his followers and critics. Even when one works through these fundamental sources, he is likely to feel that there remain many loose ends and unsettled issues. Is it true, or is it not, that a general equilibrium system derived only from the most elementary assumptions about tastes and production possibilities necessarily has an overall equilibrium solution, including full employment in an acceptable sense? More specifically, are the particular obstacles to such equilibrium that have been suggested based on logically valid considerations, or do they implicitly contradict generally accepted assumptions about economic behavior? Apart from this, what are the characteristics of general equilibrium systems, particularly of the simplified versions used for national income analysis, that are well established and beyond dispute? What issues are still open, and to what extent can the open issues be clarified and resolved into straightforward questions of fact and logic? These questions point to the main problem areas in national income analysis, for whose study an integrated and systematic treatment is needed.

Though my goals for the second edition remain basically the same as for the first, I felt that certain changes were required. For this edition the book has been completely rewritten after Chapter 3 so that parts that were universally ignored, such as the old Chapter 5 and parts of

Chapter 4, have disappeared. Scattered and disorganized discussions of important topics, such as the monetary aspect of macrotheory, now appear together, in this instance in Chapter 7. I have added new chapters on inflation and growth (4 and 5) and new material to the later chapters. I have added Mathematical Appendices to Chapters 2 and 3. The result should be a more uniformly useful work, both as a textbook and as a treatise.

Except in the instances of inflation and growth, I have resisted suggestions for new chapters—for example, to cover the interface between international trade theory and macrotheory. In this and similar cases, the material is well presented in textbooks and courses in the related fields. Many teachers of macrotheory will share my preference to let the job be done really well in those courses and to omit the material entirely from a course in macrotheory. Those who wish to cover the interface will find it at least as satisfactory to assign selected chapters from the textbook in the other field as to use the diluted version that would appear in the present work. I have also given very short treatment to deterministic growth models, derived from the growth and dynamic models of Harrod, Domar, and Samuelson. I willingly provide references but find the continued popularity of these models very hard to understand. Instead, in Chapter 11 I develop the stochastic approach that I think has the most promise and relevance.

My approach starts with clear and pertinent analytical models at the most elementary level, and I proceed as rapidly as possible to apply them to the main interesting problems. Although the text departs occasionally from the main line of thought to deal with the peripheral questions, it concentrates primarily on the substantive questions that justifiably have attracted the most attention in the fundamental sources. Accordingly, many hypothetical alternatives and problems are omitted entirely, and many others receive only brief treatment, in order to permit greater concentration on the central area of analysis and its applications.

It is obvious that a work of this kind draws heavily on the work of others, in this case particularly on the fundamental sources already mentioned. Some new material is introduced in the more advanced parts, however, particularly in Chapters 6 and 11. Concerning Chapter 9, a claim to original authorship must be shared with at least two other persons, Gary Becker and Reuben Kessel, who independently developed much of the same material for their respective courses.

The discussion is pitched partly at the intermediate level and partly at the graduate level. An intermediate course can be based on Chapters 1, 2, 3, 9, and 10. A more advanced course would pass through these chapters relatively quickly, though giving fairly full attention to Chapter

3, and would then concentrate on the remaining chapters. In both cases supplementary material would be appropriate on national income definitions and concepts and on various analytical extensions of the basic models presented here.

Grateful acknowledgment of helpful advice and suggestions is due to O. H. Brownlee, Otto Eckstein, Lloyd Reynolds, Albert Rees, Adolfo Diz, and Robert Eisner. Permission to use parts of my article "Saving and the Rate of Interest," which appeared in the August, 1957, issue of *The Journal of Political Economy*, was kindly granted by The University of Chicago Press (copyright 1957 by The University of Chicago). Parts I and II of that article, shortened and reedited, make up sections 2 to 5 of Chapter 6. Also, I am grateful to Verne Lippitt and Robert Cashner for their help with citations, revisions of statistical series, and other matters for this second edition.

Martin J. Bailey

CONTENTS

1
INTRODUCTION

Economic change, like other kinds of social change, consists of a welter of detailed movements containing certain major overall tendencies. Some industries spring up and expand while others decay; some geographical areas enjoy rapid growth and improvement while others stagnate; some individuals and groups enjoy rapid improvement in their material well-being while others do not. Sometimes nearly everyone and nearly every industry and area enjoy relatively prosperous times; other times nearly everyone and nearly every industry and area suffer relatively hard times. Some changes are brief and predictable, such as the annual pre-Christmas rush, or brief and unpredictable, such as the disruption caused by a heavy snowstorm. Some are gradual and fairly predictable, such as the growth of cities and their outlying suburbs; some are gradual and unpredictable, such as changes in the architectural style of new buildings. The more predictable changes usually receive comparatively little attention in economic analysis, because they can be taken for granted; the least predictable ones may also receive little attention if there is little hope of improving our understanding of them. The same is generally true of the most brief and of the most gradual changes.

Broadly speaking, the most interesting changes are neither very brief nor very gradual, but in between. Naturally enough, those changes are most interesting that affect nearly everyone. Finally, those changes are most interesting which seem to have some system or repetition to them, so that even if only imperfectly predictable, they offer hope of significant improvements in our understanding and ability to predict.

The economic changes that most completely fit these specifications are the movements of national income, production, employment, and prices known as recession or depression, recovery, boom, and inflation. Such movements extend anywhere from several months to several years. They affect people throughout the community in ways that are obvious and important. While each such movement is different from every other such movement, as a whole they exhibit characteristic patterns and relationships that seem to be repeated. These patterns and relationships lack the reliability that would enable us to predict the movements in question, but they are good enough to offer a definite challenge and a hope that accurate prediction and counteraction will be possible. Consequently, they have been the subject of profound speculation and controversy for generations and in various respects continue to be.

Although many issues, some theoretical and some practical, remain unsettled, the keen discussion of all aspects of economic fluctuations in the last several decades has brought greater clarity and system into their analysis. The greatest impetus toward clarity and system came from J. M. Keynes's *The General Theory of Employment Interest and Money*, even though, or perhaps especially because, it left something to be desired in both respects. The most important consequence of the publication of *The General Theory* has been the development of a single, straightforward, widely understood approach to macroeconomics, the main elements of which that work contained. The review and elaboration of this type of approach are a principal task of the present work.

Macroeconomics considers the ways that decisions by one group or sector interact with the decisions of other groups or sectors to produce an overall level and composition of national income. This stands in contrast to the theory of the firm and the theory of consumer behavior, in which the rest of the economy and its major variables are taken as given, unaffected by the actions of the firm or consumer. Although our analysis will draw on some aspects of these theories, its concerns are generally of a different, more comprehensive kind.

Many of the topics and problems we shall consider are primarily theoretical and academic in nature while some have extensive practical implications. The interrelationships between the two types of problems are so great, however, that for the most part we shall make no attempt to separate them.

2
ELEMENTS OF
NATIONAL INCOME
THEORY

1 PROCEDURE

First we shall review the most important features of the theory of national income determination. This theory uses simplified, partly illustrative assumptions about economic behavior that permit key ideas to stand out. Some aspects of the mutual dependence of households and firms are easy to grasp and are also very important. As we proceed through a series of assumptions and their consequences, we shall build up a model of the whole economy. This model, even though starkly simplified, reveals dominant relationships among the main economic aggregates. We can then consider more detailed and complex relationships among these aggregates.

The term *income* refers to the total money value of the flow of net incomes of households. Changes in its size reflect both changes in tangible standards of living and changes in the general level of prices. Changes in income with no change in the general price level, or with nonproportional changes in the general price level, are referred to as changes in real income. Since our immediate concern is with changes in real income, we begin by assuming that the general price level is constant.

2 A FIRST MODEL OF INCOME DETERMINATION

We begin with the relationship between aggregate consumption and aggregate income: when income increases, consumption does also. We shall use the simplest reasonable assumption: *consumption is a linear function of income.* That is, we have

$$C = A + bY \tag{1}$$

where A and b are constants. Moreover we shall assume that investment is a fixed quantity, say I_1. Current income consists exactly of claims to current production, made up of consumption and investment, so we write

$$Y = C + I_1 \tag{2}$$

Equation (1) shows how fast the nation's households think it prudent to absorb consumption goods as a function of their current incomes. Equation (2) is an accounting expression stating that the total of all incomes equals the sum of those arising in the production of consumption goods and those arising in the production of investment goods. I_1 is given, but consumption and income are not—they can take on a whole range of pairs of values and remain consistent with either of the equations (1) and (2) taken separately. However, only one pair of values (viz., one value of consumption combined with one value of income) is consistent with both equations at the same time, whenever $b \neq 1$. That is, we have two linear equations in two unknowns, and they determine one value for each.

If we substitute the right-hand side of (1) for the variable C in (2), we obtain

$$Y = A + bY + I_1 \tag{3}$$

from which we get the solution

$$Y_1 = \frac{A + I_1}{1 - b} \tag{4}$$

provided the constant b is not equal to 1. One can also obtain the solution value of C, that is, the value of C that is consistent with both equations (1) and (2), by substituting the solution for Y into equation (1) or equation (2).

With consumption a linear function of income and with investment given, we have obtained a single determinate value of income. For some other given value of investment, a different value of income would result.

That is, if investment equals I_2 instead of I_1, income will be

$$Y_2 = \frac{A + I_2}{1 - b} \tag{5}$$

Wherever consumption behaves as in equation (1) and our other simplifications fit the facts well, we can say that income rises and falls with investment. Indeed, we can even predict the size of the change in income, when investment changes, if we know the constant b. Subtracting (4) from (5), we have

$$Y_2 - Y_1 = \frac{A + I_2}{1 - b} - \frac{A + I_1}{1 - b}$$

$$= \frac{I_2 - I_1}{1 - b} \tag{6}$$

That is, when investment changes by an amount $\Delta I = I_2 - I_1$, the change in income will be

$$\Delta Y = Y_2 - Y_1$$

$$= \frac{\Delta I}{1 - b}$$

$$= k \, \Delta I \tag{7}$$

The constant k represents the expression $1/(1 - b)$.

The only relevant assumption is that the constant b, the marginal propensity to consume, is a positive fraction. That is,

$$0 < b < 1 \tag{8}$$

The reciprocal of a fraction is a number greater than 1; therefore k, in equation (7), is greater than 1. If b is close to 1, $1 - b$ is nearly zero and its reciprocal k will be a large number; if b is nearly zero, $1 - b$ is almost 1 and its reciprocal is only slightly greater than 1. That is, k varies directly with b. Since k is greater than 1, a change in income as indicated in equation (7) is larger than (loosely speaking, is a multiple of) the change in investment that caused it. Hence k is called *the multiplier*.

The multiplier can be derived by a different procedure, which some find helpful for getting a better grasp of the income model. First we note that whenever current income increases by some amount, say $\Delta_1 Y$, there will be a corresponding increase in consumption $\Delta_1 C$. Proceeding as in the derivation of equation (7) but using equation (1) alone, we find that

$$\Delta_1 C = b \, \Delta_1 Y$$

Further, producing consumption goods to satisfy this additional consumer demand will itself generate additional income.

If we start with an increase in investment ΔI, this gives us the first increase in income $\Delta_1 Y$. There will follow an increase in consumption $\Delta_1 C$. This implies, as just noted, a second increase in income $\Delta_2 Y$ equal to $\Delta_1 C$. This second rise in income will cause a further increase in consumption, which itself will generate income, which will imply yet another increase in consumption, and so on indefinitely. Just as the first increase in consumption is equal to b times the first increase in income, the second increase in consumption is equal to b times the second increase in income

$$
\begin{aligned}
\Delta_2 C &= b(\Delta_2 Y) \\
&= b(\Delta_1 C) \\
&= b(b \, \Delta_1 Y) \\
&= b^2 \, \Delta_1 Y \\
&= b^2 \, \Delta I
\end{aligned}
$$

and can thus be reduced to an expression in ΔI. In the same way,

$$
\Delta_3 C = b \, \Delta_2 C = b^3 \, \Delta I
$$

and so on; after j repetitions we have

$$
\Delta_j C = b^j \, \Delta I
$$

where $j = 1, 2, 3, 4, \ldots$.

Now we can obtain the total change in income that results from ΔI by summing all the changes in income contributed by these successive steps

$$
\Delta Y = \Delta_1 Y + \Delta_2 Y + \Delta_3 Y + \cdots + \Delta_j Y + \cdots
$$

where the sequence on the right continues indefinitely. Since

$$
\begin{aligned}
\Delta_1 Y &= \Delta I \\
\Delta_2 Y &= \Delta_1 C = b \, \Delta I \\
\Delta_3 Y &= \Delta_2 C = b^2 \, \Delta I \\
&\cdots \cdots \cdots \cdots \cdots \\
\Delta_j Y &= \Delta_{j-1} C = b^{j-1} \, \Delta I
\end{aligned}
$$

we have

$$
\begin{aligned}
\Delta Y &= \Delta I + b \, \Delta I + b^2 \, \Delta I + \cdots + b^{j-1} \, \Delta I + \cdots \\
&= \Delta I (1 + b + b^2 + b^3 + \cdots + b^{j-1} + b^j + \cdots)
\end{aligned}
\tag{9}
$$

The indefinitely long sum in parentheses reduces, by a theorem in high school algebra, to

$$\frac{1}{1-b} \tag{10}$$

Thus, we have

$$\Delta Y = \frac{\Delta I}{1-b} = k\,\Delta I$$

as before.

The derivation of the multiplier by an infinite sequence focuses attention on the domino-like sequence of people's decisions and offers a way of analyzing unfolding events over time. However, it should be understood that time delays and discrete steps are not a necessary part of this analysis but must be considered in their own right. The sequence just outlined, which suggests time lags between decisions, can equally well be thought of as occurring all at a single stroke.

For example, suppose some added investment activity is announced on a Saturday evening, after the end of the workweek, to commence on Monday morning. Unemployed workers are notified to return to work on Monday morning on the new investment projects. Expecting their new paychecks, they plan higher purchases than before, beginning immediately; they call their grocers and other retailers to assure credit based on their expected paychecks. These retailers shrewdly place new orders over the weekend with their wholesalers; the wholesalers similarly place increased orders with manufacturers, and the manufacturers increase their planned production runs while notifying previously laid-off workers to report to work Monday morning. These workers in turn plan increased spendings, get in touch with retailers, who call their wholesalers, who call manufacturers, who rehire workers, and so on ad infinitum. The whole process can be completed by Monday morning, so that at one stroke, income rises by the full amount of the multiplier times new investment. Indeed, all this could happen without any action by anyone to get in touch with his suppliers. Each retailer, wholesaler, and manufacturer could anticipate, without being told, what the effect on him would be, and the workers could likewise show up at their plants without being notified, in the correct expectation that work would be available.

However, cumulative changes of income usually take time to work through the system, and it is often important to take this into account in practical analysis. It is not always necessary, however; one can put time delays in or leave them out, whichever is most satisfactory for the problem at hand.

The reasoning in this section enables us to predict how much income will change when investment changes, given our narrow assumptions. Before going on, we should note what this model implies about the relationship of saving to investment.

The proposition of equation (1), $C = A + bY$, that households decide how much to consume on the basis of their current incomes, is equivalent to saying that they decide how much to add to their wealth on the basis of their current incomes. Since saving, the planned addition to wealth, is equal to the difference between current income and consumption, we can use the information in equation (1) to find out how much people will save at different levels of income.

$$S = Y - C = Y - A - bY$$
$$= -A + (1 - b)Y$$

If we look back at equation (2) and the derivation of equation (4), we find also that

$$I_1 = Y - C = -A + (1 - b)Y$$

that is,

$$I_1 = S$$

That is, whatever the level of investment, the income it determines is that level of income at which households choose to add to wealth at a rate just equal to that investment. By assumption, saving does not influence investment directly or indirectly; their only relationship is through variations in income caused by variations in investment. In fact, in every model in which government and net foreign investment are consolidated into consumption and investment, saving equals investment. In most other models, however, other variables than investment help determine income, and investment and saving are jointly dependent.

3 THE FIRST MODEL REPRESENTED GRAPHICALLY

The model of income determination given by equations (1) and (2) is illustrated in Figure 1. Equation (1), the consumption function, is the lower of the two parallel lines. Equation (3), the sum of the consumption function and the given quantity of investment, is the higher of the two lines. The two are parallel because investment is constant, that is, is assumed to be the same at every level of income. The higher line represents the total of desired expenditures—investment plus consumption—as a function of income.

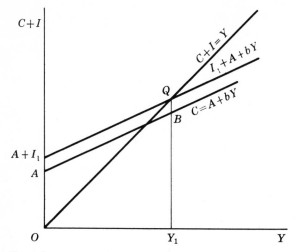

Figure 1

The line in Figure 1 that passes through the origin and bisects the right angle formed by the axes represents equation (2), the accounting identity between income and product. Since consumption, investment, and income are measured in the same units, the height of a point on this line, representing consumption plus investment, is equal to its horizontal distance from the origin, representing income. This means that the slope of the line is 45°, and it is generally called the "45° line."

The point Q at which the total expenditure line crosses the 45° line corresponds to the income Y_1 at which total expenditures equal the income that induces their consumption portion. This is the value of income obtained algebraically in equation (4) since the two lines intersect at that value of income at which equations (1) and (2) are both satisfied. The height of the point B gives consumption at this income, and the remaining height BQ is the amount of saving and investment. One way to visualize the solution in this model is to note that the income Y_1 is the only one at which the gap between the consumption function and the 45° line, which gap represents saving, equals investment I_1.

The multiplier is represented in Figure 2, in which we compare the results of two different levels of investment I_1 and I_2. When investment increases by the amount $I_2 - I_1 = \Delta I$, the total expenditure line is shifted upward by this amount. Its intersection with the 45° line moves from Q to R, and equilibrium income increases by the amount ΔY. ΔY is larger than ΔI, as it always will be when the total expenditure line slopes

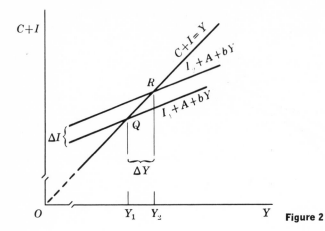

Figure 2

upward at a lower rate than the slope of the 45° line (that is, when $0 < b < 1$).

Figure 3 illustrates the larger multiplier that results when the marginal propensity to consume b is closer to 1. When the slope of the total expenditure line is very close to that of the 45° line, a given increase in investment ΔI shifts the intersection Q of the two very far to the right to R. Thus the ratio $\Delta Y / \Delta I = k$ is very large in this case.

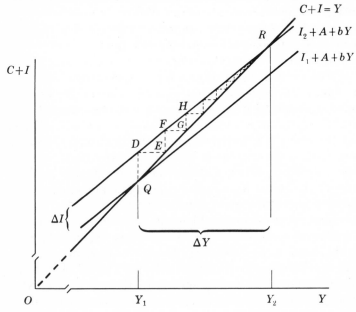

Figure 3

Figure 3 also illustrates the sequence by which the new equilibrium income Y_2 is approached, if one chooses to view it as a sequence. When the initial equilibrium, with income at Y_1 and investment at I_1, is disturbed by the increase of investment to I_2, this itself increases the expenditures people desire to make, when income is at Y_1, from its level at Q to its level at D. This additional expenditure raises income received to the level at E. At this increased level of income, however, people spend more on consumption, and, accordingly, expenditures increase to their level at F. Income is thus further increased to its level at G, which increases expenditures to their level at H, and so on. The series of steps drawn in the figure in this way converges on the new equilibrium R, the steps getting smaller and smaller as they go. They are the $\Delta_j C$ of the preceding section.

4 PROPERTIES OF THE MODEL WHEN INVESTMENT DEPENDS ON THE RATE OF INTEREST

Our next step in the analysis of national income is to consider investment as a schedule rather than as a given quantity. In particular, we assume that *the level of investment is a function of the rate of interest.*

The investment schedule is a demand schedule for resources for specific physical additions to wealth. These additions to wealth are expected to yield net income after provision for their maintenance. Against this expected income must be set either the cost of financing them, through borrowing or the sale of equities, or, if the liquid capital is already available, the income it could earn some other way. The investment a firm undertakes is determined by comparing the net incomes expected from the investment opportunities it has with the cost or "availability" of funds. Generally speaking, it will not be worthwhile to undertake all the known opportunities, given the cost or alternative earnings of investment funds. The firm will have to rank its investments by priority and cut off some of the lower priority ones. If circumstances should change so that investment with lower prospective net incomes can be considered, some additional investment will be undertaken.

There are often several ways to finance any investment, with various terms and conditions. As in other aspects of these models, we need a simplification that is both convenient and reasonably accurate. Accordingly, we assume that a good proxy variable for the combined effect of all factors involved in the cost or availability of investment funds is the rate of interest on a standard, highly marketable interest-bearing security such as a long-term government bond. This assumption serves well if variations in the overall conditions in securities markets are well correlated with variations in the interest rate selected as the proxy variable. At high rates of interest each firm will cut off its investment at a smaller amount than at low rates because of the ranking by priority or profitability.

To the extent that different rates of interest and related conditions are correlated, the volume of investment undertaken by business firms can be accurately represented by a schedule showing low investment at high rates of interest and high investment at low rates of interest. Thus in Figure 4 the downward-sloping curve $I = G_0 + G_1 i$ represents the

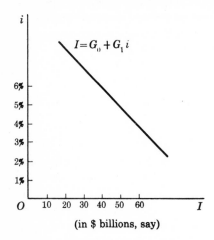

(in $ billions, say)   **Figure 4**

different amounts of investment I at different rates of interest i, where G_0 and G_1 are constants, with $G_1 < 0$. This curve is the investment function. For simplicity we assume, as in the case of the consumption function, that the investment function is linear, but its fundamental characteristic is its negative slope.

The investment function changes the income model by adding one more equation and one more variable. The model now has three equations.

$$I = G_0 + G_1 i \tag{11}$$
$$C = A + bY \tag{1}$$
$$Y = C + I \tag{2}$$

We now have three variables I, C, and Y if we take the rate of interest i_1 as given, as we had previously done for investment. In place of equation (6) we now obtain by the same procedure

$$Y_1 = \frac{A + G_0 + G_1 i_1}{1 - b} \tag{12}$$

A definite value for income is determined, as before.

Because of the similarity between (4) and (12), the multiplier is the same in this model as in the previous one. Now, however, a change in the rate of interest is a possible cause of a change in income. When the rate of interest changes from i_1 to i_2, there is a resultant change in investment given by the investment function. The change in income is still $\Delta Y = k \, \Delta I$.

We may think of the line of causation in this model as running from the rate of interest to investment to income and consumption. (Income and consumption interact with each other and so are jointly determined.) For each assumed rate of interest, there is a resultant level of income: in particular, lower rates of interest imply higher incomes, because they imply higher levels of investment, and k is positive.

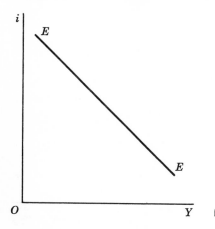

Figure 5

Figure 5 presents equation (12) graphically. The curve EE slopes downward, indicating higher incomes at lower rates of interest. The steepness with which it slopes downward is the product of two factors: the amount by which investment increases with a given fall in the interest rate, and the multiplier. That is, its slope is kG_1, referred to the vertical axis.

The curve EE tells us the level of income at each interest rate at which desired expenditures equal income. Along it consumers are satisfied with the allocation of their incomes between saving and consumption. Another way of stating this is that this curve gives the level of income at each interest rate at which investment equals desired saving. We noted the savings-investment equality at the end of section 2 above. For this reason the curve EE is sometimes designated the IS curve.

For the purposes of further analysis the curve EE will be viewed in another light. If the rate of interest i is regarded as a variable rather than as an arbitrary, given number, the three equations (11), (1), and (2) contain four variables, namely, i, I, C, and Y. These three equations in four unknowns do not determine any of the unknowns, but they combine into a single equation in any two variables. This is what was done in obtaining equation (12), which contains only the two variables Y and i (where i is now a variable).

The curve EE and the equations that underlie it will be referred to as the expenditure sector of the economy. As they stand, they represent a simplified, indeed an oversimplified, model of national income determination. From a broader point of view, they form one sector of a complete model of income determination. We now turn to the other sectors.

5 THE MONETARY SECTOR: THE DEMAND FOR AND SUPPLY OF CASH BALANCES

Each household owns a variety of assets that compose its total present wealth. Given this available total, the household must decide from time to time which assets to keep and, in particular, how much to hold in its cash balance and how much in assets yielding income or direct services. Such decisions cover the whole collection of assets, but the one concerning the proportions of their assets to hold in cash determines a demand function, in which both income and the rate of interest are variables. We assume that these are the only variables in this function. Further, *we assume that the desired aggregate quantity of cash balances increases with increasing income and decreases with increasing rates of interest.* These relationships are expressed in the function

$$M = L(i,Y) \tag{13}$$

usually called the *liquidity preference function*, because it relates to the choice between the liquid asset cash and other assets. It is illustrated in Figure 6. The figure shows a family of curves relating desired cash to the interest rate, one curve for each level of income; the higher curves correspond to higher levels of income, the lower ones to lower levels of income. That is, $Y_1 < Y_2 < Y_3$. The individual curves slope downward, showing higher cash balances demanded at lower interest rates, as assumed.

We shall review briefly the reasons for the assumed properties of the cash-balance demand function (13). The household's and firm's decision how much cash, on the average, to hold is at the same time a decision about the arrangement of cash receipts and payments. How often a house-

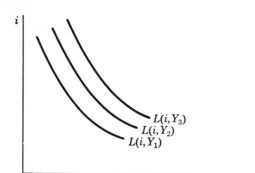

Figure 6

holder receives his paycheck—weekly, biweekly, or monthly—can be negotiated with the employing firm and does sometimes change; the same is true of other receipts.

Payment times are even more flexible. A household can, if it wishes, reduce its average cash balance almost to zero by buying virtually everything on credit and paying off debts on payday. Any excess of receipts over these debts can be invested immediately in securities or other assets. For most households, however, doing so involves more inconvenience than it is worth, and goods bought on credit generally cost more than those bought for cash. The typical household therefore chooses to hold some cash most of the time. The same is true of the typical business firm.

How large an average cash balance the household or firm chooses to hold depends, among other things, on the sacrifice of income that results from holding cash rather than other assets and on the saving that results from paying promptly rather than buying on credit. As we did with business decisions to invest, we assume that a good proxy variable for the combined effect of these factors is the standard rate of interest. When the rate of interest is high, it is generally worthwhile for firms and households to pay their debts more promptly and to press for more prompt and frequent payment of their receivables. This is particularly true of business firms, which hold a low ratio of cash balances to total cash turnover. Their cash holdings will be relatively sensitive to the related costs, because the skill with which they manage their cash has a significant effect on their profits. Accordingly, when the rate of interest is high, noncash assets are relatively attractive for everyone; people will tend to arrange their affairs so that a larger share of their assets earns income and a smaller share is in cash. When the rate of interest is low, the convenience afforded by increased cash balances costs relatively little income, so that relatively more will be held. Hence, with income fixed, the aggregate demand curve for cash balances, a function of the interest rate, will slope downward.

How much cash people hold, in preference to other assets, will depend on other factors as well, the most important of which is income. When households experience an increase in income, they typically allow some additional cash balance to accumulate before they dispose of the increased income on consumption and on noncash assets. The same is true of business firms, which will find it worthwhile to increase cash balances when the flow of transactions increases. This flow is highly correlated with income. Thus both household and business demand for cash balances will increase with increasing income.

This discussion of cash balances has assumed free choice by individual households and firms among their assets. From the point of view of each one, this assumption is correct about cash and readily marketable assets. Nothing prevents an individual household or firm from altering its cash balance at will by exchanging cash for other assets (although its willingness to do so will be affected by brokerage fees and other transaction costs).

For the community as a whole, however, such free choice is not generally possible. Although the gross amounts of various types of wealth, particularly financial claims, can to some extent be changed by financial institutions substituting one for the other, these possibilities are limited. In particular, if the monetary authorities choose to hold the total quantity of money constant, households and firms can only pass around the existing cash balances among each other and cannot all get more at once. If desired cash balances differ from actual cash balances, equalization must come about in some other way than by a change in the quantity of money, in this case.

If everyone tries at the same time to alter the composition of his assets in the direction of more cash balances, his attempt to do so by selling securities will result in a fall in security prices, which means a rise in the rate of interest. A rise in the rate of interest reduces desired cash balances toward equality with actual cash balances.

Thus, in Figure 7, if income is Y_1, the demand curve for cash balances is $L(i,Y_1)$. If the quantity of money were M_1 and the interest rate were i_2, the quantity demanded of cash balances, M_2, would exceed the actual quantity available. As everyone tries to sell securities for cash, however, the interest rate is driven up to i_1, at which point the community is satisfied with the amount of cash available, M_1.

At any given level of income, the interaction between the demand for cash balances and their supply determines the rate of interest. At a different level of income, this interaction determines a different rate of

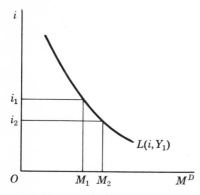

Figure 7

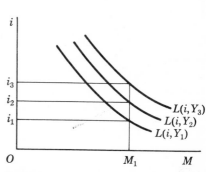

Figure 8

interest, since the demand curve for cash balances is different. In Figure 8, the interest rates which equalize the quantity demanded of cash balances to the supply M_1 at incomes Y_1, Y_2, and Y_3 are i_1, i_2, and i_3, respectively.

Generally the monetary authorities do not in fact keep the quantity of money constant. Besides permitting the quantity of money to increase in step with the growth of the economy over long periods, in short periods they have allowed it to fluctuate up and down with fluctuations in general business conditions. This is the normal reaction of the commercial banking system, if the authorities do not try to prevent it. In periods of business decline, firms generally try to reduce inventories and to repay their bank loans; their doing so extinguishes bank deposits and reduces the quantity of money. The banks themselves are likely to accept this, because in periods of poor business they want to reduce their risky commitments. This could be prevented only by an aggressive monetary policy that placed so much additional reserves in the banks as to make them willing to keep their loans and other commitments up to the old level. Although they sometimes move in this direction, the monetary authorities do not typically go this far.

The upshot is that when national income declines, both the quantity of money and the rate of interest drift downward, and when national income recovers, both drift upward. The combined actions of the monetary authorities and the banking system have the effect of producing an upward-sloping supply curve of money, as illustrated by the curve in Figure 9. This curve

$$M = h(i) \tag{14}$$

will shift from time to time with shifts in the policies of the monetary authorities, as occurs when they become alarmed about a really serious

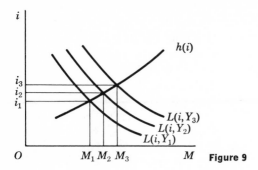

Figure 9

decline in national income or about an unusually rapid rise in the price level in prosperous times. Over a limited range of fluctuations in income, however, the curve can be regarded as a single, fixed curve. *We assume therefore that the supply of money is an increasing function of the rate of interest.*

The two equations

$$M = L(i,Y) \tag{13}$$
$$M = h(i) \tag{14}$$

contain the three variables M, i, and Y. They do not determine any of the variables but can be collapsed into one equation in two unknowns. For example, we can eliminate M simply by writing

$$h(i) = L(i,Y) \tag{15}$$

which gives us a single equation in i and Y. In Figure 9, if we consider only the intersections between $h(i)$ and successive curves of the family $L(i,Y)$, we see that equilibrium in the monetary sector occurs at higher

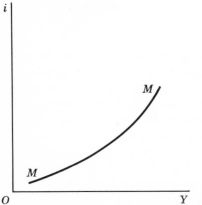

Figure 10

interest rates when income is higher and at lower interest rates when income is lower. (This follows from our assumptions about the demand and the supply of money; it is true also in Figure 8, where the supply of money is considered fixed, and it will be true for almost any likely behavior of the monetary sector.)

Equation (15) is the curve MM in Figure 10. This curve gives the value of the interest rate, for each level of income, at which the monetary sector is in equilibrium (that is, everyone is satisfied with the allocation of his wealth between money and other assets). Its upward slope indicates that this equilibrium produces higher interest rates when income is higher.

6 THE MODEL WITH EXPENDITURE AND MONETARY SECTORS

The equations of the expenditure sector and of the monetary sector are the following five relationships:

$$C = A + bY \tag{1}$$
$$Y = C + I \tag{2}$$
$$I = G_0 + G_1 i \quad \Longleftarrow \ should\ be\ i \tag{11}$$
$$M = L(i,Y) \tag{13}$$
$$M = h(i) \tag{14}$$

These contain five variables: C, Y, I, i, and M. The number of equations equals the number of unknowns; given the assumed slopes of these functions, they determine a single equilibrium value for each variable. We saw that the expenditure sector and the monetary sector each combine into a single equation in the rate of interest and income.

$$Y = \frac{a + G_0 + G_1 i}{1 - b} \tag{12}$$
$$h(i) = L(i,Y) \tag{15}$$

These together determine equilibrium values i_1 and Y_1. [The equilibrium values of the other variables can then be obtained, if desired, by letting $i = i_1$ in equations (11) and (14) and letting $Y = Y_1$ in (1).] This is illustrated in Figure 11, which puts together the curves for these two equations, which had separately been shown in Figures 5 and 10. EE is the curve representing combinations of i and Y that correspond to equilibrium in the expenditure sector, and MM is the curve representing combinations of i and Y that correspond to equilibrium in the monetary sector. Their intersection at the point A gives the one combination i_1 and Y_1 that corresponds to simultaneous equilibrium in both sectors, that is, to overall equilibrium in the whole model.

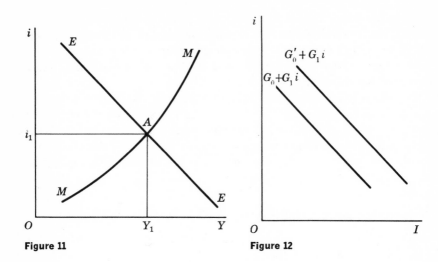

Figure 11

Figure 12

Now consider what happens to these equilibrium values when something in the model changes. For example, suppose that the investment function $G_0 + G_1 i$ shifts upward, because businessmen have become more optimistic about the prospects of their investments. The old function $G_0 + G_1 i$ shifts up to a new position $G_0' + G_1 i$, as shown in Figure 12. In equation (12) we can see that this will result in a higher equilibrium value of income for the expenditure sector at each rate of interest, because G_0' is greater than G_0. In fact, the discussion in sections 3 and 4 makes it clear that the increase in income in the expenditure sector, at any given rate of interest, is equal to the multiplier times G_0' minus G_0.

That is, the expenditure sector curve EE will shift to the right by the amount

$$
\begin{aligned}
(\Delta Y)_{i=\text{const}} &= k(\Delta I)_{i=\text{const}} \\
&= k(G_0' + G_1 i - G_0 - G_1 i) \\
&= k(G_0' - G_0) \\
&= k\,\Delta G_0
\end{aligned}
$$

This is shown in Figure 13, in which the expenditure sector curve shifts from $E_1 E_1$ to $E_2 E_2$. As a result, the overall equilibrium of the whole model will shift from the point A to the point B, at which both income and the rate of interest are higher than before.

The increase in income, from Y_1 to Y_2, is not as large as the shift in the EE curve measured in the income direction, that is, measured along a horizontal line. The upward slope of MM causes it to cut the new EE curve at a point to the left of C, that is, at a smaller income than Y_3. Had

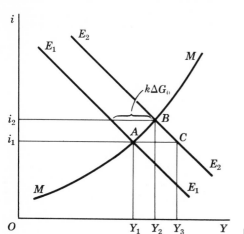

Figure 13

income increased by the full shift of the curve, from Y_1 to Y_3, its increase would be equal to the multiplier times the shift in the investment function; thus in the present model the direct use of the multiplier would result in *overstatement* of the rise in income. The multiplier plays an important secondary role in this model, however, in that it is a factor both in the slope of the EE curve and in the shift of that curve.

That the rise in income resulting from increased investment is less than the rise in investment at the initial rate of interest, is due to the damping effect on investment of the rise in the rate of interest. The rise in the rate of interest is due to the tendency of income to rise, which shifts the demand curve for cash balances to the right; the banks and monetary authorities supply the additional money demanded only at an increased rate of interest. Although investment still goes up, its rise is partly held back by the rise in the rate of interest, and therefore the total rise in expenditure, including due allowance for multiplier effects, is partly held back.

In a limited sense the multiplier still applies. Equation (12) is still part of the model, and it is satisfied both at the new equilibrium and at the old one. The reasoning initially used in presenting the multiplier, in section 2, therefore still applies; it is still formally true that $Y = k \, \Delta I$. The quantity ΔI has a new meaning, however. It is not an arbitrary or predetermined increase but that increase in investment that actually takes place as part of the simultaneous satisfaction of the whole system after the shift in the investment function. Hence the multiplier cannot provide a short-cut method for finding out the ultimate increase in income without considering the full interaction of the whole system; the size of the shift ΔG_0 in the investment function does not in general tell us what the ultimate change in investment, and therefore income, will be.

7 FURTHER PROPERTIES OF THE MORE COMPLETE MODEL OF INCOME DETERMINATION

Besides the effect of a shift in the investment function, we can analyze a shift in any of the functions in a straightforward way. For example, suppose the constant term A in the consumption function (2) increases. This constant term appears in equation (12) in a position exactly like that of G_0; the effect of its increase will therefore be the same. The expenditure curve EE will shift to the right by an amount $k\ \Delta A$, where ΔA is the increase in A. The change in equilibrium income will be less than $k\ \Delta A$, however, for the same reason that it was less than $k\ \Delta G_0$ before. This is also true of any other change in expenditure. Since government expenditures have been consolidated into consumption and investment in these models, if the government increases expenditures in some form that does not reduce or replace private expenditures of the same kind, there will be an upward shift in the consumption function or in the investment function, as the case may be, by the amount of the government's increased spending. The expenditure curve will shift to the right by the multiplier times this increase, and the overall effect will be as shown in Figure 13, that is, as implied by equations (12) and (15) combined.

Similarly, changes in the monetary sector can be analyzed in a straightforward way. Suppose the monetary authorities change their policy in the direction of encouraging a larger money supply and lower

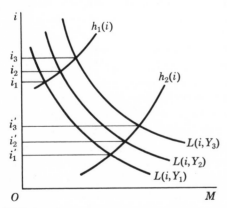

Figure 14

rates of interest than previously. This means a shift in the supply curve of money, $h(i)$, to the right, as shown in Figure 14. Under the old policy the intersections of the money supply curve with the family of demand curves $L(i,Y_1)$, $L(i,Y_2)$, $L(i,Y_3)$, . . . had occurred at i_1, i_2, i_3, . . . , respectively; under the new policy they occur at i_1', i_2', i_3', . . . , instead. Each of the new interest rates is lower than the old one, for each given level of income; that is, $i_1' < i_1$, $i_2' < i_2$, $i_3' < i_3$, and so on. Accordingly the new curve M_2M_2, showing the combinations of the interest rate and income that are consistent with equilibrium in the monetary sector under the new policy, will be below and to the right of the old curve M_1M_1, as shown in Figure 15. A tendency to easier money, that is, increased sup-

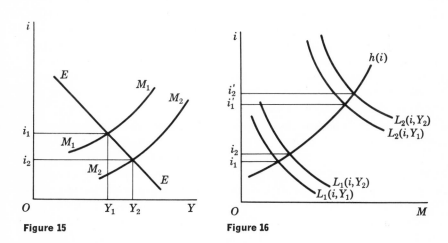

Figure 15   **Figure 16**

plies of money at given interest rates, will shift the MM curve downward and to the right; a tendency to tighter money, that is, reduced supplies of money at given interest rates, will shift the MM curve upward and to the left. The effects of these shifts on the equilibrium values of interest rates and income are also shown in Figure 15. The easy money policy, shifting the monetary sector curve from M_1M_1 to M_2M_2, lowers the equilibrium interest rate from i_1 to i_2 and increases the equilibrium level of income from Y_1 to Y_2; a shift of policy to tight money would have the reverse effects.

The effect of a change in the demand function for cash balances can be found in a similar way. In Figure 16 the demand curves $L_1(i,Y_1)$, $L_1(i,Y_2)$, . . . have shifted to the new positions $L_2(i,Y_1)$, $L_2(i,Y_2)$, . . . , respectively. This shifts the equilibrium interest rates upward from i_1, i_2, . . . to i_1', i_2', . . . , for the corresponding levels of income Y_1, Y_2, and so on. Therefore the MM curve is shifted upward and to the left, as it would be if there had been a tightening of monetary policy. The effects of the shifts in the demand function for cash balances on the equilibrium values of the interest rate and income are therefore also illustrated by Figure 15. When the demand curves for cash balances shift upward to the right, as in Figure 16, the MM curve shifts upward to the left, such as a shift from M_2M_2 to M_1M_1 in Figure 15. The interest rate rises from i_2 to i_1, and income falls from Y_2 to Y_1.

In general, the equilibrium values of the variables in the expenditure sector depend on the monetary sector, and vice versa. There is no significant sense in which the equilibrium value of income, or of any other variable, is determined by any one variable or function. In particular, it is no longer possible to predict income from knowledge of the investment schedule and the consumption function alone; it cannot be said, as it could in the first simple model considered, that investment determines income. It is true that an upward shift in the investment function will result in an increase in the equilibrium value of income, but the exact amount of the increase can be known only by taking into account the damping effects of the monetary sector.

Similarly, it is still true that saving equals investment at each position of equilibrium. Equality between the two no longer depends on variations in income alone, however, but is brought about partly through interactions with the monetary sector. For example, when the investment schedule shifts upward, we do not observe that income rises to the extent necessary to produce an increase in saving equal to the full shift in the schedule, measured at the old rate of interest; investment comes back part way to meet saving because of the increase in the rate of interest. Equality between saving and investment is brought about by variations both in income and in the rate of interest.

These properties of the model, and of the extended model of sections 9 and 10 below, are characterized as "classical." The contrasting properties when the demand curve for cash balances is horizontal are characterized as "Keynesian." Certain other cases discussed below, such as that in which the investment function is vertical, also have Keynesian characteristics.

8 PROPERTIES OF THE MODEL IN LIMITING CASES

The analysis in the preceding two sections is strictly correct only if the functions have the assumed slopes. Certain limiting cases that have been the subject of controversy will now be introduced.

We have already noted, in the preliminary discussion in section 5 on the monetary sector, that it makes no difference to the general properties of the model whether the supply curve of money is positively sloped or is vertical (denoting a fixed supply of money). Indeed, this supply curve can bend backward (have a negative slope) without affecting these properties, as long as its slope in that case is greater in absolute value than that of any of the demand curves for cash balances, measured with reference to the horizontal axis. In contrast, the general properties of the model are affected if the supply curve of money is horizontal, that is, if the monetary authorities create or destroy any amount of money that is necessary to keep the rate of interest fixed.[1]

This possibility is illustrated in Figure 17. It is evident that neither changes in income nor shifts of the demand function for money will have any effect on the rate of interest. In this case the MM curve for the

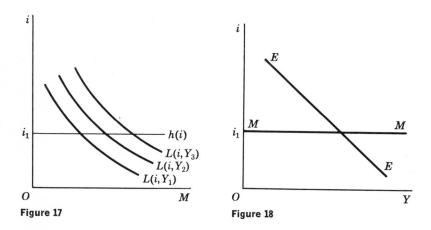

Figure 17   **Figure 18**

monetary sector will also be horizontal, as shown in Figure 18. It will remain that way, at the same rate of interest, as long as the authorities' policy remains unchanged.

In this case the properties of the model will be those of the model in which the rate of interest is given and fixed. The change in income produced by a shift in an expenditure function—the investment function or the consumption function—will equal the full shift of the EE curve. The shift of the EE curve equals $k \Delta G_0$ or $k \Delta A$, as the case may be, so the

[1] This describes the situation when the authorities peg the interest rate that prevails for government securities, as was done during and after the Second World War until 1947, and less firmly thereafter until 1951.

change in income will be equal to the full multiplier effect of the initial shift in expenditure. Interaction with the monetary sector can be disregarded.

Essentially the same conclusions follow if the demand curves for cash balances become horizontal at a single rate of interest high enough to matter. (This circumstance is called the "liquidity trap.") If, as illustrated in Figure 19, these curves run together and become horizontal

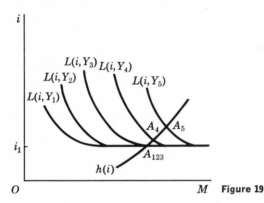

Figure 19

at the same rate of interest i_1, at which the supply curve of money cuts the ones that correspond to a certain range of incomes, then for that range of incomes the rate of interest will be fixed. This is the case for incomes Y_1, Y_2, and Y_3, since $h(i)$ cuts $L(i,Y_1)$, $L(i,Y_2)$, and $L(i,Y_3)$ at A_{123}, at which the rate of interest is i_1. For the higher incomes Y_4, Y_5, and so on, $h(i)$ cuts the corresponding demand curves at A_4 and A_5, at higher rates of interest, so that for these incomes the monetary sector reassumes the characteristics first presented.

Thus, in Figure 20, if the expenditure sector curve EE cuts MM in

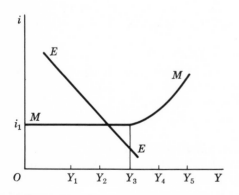

Figure 20

the range of incomes below and including Y_3, the rate of interest remains fixed at i_1, and the model has the properties of the simpler model. For this range of incomes, the multiplier analysis gives exact results. However, if the expenditure function shifts upward far enough to move EE up into the area where it intersects MM in the range above Y_3, interaction with the monetary sector affects the outcome, and the analysis of the preceding two sections becomes applicable.

When the situation is strictly as shown, it will also be true that changes in monetary policy will have no effect as long as the EE curve continues to cut the MM curve in its horizontal part. If the supply curve of money $h(i)$ is shifted to the right, in Figure 19, the range of incomes will be increased for which $h(i)$ cuts the demand curves for money in their horizontal sections. This will shift to the right the rising section of the monetary sector curve, extending the horizontal part as shown in Figure 21. A change to an easier monetary policy, shifting $h(i)$ in Figure 19 to the right, shifts the monetary sector curve in Figure 21 from M_1M_1 to M_2M_2; a change to a tighter monetary policy will have the reverse effect. Neither change will have any effect on the equilibrium income and rate of interest, as long as the expenditure sector curve EE cuts the monetary sector curve in its horizontal section.

Another special case occurs if investment is completely insensitive to the interest rate. If, as in Figure 22, the investment schedule is a vertical line (that is, $G_1 = 0$), indicating that investment will be constant at G_0 regardless of the interest rate, the equilibrium value of income also will be constant.

$$Y_1 = \frac{a + G_0}{1 - b}$$

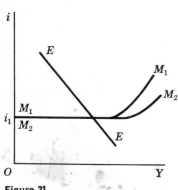

Figure 21

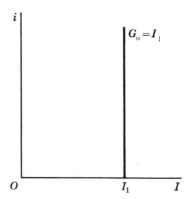

Figure 22

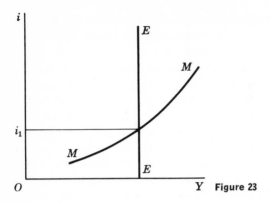

Figure 23

Accordingly, the *EE* curve will be a vertical line over Y_1, as shown in Figure 23. The interest rate can be said to depend on interaction between the expenditure sector and the monetary sector, in this case, but income does not. Neither a change in monetary policy nor any other change in the monetary sector will affect the equilibrium value of income but will only change the interest rate. In this case also the multiplier analysis applies exactly; any shift in an expenditure functon will increase income by the full shift in the *EE* curve, as given by the multiplier. The interest rate will rise or fall, according to whether the shift is to the right or to the left, but income is unaffected by this rise or fall.

9 THE PRICE LEVEL

Up to this point we have assumed that the price level is given and constant. On this assumption, the number of equations has been exactly enough to determine all the unknowns, except in special cases. If the price level is considered an undetermined variable, the model is incomplete. Now let us consider in detail how the model is modified by the introduction of the price level as a variable.

We assume that *when the price level changes all prices change in the same proportion.* This is not strictly accurate, since changes in other variables affect relative prices; for example, a change in the rate of interest will among other things imply changes in the prices of capital-intensive goods relative to labor-intensive ones. Effects of this kind are immaterial to the problems and issues to be considered here, however, and will be disregarded. We shall also suppose that contracts, pensions, and other assets and income flows normally thought of as fixed in money terms are all adjusted proportionately with the price level, so that there are no distributional effects.

Consider first the equations of the expenditure sector. There is no reason, as a first approximation, to suppose that the relationship between consumption and income will be affected by the price level. Since by assumption all prices, contract incomes, and so on change in the same proportion, the bill of goods each household can command and can expect to command in the future will be entirely unaffected. It is reasonable to suppose, therefore, that *each household will make the same allocation of income as before between current consumption and saving in real terms, if real income is unchanged.* Accordingly, we write

$$c = a + by \tag{16}$$

where lowercase letters represent real (deflated) counterparts to the current values previously expressed with capital letters.

$$c = \frac{C}{P} \qquad a = \frac{A}{P} \qquad y = \frac{Y}{P}$$

Equation (16) expresses the consumption function explicitly in real terms. When the price level changes, the quantities C, A, and Y, which are expressed as money values per unit time, will change in the same proportion, since the price of everything included in each of them will have changed in the same proportion. Hence the ratios C/P, A/P, and Y/P will be invariant for changes in the price level, when the real quantities are unchanged.[1]

Similar considerations apply to investment. Under the assumed conditions there is no reason to suppose either that the expected rate of profit or the risk connected with any investment will be changed by changes in the price level. (This is contingent also on the assumption about expectations made below.) Accordingly, the willingness of firms, financial intermediaries, and households to borrow and lend for productive investment will not be affected, and we can write

$$z = g_0 + g_1 i \tag{17}$$

where $z = \dfrac{I}{P}$

$$g_0 = \frac{G_0}{P}$$

$$g_1 = \frac{G_1}{P}$$

---

[1] Since the constant A was first introduced as a magnitude expressed in money terms, consistency requires that it be converted to real terms. The same is true of G_0 and G_1, in (17).

Again a change in P carries with it a change in every element of I in the same proportion; the ratio I/P is invariant with respect to the price level, as long as the physical quantities in it are unchanged.

The accounting identity for national income remains an identity when each of its components is divided by the same number, so that

$$y = \frac{Y}{P} = \frac{C + I}{P} = c + z \tag{18}$$

automatically holds for every price level.

In contrast to equation (18), writing equations (16) and (17) as we did involves more than the formal operation of dividing the value magnitudes in the corresponding equations (2) and (11) by the price index P. It implies that the same real quantities will always satisfy the relationships indicated, that is, that households and firms will continue to buy the same physical quantities of all goods and services, whatever the price level, for any given interest rate. Equation (18) would be true whether the others were accurate descriptions of behavior or not.

In the monetary sector we must make an assumption about the prevailing expectation of the future course of the price level. For simplicity in the present context we assume that everyone expects the price level to remain where it is. *Whether the price level doubles or falls by half, we assume that people expect it to remain at its new level indefinitely.*

When this is true, it is reasonable to suppose that households and firms regard the quantity of goods and services that a given cash balance will command in the same light as any other real or physical quantity. The reasons for holding cash, including both routine payments and possible unexpected outlays, will rise in money value in direct proportion to the price level. *The cash that is necessary or desirable to hold for all contingencies for given real income and wealth will rise in the same proportion as the price level.* This means that we can write

$$m = \frac{M}{P} = L(i,y) \tag{19}$$

This demand function is analogous to the new versions of the consumption and investment functions, equations (16) and (17). As in those equations, if the price level is changed and if the real magnitudes involved remain the same, equation (19) will continue to be satisfied; M demanded will rise in the same proportion as the price level when real income and i remain constant.

Concerning the supply of money, it is less easy to specify its behavior with changes in the price level. There are several possible ways the monetary authorities might respond to changes in the price level, and there is little clear evidence on what they do. The simplest assumption, which will serve adequately for now, is that *the authorities hold constant the supply curve of cash balances in nominal terms;* that is, in effect they do not react in any way to unsystematic changes in the price level. Stated differently, a given upward shift in the demand for cash will bring forth the same responses from the monetary institutions and authorities whether the shift is due to a rise in real income with prices constant or to a rise in the price level with real income constant. (Even if this is only approximately correct, the accuracy of our main analysis will not be affected.) In this case we keep the supply equation

$$M = h(i) \tag{14}$$

and divide both sides by P in order to have the same variable on the left as in equation (19).

$$m = \frac{1}{P} h(i) \tag{20}$$

The equations representing the model of income determination are now the following:

$$c = a + by \tag{16}$$
$$z = g_0 + g_1 i \tag{17}$$
$$y = c + z \tag{18}$$
$$m = L(i,y) \tag{19}$$

$$m = \frac{1}{P} h(i) \tag{20}$$

In place of the previous variables C, Y, I, i, and M, we now have the variables c, y, z, i, and m, respectively, and in addition, since P appears on the right-hand side of (20), we have P as a separate variable. Thus we have six variables and only five equations.

Since the price level does not affect the equations of the expenditure sector, which contain real variables and the interest rate only, this sector combines as before into a single equation in the two variables, real income and the interest rate.

$$y = \frac{a + g_0 + g_1 i}{1 - b} \tag{21}$$

The monetary sector, however, simplifies into one equation in *three* variables, namely, real income, the interest rate, and the price level.

$$\frac{1}{P} h(i) = L(i,y) \tag{22}$$

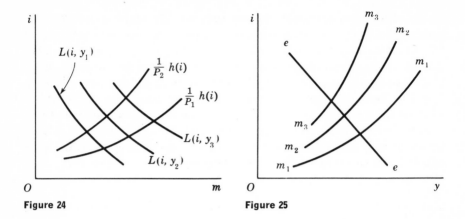

Figure 24   **Figure 25**

The monetary sector, under the present assumptions, is illustrated in Figure 24. The horizontal axis now measures real cash balances m, rather than nominal cash balances. The demand function for real cash balances is the same as before, with a different curve for each level of real income. It is now necessary, however, to draw the supply function of money as a family of curves, instead of only one curve. Each curve corresponds to a different price level, as indicated, where $P_2 > P_1$.

It can be seen that a rise in the price level from P_1 to P_2 has the same general effect on the supply of real cash balances as would a shift to tighter monetary policy at a constant price level. The shift to the left of $(1/P)h(i)$, because of the rise in the price level, raises the interest rate at which it intersects with each of the demand curves for real cash balances. Therefore, the curve representing equilibrium in the monetary sector, relating the interest rate to real income, is shifted to the left. This is illustrated in Figure 25. For each price level, P_1, P_2, P_3, there will be a different monetary sector curve, m_1m_1, m_2m_2, and m_3m_3, respectively. The expenditure sector curve, representing equation (21), is a single curve ee as before.

The combination of the monetary and expenditure sectors no longer determines a single value each for the rate of interest and income. Depending on the price level any combination of the rate of interest and income along the expenditure sector curve can be consistent with simultaneous equilibrium in both sectors, and the price level is indeterminate.

10 THE PRODUCTION–EMPLOYMENT SECTOR

The model is indeterminate with the price level as a variable, because it is incomplete. We get a complete enough model for addressing the major issues of national income determination when we introduce the sector relating employment and real wages to national income and product.

For the present, we assume that *employment is related in a simple and direct way to production, such that the two rise and fall together and such that employment is always the same at any given level of production, and vice versa.* Recalling that income always equals production, we write

$$y = f(N) \tag{23}$$

where N represents total employment. The function $f(N)$ is a simplified version of the production function; it is an aggregate of the corresponding functions for individual firms. We further assume that *hiring by firms is competitive, so that each firm will hire up to the point at which the real wage is equal to the marginal product of labor*

$$w = f'(N) \tag{24}$$

where w is the real wage rate and where $f'(N)$, the first derivative of the production function, is labor's marginal product in generalized units of product.

Finally, we assume that *the supply of labor can be expressed as a simple function of the real wage*

$$N = j(w) \tag{25}$$

This means either that labor is supplied competitively or where it is not the demand curve it faces shifts in such a way as to give a simple relation between the real wage and the quantity of employment.

The three equations of the production and employment sector appear in Figure 26(a) and (b). In Figure 26(a) we have the supply and demand curves for labor. The supply curve is drawn backward-bending,

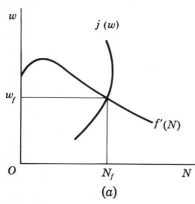
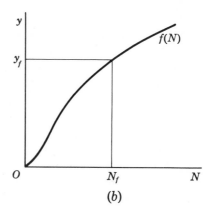

(a)   (b)

Figure 26

although it does not necessarily have this characteristic. The demand curve, that is, the marginal-productivity curve, slopes downward in the relevant part of its range. Their intersection determines that real wage w_f and that level of employment N_f which correspond to equilibrium in the labor market, that is, to full employment. Carrying N_f into part (b) of Figure 26, we obtain from the production function $f(N)$ the level of real income and production y_f that corresponds to full employment.

The solutions are final, because the three equations (23) to (25) contain only three variables. The two equations (24) and (25) determine their two variables, including the full-employment level of employment; this result, introduced into equation (23), gives full-employment real income. Full-employment real income is a constant with respect to the variables in the expenditure and monetary sectors and in particular with respect to the rate of interest. We introduce this result into the diagram representing those two sectors by using a vertical line over full-employment real income, in Figure 27. The curves for the other sectors duplicate those in Figure 25.

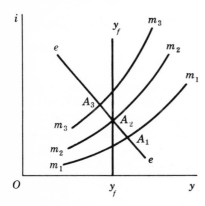

Figure 27

The model combining all three sectors is fully determinate, except in limiting cases such as those mentioned in section 8; there is only one price level at which the monetary and expenditure sectors can be in simultaneous equilibrium at the full-employment level of real income. When the relationships are shown in Figure 27, that price level is P_2. At the lower price level P_1, the monetary sector curve m_1m_1 intersects the expenditure sector curve at the point A_1, at which income is higher than the full-employment level. This implies that the price level will rise; and since there is only one equilibrium level for real wages, money wages will rise in step with the price level. [It can be seen in Figure 26(a) that when the prices of consumption and investment goods and services rise, lowering real wages, the demand for labor will exceed its supply; this implies a rise in money wages.] Equilibrium will prevail throughout the system when the price level reaches P_2.

At the higher price level P_3, the monetary sector curve m_3m_3 intersects the expenditure sector curve at the point A_3, at which income is lower than the full-employment level and the interest rate is higher. At this point aggregate demand is less than the aggregate supply of goods and services. The price level will tend to fall, including money wages. Both will continue to fall until equilibrium prevails at the price level P_2.

In summary, the equations of the model of national income determination are the following:

The expenditure sector:

$$c = a + by \qquad (16)$$
$$z = g_0 + g_1i \qquad (17)$$
$$y = c + z \qquad (18)$$

The monetary sector:

$$m = L(i,y) \qquad (19)$$
$$m = \frac{1}{P} h(i) \qquad (20)$$

The production-employment sector:

$$y = f(N) \qquad (23)$$
$$w = f'(N) \qquad (24)$$
$$N = j(w) \qquad (25)$$

Each of the sectors can be collapsed into a single equation in two, three, and one variable(s), respectively.

The expenditure sector:

$$y = \frac{a + g_0 + g_1i}{1 - b} \qquad (21)$$

The monetary sector:

$$\frac{1}{P} h(i) = L(i,y) \qquad (22)$$

The production-employment sector:

$$y = f(N_f) = y_f \qquad (26)$$

These three equations are the curves in Figure 27.

11 ECONOMIC LINKS BETWEEN SECTORS

Consider an apparent puzzle in the properties of the complete model. We have noted that only real variables, and not the price level or the quantity of real cash balances, appear in the equations of the expenditure sector and of the production-employment sector. The price level and real cash balances appear as variables only in the monetary sector equations. The price level, however, is made up of the prices of current goods and services in the expenditure sector; a disequilibrium in the price level must be corrected by changes in these prices. If the price level is not a variable in the expenditure sector, how can there be a tendency toward equilibrium in the price level? More particularly, if a given combination of the interest rate and real income is consistent with the expenditure sector regardless of the price level, a change in the price level does not disturb the consistency of this combination; similarly, a given combination of the interest rate and real income that is inconsistent with the expenditure sector remains inconsistent regardless of any change in the price level. If the price level does not affect these relationships in the expenditure sector, how can the expenditure sector affect the price level?

This puzzle disappears, however, when we note that each market in the expenditure sector and the production-employment sector drives its price and so affects the price level. At a rate of interest below its equilibrium value, every such market might have unsatisfied demand, and every price would rise. When every price rises, however, every demand curve and supply curve shifts upward, so that their intersection runs away from the price as fast as it rises, unless the interest rate changes. The interest rate does change, because the rise in the price level increases the interest rate that balances supply with demand in the monetary sector. This reaction through the monetary sector cuts back the upward shift in the demand curve for each good and service, so that its price closes the gap to the intersection of the demand curve and supply curve. Thus the expenditure sector and the production-employment sector drive the price level, through ordinary demand-supply relationships, even though a proportionate change in every price leaves every excess demand where it was until and unless the interest rate changes. The change in the interest rate comes from the monetary sector, in reaction to the change in the price level.

The transition to equilibrium involves a series of interactions among all three sectors, if we choose to view it as a sequence analogous to that in the development of the multiplier. With a price level that is initially too low, the monetary sector produces an interest rate that is too low for equilibrium in the other sectors: desired expenditures exceed available supplies and resources, whose prices therefore rise. The price level rises, and the monetary sector now produces an interest rate that is closer to the equilibrium one than before: the excess of desired expenditures over supplies and resources is less than previously. The price level continues to rise until it reaches the equilibrium level.

The appearance of paradox or puzzle comes from a difference between the mathematical interpretation and the economic interpretation of the model. Mathematically, the expenditure sector and the production-employment sector determine the interest rate and have nothing to do with the price level, which does not appear as a variable in their equations. Mathematically, the monetary sector has the interest rate given by the other two sectors and, subject to this rate, determines the quantity of money and the price level.

Economically, however, the expenditure sector and the production-employment sector help determine the prices of their goods and services. The model fails to reflect this economic aspect of these sectors because it aggregates the markets for goods and services and disregards individual prices. In a parallel way, economically the monetary sector acts on the interest rate, which is the price that equates supply and demand for cash balances as a part of the economy's portfolio.

But just as the price level that the nonmonetary sectors set for goods and services depends on the interest rate, so also the interest rate that the monetary sector sets depends on the price level. The interest rate it "determines" is driven by the price level to the full-employment rate, given by the other two sectors. This interaction reconciles the mathematical and economic interpretations of the model.

12 COMPARATIVE STATICS OF NATIONAL INCOME

The national income model assembled in the preceding sections, as it stands, is probably the most enlightening and generally applicable representation of the economy among the many that have come into use. It is important to acquire a good grasp of its characteristics and implications. Not only does it have a very general usefulness in and of itself, but it provides a good point of departure for the analysis of more complicated or specialized questions than the model itself can answer.

The model shows what happens to the equilibrium values of different variables when some function shifts. This use of it is *comparative statics*, so called because it involves the comparison of different static positions of equilibrium. Our analysis has used comparative statics throughout, and we shall consider four more examples now, with the complete model.

A SHIFT OF A FUNCTION IN THE EXPENDITURE SECTOR

Suppose that either the consumption function or the investment function shifts upward, so that at any given rate of interest expenditure is higher than before. We have seen that this implies a shift to the right of the aggregate expenditure function, as illustrated in Figure 28, from e_1e_1 to e_2e_2, where the shift equals the product of the multiplier times the shift in the consumption or investment function.

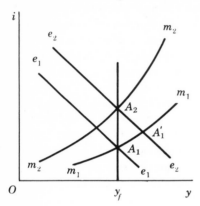

Figure 28

The result of this shift is that the new expenditure sector curve intersects the monetary sector curve at A_1' instead of A_1, at a greater than full-employment level of real income; thus the price level is below its equilibrium level. As noted in the preceding section, the price level will rise, shifting the monetary sector curve from m_1 to m_2, so that it intersects the expenditure sector curve at the full-employment level of real income, at A_2.

Now the interest rate and the price level are higher than before. If the upward expenditure shift was in investment, consumption is the same as before, as real income is unchanged (and we have assumed that consumption depends only on income, not on the interest rate). Therefore, since saving equals investment both before and after the shift and since saving is unchanged, investment is unchanged; the rise in the rate of interest chokes investment back to its old level, fully offsetting the upward shift in the investment function. If the upward expenditure shift were in consumption, consumption will be higher by the full amount of the shift measured at full-employment income; investment will be reduced by this amount because of the rise in the rate of interest. Because of the rise in the rate of interest and the rise in the price level, equilibrium real cash balances will be less than before. Real wages and employment are unaffected.

A CHANGE IN MONETARY POLICY

Suppose the monetary authority shifts to a tighter monetary policy, that is, shifts $h(i)$ to the left. We have seen that this implies a shift to the left of the monetary sector curve, so that it intersects the expenditure sector curve at an income below the full-employment level. As in the preceding section this means that the price level is above the equilibrium level. The price level will tend to fall, shifting the monetary sector curve back to its intersection with full-employment real income. The supply curve of real cash balances intersects, at the same point as before, the demand curve for real cash balances at full-employment real income.

The result is that real cash balances, real income, the interest rate, and all other variables except the price level will be the same in new equilibrium as in the old one. The price level will fall by the proportion by which the money supply was reduced (in nominal terms) at the equilibrium rate of interest.

A SHIFT IN THE LIQUIDITY PREFERENCE FUNCTION

Suppose that the public reduces the real cash balances it desires to hold, other things equal, either by a change in tastes or by improvements in the means of making payments. We have seen that this implies a shift to the right of the monetary sector curve. Thus the price level is below its new equilibrium level. The price level will rise, shifting the supply curve of real cash balances to the left and shifting the monetary sector curve back to its old intersection with the expenditure sector curve.

The shifts in the monetary sector are illustrated in Figure 29. Only the demand curve for real cash balances at full-employment real income is

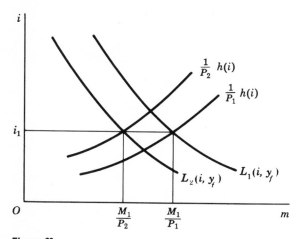

Figure 29

shown. This curve shifts from $L_1(i,y_f)$ to $L_2(i,y_f)$. (The effect of the shift on the monetary sector curve is discussed and illustrated in section 7.) The consequent rise in the price level shifts $(1/P_1)h(i)$ to $(1/P_2)h(i)$, although $h(i)$ itself has not shifted. Overall equilibrium will occur at the old rate of interest, so that the nominal supply of money is the same as before, at M_1. Real cash balances fall from M_1/P_1 to M_1/P_2, by the same proportion as the shift to the left of the demand curve (at full-employment real income) for real cash balances; the price level rises by the inverse proportion.

A SHIFT IN THE PRODUCTION FUNCTION

Suppose that the production function shifts upward, so that the same employment produces more. Suppose also that the investment schedule is unaffected, so that the expenditure sector curve remains unchanged.

This shift is illustrated in Figure 30, showing the production function; $f_1(N)$ has shifted upward to the new position $f_2(N)$. Full-employment real income is increased by the amount of the upward shift of the production function at N_f, from y_1 to y_2, plus a possible adjustment for a change in the full-employment value of N_f.

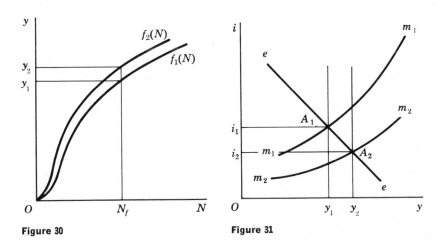

Figure 30

Figure 31

The interaction of this change in the production-employment sector with the other sectors appears in Figure 31. The shift to the right of full-employment real income moves it away from the intersection of the curves for the monetary sector and the expenditure sector. Then the price level is above its equilibrium level; it must fall. The resultant fall in the price level shifts the monetary sector curve to the right, from m_1 to m_2, so that it intersects the expenditure sector curve at A_2, at which real income has risen to its new full-employment level y_2 and the rate of interest has fallen from i_1 to i_2.

The following changes have resulted: the rate of interest and the price level are lower; real consumption, real investment, real income, and real cash balances are all higher.

These four examples cover the main shifts that the model can be used to analyze. We have considered two shifts in the monetary sector and one shift each in the expenditure and the production-employment sectors. These illustrate certain general properties of the model, within that range in which none of the limiting cases of section 8 applies.

Since the production-employment sector is self-contained, with the number of variables in it equal to the number of equations, the equilibrium values of the variables in this sector are independent of shifts in the other sectors. Similarly, since only three variables besides real income appear in the expenditure sector, namely real consumption, real investment, and the rate of interest, there is a total of six variables in the two sectors combined, equal to the number of equations in both combined. Hence the equilibrium values of these three additional variables are independent of shifts in the monetary sector. The monetary sector, by contrast, has too many variables to determine anything except when it is combined with the whole model; hence the equilibrium values of real cash balances and of the price level will be affected by shifts in all three sectors.

These characteristics of the model depend on some key assumptions. For example, that the equilibrium values of all the variables appearing in the two nonmonetary sectors should be independent of all shifts occurring in the monetary sector depends critically on the assumption that each of the equations in those two sectors is independent of the price level of all goods and services. Some of these key assumptions, and the effects they have on the properties of the national income model, are the subject of the next chapter.

BIBLIOGRAPHY

Brownlee, O. H.: "The Theory of Employment and Stabilization Policy," *Journal of Political Economy*, vol. 58 (1950), pp. 412–424.

Hansen, Alvin H.: *A Guide to Keynes* (New York, McGraw-Hill Book Company, 1953).

Hicks, J. R.: "Mr. Keynes and the Classics: A Suggested Interpretation," in American Economic Association, *Readings in the Theory of Income Distribution* (New York, McGraw-Hill Book Company, 1946), parts I–III, pp. 461–472.

Keynes, J. M.: *General Theory of Employment, Interest and Money* (London, Macmillan & Co., Ltd., 1936).

Lerner, Abba P.: "Saving and Investment: Definitions, Assumptions, Objectives," in American Economic Association, *Readings in Business Cycle Theory* (New York, McGraw-Hill Book Company, 1944).

Lutz, F. A.: "The Outcome of the Saving-Investment Discussion," in American Economic Association, *Readings in Business Cycle Theory* (New York, McGraw-Hill Book Company, 1944), chap. 6.

Modigliani, Franco: "Liquidity Preference and the Theory of Interest and Money," in American Economic Association, *Readings in Monetary Theory* (New York, McGraw-Hill Book Company, 1951), chap. 11.

Ruggles, Richard, and Nancy D. Ruggles: *National Income Accounts and Income Analysis*, 2d ed. (New York, McGraw-Hill Book Company, 1956).

Tarshis, Lorie: "The Flow of Business Funds, Consumption and Investment," chap. 14 in Kenneth Kurihara (ed.): *Post Keynesian Economics* (New Brunswick, N.J., Rutgers University Press, 1954).

A APPENDIX

MATHEMATICAL APPENDIX TO CHAPTER 2

The national income model developed in this chapter, in its consolidated sector form, consists of the three equations

$$y = \frac{a + g_0 + g_1 i}{1 - b} \tag{21}$$

$$\frac{h(i)}{P} = L(i,y) \tag{22}$$

$$y = f(N_f) = y_f \tag{26}$$

Substituting y_f into the first equation (21) yields the equilibrium value of the rate of interest i_f; substituting both into (22) yields the equilibrium price level P_f:

$$P_f = \frac{h(i_f)}{L(i_f, y_f)}$$

For comparative statics of changes in the expenditure and monetary sectors, we take differentials after first noting that for all such changes we have from (26)

$$\delta y = 0$$

because y_f is a constant. For a change in the constant term in the consumption function $\delta a \neq 0$, we have from (21)

$$0 = \frac{\delta a + g_1 \, \delta i}{1 - b}$$

which gives

$$-g_1 \, \delta i = \delta a$$

As a result, investment falls by exactly the amount of the upward shift in consumption, through the interest-rate effect

$$\delta z = g_1 \, \delta i = -\delta a$$

The rise in the interest rate is just enough to give that result. For the monetary sector, we write

$$h(i) = PL(i,y)$$

from which we have

$$h' \, \delta i = L \, \delta P + PL_i \, \delta i$$

This gives

$$\delta P = \frac{h' - PL_i}{L} \, \delta i$$

or

$$\frac{\delta P}{P} = \frac{h' \, \delta i - PL_i \, \delta i}{PL} = \frac{h' \, \delta i - PL_i \, \delta i}{h(i)}$$

$$= \frac{\delta M^S - \delta M^D}{M} \qquad\qquad \text{(A-1)}$$

where M is the original quantity of cash, $\delta M^S = h' \, \delta i$, and $\delta M^D = PL_i \, \delta i$. In (A-1) we have in the numerator the excess supply of cash balances induced by the change in the interest rate. For example, if the interest rate rises, the quantity of cash supplied increases by the amount $h' \, \delta i$ while the quantity demanded decreases by the amount $PL_i \, \delta i$. With the minus sign the quantity in the numerator sums their absolute values and measures the discrepancy between supply and demand at the higher interest rate and the old price level. The price level must rise just enough to eliminate this discrepancy in real terms, that is, by the proportion it bears to the original money stock. Therefore, if the rise in the equilibrium interest rate creates an excess supply of money equal to 1 percent of the original money stock, the price level must rise 1 percent to restore equilibrium. (The above results are identical throughout for a change in the constant g_0 in the investment function.)

The result in equation (A-1) partly anticipates those we get for shifts in the monetary sector. For such shifts, all the parameters in the expenditure sector remain unchanged, so that $\delta i = 0$. For a shift in the supply curve $\delta h \neq 0$, we have

$$\delta h = L \, \delta P$$

and

$$\frac{\delta P}{P} = \frac{\delta h}{PL} = \frac{\delta h}{h} = \frac{\delta M^s}{M} \tag{A-2}$$

The price level rises (falls) by the same proportion as the money supply increases (decreases), at the equilibrium interest rate. For a shift in the demand curve $\delta L \neq 0$ we have

$$0 = L \, \delta P + P \, \delta L$$

and

$$\frac{\delta P}{P} = \frac{-\delta L}{L} \tag{A-3}$$

The price level falls (rises) by the same proportion as the demand for money increases (decreases), at the equilibrium interest rate. The result (A-2) is that given by the quantity theory of money. Results (A-1) and (A-3) parallel (A-2).

Finally consider a change in full-employment real income because of changed technology or factor inputs

$$\delta y_f > 0$$

Then from (21) we have

$$\delta y = \frac{g_1 \, \delta i}{1 - b} = k g_1 \, \delta i$$

and

$$\delta i = \frac{\delta y}{k g_1} < 0 \qquad \text{because } g_1 < 0$$

From (22) we have

$$h' \, \delta i = L \, \delta P + P(L_i \, \delta i + L_y \, \delta y)$$

and

$$\frac{\delta P}{P} = \frac{h' - PL_i}{h} \, \delta i - \frac{L_y \, \delta y}{L} \tag{A-4}$$

The terms that multiply δi in (A-4) are all positive, while δi is negative; the terms that multiply δy, taken separately, are all positive, as is δy, and they have a minus sign. Thus both parts of δP are negative, so the price level necessarily falls when full-employment real income rises.

The terms in δi in (A-4) are the same as the expression that led to (A-1) and have the same interpretation. δP now has the additional term in δy, which is the additional proportion demanded of cash balances due to the increase in full-employment real income. Thus the proportionate fall in the price level is the proportion of excess demand for cash due to (1) the reduced supply due to the fall in the interest rate, (2) the increased demand due to this same fall, and (3) the increased demand due to the rise in income.

3

ADVANCED ANALYSIS OF NATIONAL INCOME

1 INTRODUCTORY REMARKS

Although Chapter 2 introduced national income analysis, it gave scant treatment to several important questions, some of primarily academic interest and some of practical interest. We shall now take up the more significant of these. Some of these questions involve special or limited cases of the model in Chapter 2; others involve modification of the assumptions used there.

2 INCONSISTENT EQUATIONS

Several authors debated in the 1930s and 1940s whether the equations of the national income model have a full-employment solution, that is, are consistent with each other. This question must be resolved by experience, not by reasoning from basic principles. Equality between the number of equations and the number of unknowns is not enough to guarantee a single set of values, one for each unknown, that will simultaneously satisfy all the equations. (Consistency is still less certain if we insert an additional equation in the same variables.) Three significant instances appear in Keynes's *General Theory*.

(1) Wages might be set too high to be consistent with full employment, where full employment means that every qualified worker willing to work at the going wage is able to find a job. The wage might be higher because of noncompetitive conditions in the production-employment sector; if so, employment would be lower than it would be under perfect competition in this sector.

If money wages are fixed, we must write for the labor supply function

$$W = W_0 \tag{27}$$

a constant, in place of the previous function

$$N = j(w) \tag{25}$$

With this substitution, the model's solution has different properties in some respects from those mentioned at the end of Chapter 2. It will be inconsistent with equation (25); a model containing both equations at once will be inconsistent.

This situation is illustrated in Figure 32. Suppose that the labor force that would be available at different real wages is still given by the function $j(w)$; but because of the setting of the money wage at W_0,

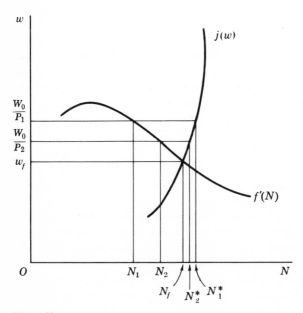

Figure 32

none is available at any lower money wage. The supply of labor at each price level P is given by a horizontal line at the height W_0/P extending from the vertical axis out to the amount of employment given by $j(w)$ for that real wage. Thus we have a family of labor-supply curves in this figure, one for each price level. If the price level is at the low value P_1, at which real wages are relatively high, the labor supply is the horizontal line at W_0/P_1, up to a maximum labor supply offered at N_1^*; but only N_1 of labor will be demanded by business firms. At the relatively higher price level P_2, the labor supply up to a maximum of N_2^* is given by the horizontal line at W_0/P_2; here the demand for labor is N_2. For each of these amounts of labor demanded there will be a different total production and income, given by the production function.

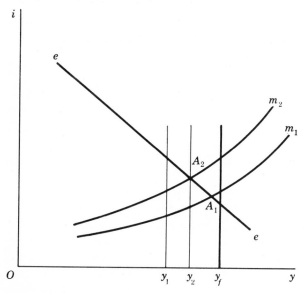

Figure 33

With a fixed money wage, we get a sequence of values of equilibrium real income, one for each price level, just as there is a family of monetary sector curves, one for each price level. This is illustrated in Figure 33. At the low price level P_1 the real income y_1 given by the production-employment sector is lower than the intersection of the monetary sector curve m_1 with the expenditure sector curve ee at A_1. The price level will tend to rise. A rise in the price level to P_2 increases the real income given by the production-employment sector to y_2 and shifts the monetary sector curve to the left to m_2. Their new intersection at A_2 is consistent with equilibrium all around. Real income is below the full-employment level as previously defined, and employment at N_2 is less than the maximum willing supply of labor N_2^*.

A way to restore equilibrium at full employment, on the function $j(w)$, is to increase the supply of money enough to lower W_0/P to w_f, by driving up the price level. This step removes the inconsistency in the model that has both the fixed money wage and the previously defined labor supply function, by making W_0/P pass through the intersection of $j(w)$ and $f'(N)$. Employment rises to N_f, and production rises to full-employment real income y_f.

However, increasing the money supply will fail to restore full employment if we assume a fixed real wage, rather than a fixed money wage, at too high a level for full employment. This assumption better represents any monopoly power exercised by unions; their ability to extract high real wages is not affected by changes in the price level. That the union has the right to reopen wage negotiations at any time—regardless of what the agreement may say—implies that the union can maintain the initial real wage regardless of monetary policy. Frequent cost-of-living adjustments, if specified in the wage agreement, also have the same effect. There is only one level of production consistent with equilibrium in the production-employment sector—that determined by the high fixed real wage and the corresponding low employment. An easy money policy in this case will simply raise the price level without changing production and employment.

From a practical point of view an intermediate case may also be important, in which unions periodically exercise monopoly power in arriving at a wage agreement that in part has the character of a long-term contract. Such an agreement may specify a *money* wage that implies low employment at the prices then prevailing. An easy money policy will then increase employment during the term of the wage agreement, if the agreement is not revised before it expires. When a new agreement is negotiated, real wages and employment will again presumably go back to the levels implied by the unions' monopoly power. Indeed, the union may choose to set an even higher real wage, nonoptimal for its members because it causes too much unemployment, if they expect it to be undone partly by subsequent inflation. In such a situation we can say that the rate of inflation will be determined by monetary policy, while the average level of employment and the movement around this average will be determined by the length of term of the wage agreement and by the extent to which the unions anticipate further inflation in their wage settlements.

In summary, *if the monetary authority rests content in letting employ-*

*ment stay at the low level implied by the initial exercise of the supposed
monopoly power of the unions, there will be no continuing inflation.* If in
contrast the authorities try to increase employment through an inflationary policy, they will partially succeed until such time as unions begin
to anticipate further inflation in their wage settlements. When they do,
the situation will be one of inflation *and* low employment, unless the
inflation outstrips the unions' expectations by proceeding at an ever-
increasing rate.

(2) A second possibility of inconsistency arises in connection with a
limiting case discussed in section 8 of Chapter 2, in which the demand
curves for real cash balances, or the supply curve, imply a horizontal
monetary sector curve over the relevant range at too high a rate of interest. This type of monetary sector curve results either if the monetary
authority pegs the rate of interest or if the demand curves for real cash
balances are all horizontal over a certain range. The monetary sector
curve also may merely be nearly horizontal and still be inconsistent with
equilibrium as would happen, for example, if the demand curves remain
asymptotically above an interest rate too high for equilibrium.

If so, and if the minimum rate of interest set by the monetary sector
curve is higher than the rate at which the expenditure sector curve
reaches full-employment real income, there will be no price level at which
the three curves can intersect in the same point. Such a situation is illustrated in Figure 34. If the rigidity in the monetary sector is due to the
pegging of the interest rate by the monetary authority, there is no rising
section of the monetary curve; if it is due to the shape of the demand
curves for real cash balances, the rising section of the monetary sector
curve will shift to the right as indicated, as the price level falls, without
affecting the inconsistency of the system. No matter how far the price

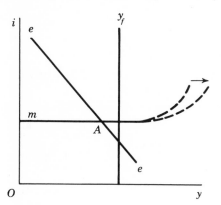

Figure 34

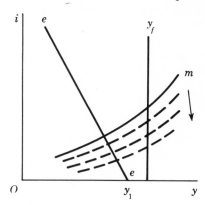

Figure 35

level falls, the monetary sector curve will intersect the expenditure sector curve at the point A, at a lower real income than the full-employment level.

(3) The third possibility of inconsistency is that the expenditure sector curve never reaches the full-employment level of real income at any positive rate of interest. Although this curve slopes down, this slope does not assure that the expenditure sector's equilibrium real income will rise to the full-employment level at any positive interest rate. This situation is illustrated in Figure 35. The expenditure sector curve intersects the horizontal axis at y_1, a real income below the full-employment level. Even if the monetary sector curve converges on the horizontal axis as the price level falls, it stays above the axis. Its intersection with the expenditure sector curve will therefore always be to the left of full-employment real income.

A failure of the expenditure sector curve to reach full-employment real income at any positive rate of interest would be due to poor investment prospects. At the equilibrium in the expenditure sector for each interest rate, income is just enough to make desired saving equal investment. The failure of this sector ever to reach full-employment real income means that investment at any positive interest rate is less than what saving would be at full-employment real income.

Examples 2 and 3, just given, differ from each other with respect to the minimum rate of interest. In both cases this minimum is too high to permit the attainment of overall equilibrium. They are distinct in principle, however, because each of them raises a different set of issues. Both these cases represent potential inconsistencies in the national income model as set out in Chapter 2. Example 1, in contrast, is an inconsistency introduced by the insertion of another equation in addition to the ones already there.

3 REAL CASH BALANCES AND CONSUMPTION

Consider now how the model changes if the quantity of real cash balances is a variable in the consumption function. The effect of cash balances on consumption is known as the *Pigou effect*, or the *real balance effect*. It asserts that a nonrecurrent change in real cash balances held by the private sector of the economy, such as that caused by a change in the price level, will induce a change in consumption. It does not depend on expectations of further change in the price level.

If the quantity of real cash balances is a variable in the consumption function, as, for example, in the form

$$c = a + b_1 y + b_2 m$$

where b_2 is a positive constant, the equation of the expenditure sector becomes

$$y = \frac{a + g_0 + g_1 i + b_2 m}{1 - b} \tag{28}$$

With this new variable in the expenditure sector, its three equations contain five variables; these three equations simplify into (28), which has three variables, rather than two. It can no longer be represented by a single curve but must be represented by a family of curves, one for each price level. This is illustrated in Figure 36, which has a family of curves

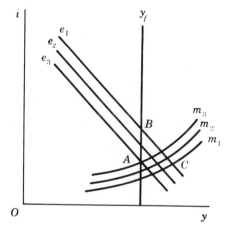

Figure 36

for the expenditure sector, one for each price level, as does the monetary sector. If the price level is P_1, the monetary and expenditure sector curves intersect at C, at a higher than full-employment real income, and the price level will tend to rise. As this rise reduces real cash balances, consumption will fall, and the expenditure sector curve shifts downward to the left. Equilibrium is reached at a price level P_3 at which the corresponding monetary and expenditure sector curves intersect at the point A, at full-employment real income.

Putting real cash balances in the consumption function changes one of the previous main properties of the system. Under the old assumptions, the equilibrium values of the variables in the nonmonetary sectors of the economy were independent of all shifts in the monetary sector. This is no longer true. For example, suppose an initial equilibrium at the point B, with price level P_1, has been disturbed by a shift in the demand function for cash balances toward smaller real cash balances, shifting the monetary sector curve for P_1 to the position m_1 shown in Figure 36. The resulting new equilibrium, at the point A with price level P_3, involves a lower interest rate than before and a changed mix of consumption and investment. The equilibrium values of the nonmonetary variables and of the rate of interest are no longer independent of events in the monetary sector.

In this model, a shift in monetary policy has no effect on any variable in the system except the price level, as before, because the change in monetary policy does not affect the equilibrium value of real cash balances. (Government bonds, deflated by the price level, might plausibly also appear in the consumption function; in that case even a change in monetary policy will affect the equilibrium values of the rate of interest and other variables. See Chapter 9.)

The real balance effect offers a possible route to overall equilibrium in a system in which the expenditure sector curve at first falls short of the full-employment level of real income even at a zero rate of interest. With this effect, a fall in the price level shifts the expenditure sector curve upward and might eventually shift it far enough to make it reach full-employment real income at a positive rate of interest. However, the existence of the real balance effect is doubtful, and it is even more doubtful that the effect is strong enough to guarantee equilibrium.

4 REAL CASH BALANCES AND PRODUCTION

Whether or not cash balances help determine consumption, they assuredly are a factor of production. Since people willingly hold cash balances at a sacrifice, it can be inferred that cash balances yield equivalent value. Whether or not this value appears in tangible production or comes as a direct yield of satisfaction to households, total product changes when real cash balances change. For example, if the householder had more frequent, smaller receipts and payments for the same income stream, he would have to spend more of what would otherwise be his leisure time making transactions. Also, the householder holds cash balances because of the security they give him against unforeseen contingencies. (Other assets can be sold to meet such contingencies but at an inconvenience and possible loss.) This security, whose value to the householder can be measured by straightforward imputation, is an element of both income and consumption, similar to leisure.

It follows that full-employment real income depends on the monetary sector; it has a different value for each quantity of real cash balances. Real cash balances will appear in the production function, so that it becomes

$$y = f(N,m) \tag{29}$$

The marginal productivity of labor will also depend on this variable, that is,

$$w = f_N(N,m) = \frac{\partial f(N,m)}{\partial N} \tag{30}$$

Hence equilibrium real wages and employment depend on real cash balances, and no longer have a self-contained system. A different equilibrium value of each of the variables in this sector will correspond to each different value of real cash balances.

When a shift in either the expenditure sector or the monetary sector changes equilibrium real cash balances, full-employment real income will also change. This change, to a first approximation, equals the product of the average rate of return on other assets and the change in equilibrium real cash balances. Full-employment real income is no longer a single value, that is, not a single vertical line in Figure 37, but a family of

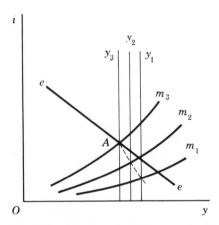

Figure 37

vertical lines. When real cash balances are above their equilibrium level, at a price level P_1, the price level will tend to rise, shifting both the monetary sector curve and full-employment real income to the left. Equilibrium is reached at the higher price level P_3, at which all three sector curves intersect at the same point A. (For simplicity, the expenditure sector function has been drawn as a single curve.) As when real cash balances are in the consumption function, this equilibrium point shifts if a shift in the monetary sector changes the equilibrium value of real cash balances.

Although real cash balances are certainly a factor of production they need not enter the consumption function. Where the income from cash balances is partly imputed and enters into imputed consumption, this need not affect the relation between consumption and income. The consumption imputed from real cash balances will not in general be the fraction b of the total income produced by and imputed from them, but other consumption will bring the aggregate relationships into conformity with the consumption function.

5 CONSUMPTION AND THE RATE OF INTEREST

Although it is generally assumed that consumption depends in some way on the rate of interest, we have ignored its effect for the sake of simplicity. To correct the omission, we write a revised consumption function

$$C = a + b_1 y + b_2 i \tag{31}$$

where b_2 is a constant. The expenditure sector function then becomes

$$y = \frac{a + g_0 + g_1 i + b_2 i}{1 - b} \tag{32}$$

As the rate of interest appears in the investment function, and was therefore already present in the expenditure sector function, the new form (32) of this function is still an equation in two variables, a single curve. (With a real balance effect it would be an equation in three variables, as before.) The slope of the curve, referred to the interest-rate axis, is now the product of the multiplier times the sum of the change in investment and the change in consumption induced by the interest rate.

6 REAL INCOME IN THE INVESTMENT FUNCTION

In the discussion of the investment function in Chapter 2, the shape and position of this function came from business investment opportunities, with business expectations taken as fixed. While business expectations are notoriously unpredictable, they seem to depend in part on the way things are actually going, for example, on the level of current real income. One way to allow for this possibility is to include real income as a variable in the investment function:

$$z = g_0 + g_1 i + g_2 y \tag{33}$$

In this case the investment function becomes a family of curves, as shown in Figure 38, the higher curves corresponding to higher real income.

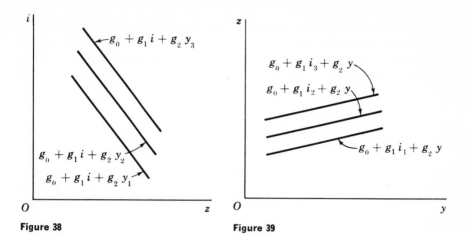

Figure 38   Figure 39

A preferable way to present the function, however, with a view to combining it with the other functions of the expenditure sector, is shown in Figure 39; investment is plotted against income, holding the rate of interest constant along each curve. Viewed in this way, the investment function is fully analogous to the consumption function. So also is the sum of the consumption function and the investment function, total desired expenditure. This curve is shown in Figure 40, cutting the 45° line at the point A. Note that it slopes up more steeply than the consumption function below it, because investment also increases with income.

The two curves are shown for a single real rate of interest i_1; for a different rate of interest, the intersection point will be different. In this

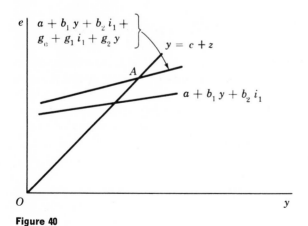

Figure 40

respect, the analytical properties of the system are the same as before; the single equation condensed from the functions of the expenditure sector is one equation in two variables and can be represented as a single curve. Proceeding as before, we have

$$y = \frac{a + g_0 + g_1 i + b_2 i}{1 - b_1 - g_2} \tag{34}$$

There is one respect, however, in which (34) differs markedly from all earlier versions of the expenditure sector curve. Previously the expenditure sector curve necessarily had a negative slope, because $g_1 < 0$ and $b_1 < 1$. In contrast, the slope of (34) can be positive, zero, or negative. Its shift characteristics can also vary in the same way.

The key to the properties of the sector is the multiplier. Consider the effect of a shift in either the consumption or the investment function. Denote the size of the shift for given real income and interest rate by Δx, and note that the effect of a change in real income on real investment (the slope of the relevant curve in Figure 39) is g_2. Taking the difference between the new and old equilibrium values satisfying equation (34), we have

$$\Delta y = \frac{\Delta x}{1 - b_1 - g_2} = k' \Delta x \tag{35}$$

If we define a marginal propensity to spend $s = b_1 + g_2$, the amount of new spending on both consumption and investment induced by a dollar increase in income, we have

$$k' = \frac{1}{1 - s} \tag{36}$$

which, formally speaking, is analogous to k.

Its analogy to k also extends to the characteristics of the expenditure sector curve (34), whose slope is equal to the product of k' times the additional expenditure—consumption plus investment—directly induced by the rate of interest. However, the assurance that $b < 1$ does not assure $s < 1$. It can be seen in equation (35) that if the marginal propensity to invest g_2 is greater than the marginal propensity to save $1 - b$, then k' is negative. No principle of economic behavior assures that this cannot happen. If it does happen, the expenditure sector curve will slope upward rather than downward and will shift in the opposite direction to a shift of any of the functions in the expenditure sector.

A negative multiplier presents special problems of interpretation. If we attempt to derive it in terms of a spending-responding sequence of the type introduced in Chapter 2, section 3, we get an entirely different result. Proceeding as in that section, we have an ultimate change in income Δy, resulting from a shift in expenditure Δx, equal to

$$\Delta y = \Delta x(1 + s + s^2 + s^3 + s^4 + \cdots) \tag{37}$$

If $s > 1$, however, the expression in parentheses does not converge to any finite number but rises without limit as additional powers of s are included. Each round of increased spending in turn provokes a still larger increase, and so on without limit. Looked at in this way, the multiplier is positive and infinite, not negative.

However, the derivation in equations (35) and (36) is a valid case of comparative statics, as is the use of the expenditure sector curve (34) in a model complete with all three sectors, regardless of whether k' as defined in equation (36) is positive, negative, or infinite. The arguments concerning the direction and mechanism of pressure on the price level, and its presumptive tendency to restore overall equilibrium, still apply.

If the expenditure sector curve slopes upward, we can say that the tendency for desired real expenditures to exceed full-employment real income, when the price level is too low, appears to be boundless. This boundless tendency might mean that equilibrium, if attained, is unstable; it depends on our assumptions about dynamic adjustments. Most dynamic models use the sequence approach, which here gives an infinite multiplier when $s > 1$; such a case may nevertheless be tractable if some barrier, such as full employment, modifies the multiplier process after a certain point.[1]

7 THE REAL WAGE RATE IN THE INVESTMENT FUNCTION

A variable not yet considered that almost certainly affects investment is the real wage rate. The rate of profit a business firm can expect on a given investment opportunity will depend on the costs of the resources that will cooperate with the new capital, and the most important of these costs is the cost of labor. The higher the real wage rate, the less profitable the opportunity will be, at a given rate of interest. It follows that when any shift changes the equilibrium real wage rate, the investment function will be shifted. This approach is an alternative to using real income as a variable in this function. We have

$$z = g_0 + g_1 i + g_2 w \tag{38}$$

Accordingly, even if real cash balances are not a variable in the con-

[1] Extensive treatment of cases of this kind appears in J. R. Hicks, *A Contribution to the Theory of the Trade Cycle* (New York, Oxford, Clarendon Press, 1950).

sumption function, the expenditure sector function is a family of curves rather than a single curve, depending on the real wage rate.

Now consider again the effects of a shift in the production function, analyzed in the last section of Chapter 2. There it was assumed that the shift was such as to leave the investment schedule unchanged. Here we shall consider a more general kind of shift. Ordinarily an upward shift in the production function will improve investment opportunities and will increase real wages. Other outcomes are possible but unlikely.

The shifts in the production-employment sector appear in Figure 41(a) and (b). Both the marginal-productivity schedule, in (a), and the

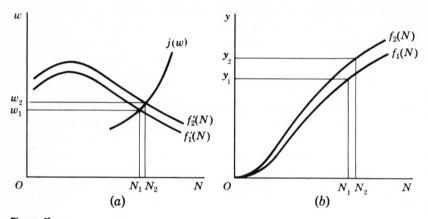

Figure 41

production function, in (b), appear with an upward shift throughout. In this example equilibrium employment increases from N_1 to N_2, the equilibrium real wage rate from w_1 to w_2, and equilibrium real income y_1 to y_2.

The investment function is now subject to two opposite directions of shift: the shift in the production function tends to increase investment opportunities at a given real wage, real income, and rate of interest; but the rise in the real wage tends to reduce real investment, as just indicated. Ordinarily one would expect that the upward shift in the production function will dominate, because technological advance usually does seem to result in substantial new investment, which precedes and helps drive up income and wages. Accordingly, in Figure 42 the expenditure function shifts to the right. A smaller shift to the right is shown for full-employment real income, again a plausible but not certain outcome; in this case the equilibrium of the nonmonetary sectors is moved from the point A to the point B, at which the equilibrium rate of interest is higher than

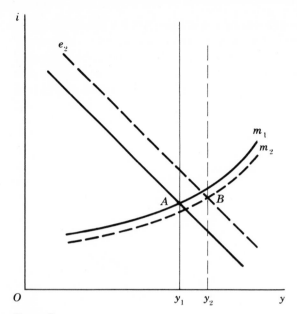

Figure 42

before. As the point B is below the old monetary sector curve, a fall in the price level is required to achieve overall equilibrium, though not so great a fall as was implied in the example at the end of Chapter 2. If investment takes time to increase potential full-employment real income, the effect at first is merely that of an upward shift in the investment schedule, which drives up the rate of interest without increasing equilibrium income.

The direction of change for every variable is in fact uncertain, although probable directions can be indicated for most of them. Real income will almost certainly rise when the production function shifts upward, although a sharply backward-bending supply of labor could conceivably reduce it. The other variables also have probable but uncertain directions of change. The real wage rate, real investment, the interest rate, the nominal quantity of money, and consumption will probably, but not necessarily, rise. The price level may either rise or fall: we expect it to rise at first when the upward shift of investment dominates the picture, but we expect that the new production methods brought in with this investment will lower the prices of the affected goods and services. When their prices fall and their output increases, the general price level will fall, possibly below its old level.

These remarks suggest a two-stage shift. First, the investment schedule shifts upward without any change in full-employment real income. This shift appears in Figure 43(a), which is the same as Figure 28 of Chapter 2. As noted there, the interest rate and the price level rise, while nothing else changes in the real sectors (although if consumption and investment both depend on the interest rate the mix of the two at

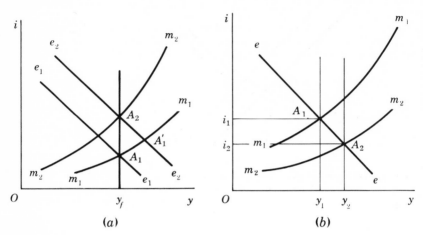

(a)   (b)

Figure 43

the same full-employment real income will change). Then when full-employment real income increases, we have the shifts shown in Figure 43(b), which is the same as Figure 31 of Chapter 2. Now the price level and the interest rate fall, while consumption, investment, and real income all increase, as noted there. Figure 42 is a possible result of combining the two halves of Figure 43.

BIBLIOGRAPHY

Allen, R. G. D.: *Mathematical Analysis for Economists* (London, Macmillan & Co., Ltd., 1938), chap. 14.

Duesenberry et al.: *The Brookings Quarterly Econometric Model of the United States* (Chicago, Rand McNally and Company, 1965).

Haberler, Gottfried: "The General Theory (4)," in Seymour Harris (ed.): *The New Economics* (New York, Alfred A. Knopf, Inc., 1947).

Hicks, J. R.: "Mr. Keynes and the Classics: A Suggested Interpretation," in American Economic Association, *Readings in the Theory of Income Distribution* (New York, McGraw-Hill Book Company, 1946), part IV.

Kaldor, Nicholas: "On the Theory of Capital: A Rejoinder to Professor Knight," *Econometrica*, vol. 6 (1938), p. 163.

Kaldor, Nicholas: "The Recent Controversy on the Theory of Capital," *Econometrica*, vol. 5 (1937), p. 201.

Klein, Lawrence: *The Keynesian Revolution* (New York: The Macmillan Company, 1947).

Knight, Frank H.: "On the Theory of Capital: In Reply to Mr. Kaldor," *Econometrica*, vol. 6 (1938), p. 63.

Lange, Oscar: "The Rate of Interest and the Optimum Propensity to Consume," in American Economic Association, *Readings in Business Cycle Theory* (New York, McGraw-Hill Book Company, 1944).

McKenzie, Lionel: "On Equilibrium in Graham's Model of World Trade and Other Competitive Systems," *Econometrica*, vol. 22 (April, 1954), pp. 147–161.

Metzler, Lloyd: "Wealth, Saving, and the Rate of Interest," *Journal of Political Economy*, vol. 59 (April, 1951), pp. 93–116.

Mueller, M. G. (ed.): *Readings in Macroeconomics* (New York, Holt, Rinehart and Winston, Inc., 1967).

Patinkin, Don: "The Indeterminacy of Absolute Prices in Classical Economic Theory," *Econometrica*, vol. 17 (1949), p. 1.

Patinkin, Don: "The Invalidity of Classical Monetary Theory," *Econometrica*, vol. 19 (1951), p. 135.

Patinkin, Don: *Money, Interest and Prices*, 2d ed. (New York, Harper and Row Publishers, Incorporated, 1962), chaps. 9–15.

Patinkin, Don: "Price Flexibility and Full Employment," in American Economic Association, *Readings in Monetary Theory* (New York, McGraw-Hill Book Company, 1951), chap. 13.

Patinkin, Don: "Relative Prices, Say's Law, and the Demand for Money," *Econometrica*, vol. 16 (1948), p. 135.

Pigou, A. C.: "The Classical Stationary State," *Economic Journal*, vol. 53 (1943), pp. 343–351.

Robertson, Dennis H. (ed.): "A Survey of Modern Monetary Controversy," *Readings in Business Cycle Theory* American Economic Association (Homewood, Illinois, Richard D. Irwin, Inc., 1951), chap. 15.

Samuelson, Paul A.: "The Simple Mathematics of Income Determination," part I, chap. 6 in Lloyd Metzler et al.: *Income Employment and Public Policy* (New York, W. W. Norton and Company, Inc., 1948).

Williams, Harold R. and John D. Huffnagle (eds.): *Macroeconomic Theory: Selected Readings* (New York: Meredith, 1969).

A APPENDIX

MATHEMATICAL APPENDIX TO CHAPTER 3

1 A RISE IN THE MONEY WAGE

We begin with the same equations of the three sectors as we had in Chapter 2.

$$y = \frac{a + g_0 + g_1 i}{1 - b} \tag{21}$$

$$\frac{h(i)}{P} = L(i,y) \tag{22}$$

$$y = f(N_f) = y_f \tag{26}$$

Now if the wage level is arbitrarily increased above the full-employment real wage, where we ignore the supply curve of labor $j(w)$, we have

$$\delta w = \delta\left(\frac{W}{P}\right) > 0 \qquad \delta w = f'' \, \delta N \qquad \text{or} \qquad \delta N = \frac{\delta w}{f''} < 0$$

because in equilibrium $f'' < 0$. Then

$$\delta y = f' \, \delta N = \frac{f'}{f''} \, \delta w < 0 \tag{A-1}$$

The effect of the decline in real income carries into the other sectors as in Chapter 2, and we have from its Mathematical Appendix that

$$\delta P = \frac{h' - PL_i}{L}\, \delta i - \frac{P}{L} L_y\, \delta y$$

$$= \left(\frac{h' - PL_i}{Lkg_1} - \frac{P}{L}L_y\right) \delta y > 0 \tag{A-2}$$

The ultimate change in real wage, for given δW, is

$$\delta w = \delta\left(\frac{W}{P}\right) = \frac{P\,\delta W - W\,\delta P}{P^2} \tag{A-3}$$

Equations (A-1), (A-2), and (A-3) are a set of three independent linear equations in the three variables δw, δy, and δP, and so determine all three as a function of δW. They reflect the feedback to the production-employment sector of the induced rise in the price level, which cancels out part of the real effect of the initial rise in the money wage. But we know that it does not cancel it out completely; if it did $\delta w = 0$ would make $\delta y = 0$ through (A-1), which would imply through (A-2) that δP was also zero, a contradiction. In the final equilibrium the net changes still have the signs indicated by the discussion leading up to (A-1) and (A-2), as can be verified by solving the three equations and evaluating signs. Therefore, raising the money wage above its equilibrium value raises the real wage and the price level, lowers aggregate real income and employment, and raises the interest rate.

2 THE PIGOU EFFECT

Consider now the impact of the real balance effect, or Pigou effect, on the comparative statics of the system. The consumption function becomes

$$c = a + b_1 y + b_2 m$$

and the equation of the expenditure sector changes from (21) to

$$y = \frac{a + g_0 + g_1 i + b_2 m}{1 - b} \tag{28}$$

Equations (22) and (26), for the other two sectors, remain unchanged.

If the consumption function shifts, we have $\delta a \neq 0$, and $\delta y = 0$, as in the simpler system in Chapter 2. Then

$$0 = \frac{\delta a + g_1\, \delta i + b_2\, \delta m}{1 - b}$$

From the demand function for money $m = L(i,y)$ we have

$$\delta m = L_i \, \delta i$$

so that

$$\delta a + g_1 \, \delta i + b_2 L_i \, \delta i = 0$$

or

$$\delta i = - \frac{\delta a}{g_1 + b_2 L_i}$$

Because both terms in the denominator are negative,

$$\delta i > 0 \qquad \text{when } \delta a > 0$$

as in Chapter 2. The term $b_2 L_i$, which did not appear in the corresponding result in the appendix to Chapter 2, increases the absolute value of the denominator, so that δi is smaller than before. The Pigou effect dampens the effect of the expenditure shift on the interest rate.

For the price-level effect of the shift in consumption, we have from (22)

$$h' \, \delta i = P L_i \, \delta i + L \, \delta P$$

and

$$\frac{\delta P}{P} = \frac{1}{L} \left(\frac{h'}{P} - L_i \right) \delta i = \frac{\delta M^S - \delta M^D}{M} > 0$$

when $\delta a > 0$. The price level rises as in Chapter 2, by just enough to eliminate the initial excess supply of cash. However, because the rise in the rate of interest is smaller, the excess supply and the price rise are also smaller.

If the supply of money shifts in this sytem $\delta h \neq 0$, we still have $\delta y = 0$, and

$$g_1 \, \delta i + b_2 \, \delta m = 0$$

As before

$$\delta m = L_i \, \delta i$$

so that

$$(g_1 + b_2 L_i) \, \delta i = 0$$

Inasmuch as both terms in parentheses are negative, it follows that

$$\delta i = 0$$

From (22) we have

$$h' \, \delta i + \delta h = P L_i \, \delta i + L \, \delta P$$

and because $\delta i = 0$,

$$\delta h = L \, \delta P$$

or

$$\frac{\delta P}{P} = \frac{\delta h}{LP} = \frac{\delta h}{h}$$

as in Chapter 2. The price level still increases in the same proportion as the money supply, and the real variables of the system are unaffected.

However, we get new results for a shift in the demand curve for money, $\delta L \neq 0$. As in the case of the supply shift

$$g_1 \, \delta i + b_2 \, \delta m = 0$$

but now

$$\delta m = L_i \, \delta i + \delta L$$

giving

$$\delta i = \frac{-b_2 \, \delta L}{g_1 + b_2 L_i} \tag{A-4}$$

which has the same sign as δL. If the demand for money shifts upward (downward), the interest rate rises (falls). In Chapter 2 only the price level was affected by this demand shift. Now for the price level change we obtain from (22)

$$h' \, \delta i = PL_i \, \delta i + P \, \delta L + L \, \delta P$$

which gives

$$\delta P = \frac{(h' - PL_i) \, \delta i - P \, \delta L}{L} \tag{A-5}$$

Substituting (A-4) into (A-5), we have

$$\delta P = \frac{b_2(h' - PL_i) + P(g_1 + b_2 L_i)}{-(g_1 + b_2 L_i)L} \, \delta L$$

$$= \frac{b_2 h' + g_1 P}{-(g_1 + b_2 L_i)L} \, \delta L \tag{A-6}$$

The sign of (A-6), when $\delta L > 0$, is the sign of the numerator, which contains the positive expression $b_2 h'$ plus the negative term $g_1 P$. Thus the price level can either rise or fall. The expression $b_2 h'$ reflects increased consumption due to the increased cash supplied through the movement along the supply curve, whereas $g_1 P$ reflects reduced investment, both for a given rise in the interest rate. If the consumption effect is larger, the price level rises, whereas if the investment effect is larger (in absolute value) it falls. Note that if the supply of money is a fixed quantity h_0, then $h' = 0$, and the price level necessarily falls.

3 REAL BALANCES IN THE PRODUCTION FUNCTION

Consider now the comparative statics of a system with real balances in the production function. For the production-employment sector we have

$$y = f(N,m) \tag{29}$$
$$w = f_N(N,m) \tag{30}$$
$$N = j(w) \tag{25}$$

Whenever a shift changes equilibrium real balances, we have

$$\delta y = f_N \, \delta N + f_m \, \delta m$$
$$\delta w = f_{NN} \, \delta N + f_{mN} \, \delta m$$
$$\delta N = j' \, \delta w$$

Solving these for δy gives

$$\delta y = \frac{j' f_N f_{Nm} + f_m - j' f_m f_{NN}}{1 - j' f_{NN}} \, \delta m \tag{A-7}$$

whose sign is indeterminate if the sign of j' is unknown or negative. When the sign of δy is indeterminate, so are the signs of all other variables. They can be determined only by using numerical values of the parameters and derivatives of the system. Moreover, even having the sign of δy is little help.

Consider the following case. If $j' = 0$, that is, if the supply of labor is fixed, (A-7) simplifies to

$$\delta y = f_m \, \delta m \tag{A-8}$$

which has the same sign as δm, because the marginal productivity of cash f_m is positive. Moreover, at the equilibrium of the firm the law of variable proportions applies, so that we have $f_{Nm} > 0$ and $f_{NN} < 0$. Therefore if $j' > 0$ all the terms in the numerator and denominator of (A-7) are positive, so that in this case also δy has the same sign as δm. It has the same sign also if the supply curve of labor bends backward only slightly, that is, if j' is near zero though negative.

To illustrate our problem, we will use (A-8) and the case of a shift in the consumption function $\delta a \neq 0$.

Now from (21) we have

$$\delta y = kg_1 \,\delta i + k \,\delta a$$

and from the demand curve for money we have

$$\delta m = L_i \,\delta i + L_y \,\delta y$$

Using (A-8), we obtain

$$f_m \,\delta m = kg_1 \,\delta i + k \,\delta a$$

and

$$\delta m = L_i \,\delta i + L_y f_m \,\delta m \qquad \text{(A-9)}$$

$$= \frac{L_i \,\delta i}{1 - L_y f_m} \qquad \text{(A-10)}$$

(A-9) and (A-10) combine to give

$$\frac{f_m L_i}{1 - L_y f_m} \,\delta i = kg_1 \,\delta i + k \,\delta a$$

and

$$\delta i = \frac{(1 - L_y f_m)k \,\delta a}{f_m L_i - (1 - L_y f_m)kg_1} \qquad \text{(A-11)}$$

The sign of (A-11) is indeterminate without specific numerical values for the derivatives. Whenever

$$L_y f_m < 1$$

the denominator of (A-11) can be of either sign.

For very small values of f_m

$$\lim_{f_m \to 0} \delta i = -\frac{\delta a}{g_1}$$

which is the value we obtained for δi in the appendix to Chapter 2. Equilibrium of the firm implies

$$f_m = i$$

which is a small number, e.g., 6 percent per year. Moreover, the difference between the present model and that in Chapter 2 centers on

$$\delta y = f_m \,\delta m$$

whose size also depends on the size of δm. In every country total real balances are a fraction of annual income, and the changes in these balances in response to ordinary changes in the variables of the system are a small fraction of their total. This compounding of fractions suggests intuitively that real balance effects are small enough to disregard in the comparative statics of the system.

However, the above reasoning fails in case of positive expected inflation, discussed below in Chapter 4. In that case the money rate of interest is

$$i = r + \frac{\Delta P^e}{P} \qquad (39)$$

which can rise to any height, and the comparative statics of the system becomes unpredictable. Thus the dynamic equilibrium described in Chapter 4 can be complicated by perverse (and possibly dynamically unstable) properties of the system.

One feature still remains, however. If the supply of money shifts by a given proportion the price level changes in the same proportion, as it does in all the other models we have considered, with no change in the real variables. This can be verified by supposing it to be true and then checking that the differentials reconcile.

4 CONCLUSION

When we depart from the simple national income model of Chapter 2 to add new variables in the various functions its simple comparative statics disappears, except for changes in the supply of money. For these changes, the price level always changes in the same proportion, provided that expectations of price stability or inflation don't change. But for all other changes the signs of the changes in dependent variables are unpredictable without specific knowledge of the parameters and derivatives of the system. These uncertainties also apply to the last two models presented in Chapter 3, in which real income and real wages appear in the investment function.

4

THE PRICE LEVEL
AND
INFLATION

1 INTRODUCTION

Chapters 2 and 3 provide us with a theory of the price level, but
not with a theory of inflation or deflation. We have found repeatedly
that each complete model of the economy has a solution for the price
level, if the equations of the model have an overall solution. Moreover,
shifts in particular equations of the model imply price level changes that
can be specified exactly in terms of the parameters of the model. However, all the analysis depended on the stated assumption that households
and firms expect the price level to remain unchanged, regardless whether
it has recently changed or not. It would be misleading to analyze inflation
in these terms. Instead we shall introduce expected change in the price
level as a variable.

With the assumption that households and firms expect no change in
the price level, we found that the price level changes in the same proportion as the quantity of money for every shift in the supply of money.
The equilibrium real rate of interest is invariably unaffected by shifts in
this supply,[1] and therefore the equilibrium quantity of real cash balances

[1] Except when government bonds are also a variable in the system. See the last
section of Chapter 9.

is unchanged. Any shift that leaves this quantity unchanged must lead to equiproportionate changes in the quantity of money and the price level, if they change at all. This statement in itself provides a primitive theory of inflation, identified historically with the quantity theory of money: the price level changes in the same proportion as the quantity of money, if other things are equal.

Dropping the assumption that households and firms expect no change in the price level leads to the conclusion that the price level does not, in general, change in the same proportion as the quantity of money. Whether it affects the comparative statics of the national income model in any other way depends on whether the model includes a real balance effect. If it has no real balance effect, price level expectations affect only the price level; if it has a real balance effect, they also affect the real variables of the model. Taking account of these effects provides a theory of inflation that is as nearly complete as is our theory of real income; but both suffer from the lack of a reliable theory of dynamics.

2 EXPECTED CHANGE IN THE PRICE LEVEL AS A VARIABLE

Expected change in the price level, like the price level itself, can be left out of the real equations of the model and confined to the monetary sector. Employment, real wages, real investment, real consumption, and real income can all be analyzed without reference either to the price level or to expectations about it. Superficially this statement might seem false. Won't firms invest more, and hire more labor, if they expect the price level to rise; and won't households consume more and save less? Not necessarily. Firms will invest more if they expect the price level to rise and they do not have to pay a correspondingly higher rate of interest, or its equivalent, for the capital to invest. They will hire more labor if the price level rises more than the wage level. But whether they have to pay a higher rate of interest depends on expectations in the money market; if they do have to pay a rate of interest that rises by just the same amount as the expected rise in the price level, they have no incentive to invest more than they would otherwise. Also, whether money wages rise as fast as the price level depends on the speed of adjustment of the labor market; for present purposes, it is best to assume that wages neither lead nor lag the price level, so that changes in the price level and changes in the expected rate of change of the price level have no effect on employment. Although this assumption disagrees with historical experience, to some extent, dropping it would involve dynamics, which we defer until a later chapter.

To illustrate the idea of the independence of investment from price-level expectations, consider a firm that borrows no funds at fixed interest, so that all its capital is equity capital. If all prices and wages rise in the same proportion, profits rise in this proportion also compared to what they otherwise would be, so that real profits are unaffected. Apart from real balance effects, this firm has no incentive to invest differently or do anything else differently if it expects prices to rise than if it doesn't. If it has shares that are traded, these have the same present value whether inflation is expected or is not, in terms of current relative prices. The expected yield on these shares is the real rate of interest, adjusted for risk, and is independent of expected changes in the price level.

Similar reasoning applies to the household. The savings of the household have the same real prospective yield for every expected change in the price level if the household buys shares in the above firm, or if the household invests in other ways that are unaffected in real terms by changes in the price level. Therefore the household has no incentive to change its choice between consumption and saving when it changes its expectation about changes in the price level.

The one inevitable effect of an expected change in the price level concerns bonds and other obligations fixed in money terms. With each 1 percent rise in the price level a bond, any other money obligation, and a cash balance lose 1 percent in real value. If the prospective holder compares any of these assets with a corporate share when he expects a 1 percent annual rise in the price level, he needs no extra yield on the share but an extra 1 percent annual yield on each of the money obligations to maintain the same expected real yield on each. In the case of the cash balance, all he can do is reduce his balance until its marginal convenience yield rises by 1 percent, to match the annual loss of 1 percent in real value. The borrower who issues bonds or other money obligations will be willing to pay the extra 1 percent if he also expects that annual price rise; his real yield on investment is the same as before, and he can afford to pay the same real yield on his obligations. Thus a rise in the rate of interest on bonds and other money obligations just equal to the expected rate of inflation satisfies both borrowers and lenders. When they compare these obligations with either shares or real assets, their choice will then be what it was without the expectation of inflation.

We can represent the adjustment to expected inflation by a difference between the money rate of interest and the real rate equal to the expected rate of inflation. The real rate enters into all the equations of the system except those of the monetary sector. Bonds and other money obligations involve only the monetary sector, in which the money rate of interest enters as a variable.

3   INFLATION SEMIDYNAMICS

Suppose that the prevailing expectation in the community is a certain rate of price rise per period $\Delta P^e/P$. Although we disregard how people form their expectations, we assume that when the expectation is fulfilled it doesn't change; that is, expectations are in equilibrium when a constant actual rate of price rise equals the expected rate. With this expectation, lenders charge higher interest and borrowers are willing and able to pay the extra interest. Because borrowers and lenders agree, the market rate of interest per period will rise by the amount of the expected rate of price rise, as we noted above. Hence

$$i = r + \frac{\Delta P^e}{P} \tag{39}$$

where i is the money rate of interest and r is the real rate, the expected real productivity of investment.

We have seen that the investment function is properly expressed in terms of the real rate of interest and is independent of the expected rate of inflation.

$$z = g_0 + g_1\left(i - \frac{\Delta P^e}{P}\right) = g_0 + g_1 r \tag{40}$$

Therefore the expenditure sector curve also depends only on the real rate.

$$y = \frac{a + g_0 + g_1 r}{1 - b} \tag{41}$$

For the holder of cash balances, however, it is the money rate of interest that matters. He sacrifices the money rate when he holds money instead of bonds, where both will lose real value due to inflation. Holding cash rather than stocks or real assets implies the same sacrifice, made up of their real yield plus the loss of real value of the cash due to inflation. Thus the demand for cash balances will be a function of the money rate of interest as given before.

$$m = L(i,y) = L\left(r + \frac{\Delta P^e}{P}, y\right) \tag{19}$$

We assume that the supply of money also is the same function of the money rate of interest as in our previous analysis, except that inflationary equilibrium requires that this function shift to the right at the expected (and actual) rate of inflation. We have

$$m = \frac{1}{P} h_t(i) = \frac{1}{P} h_0\left(r + \frac{\Delta P^e}{P}\right) \exp\left(t\frac{\Delta P^e}{P}\right) \tag{20}$$

Consider a situation in which the expected rate of inflation is zero, and in which the system is in overall equilibrium. In this case $r = i$, and we can draw the expenditure sector curve in terms of i using this substitution, as shown in Figure 44. Now if expectations change, so that a positive rate of inflation is expected, i becomes greater than r; since the expenditure sector is defined in terms of r, which doesn't change, this shifts the expenditure sector curve upward in terms of i. That is, for each value of r the level of real income that is consistent with equilibrium in the expenditure sector is the same as before, and this value of r corresponds to a value of i higher by the amount of the expected rate of inflation. The upward shift is constant along the length of the curve, as shown in the shift from e_1 to e_2 in Figure 44. Meanwhile the monetary sector curve m_1 is the same as before, in terms of i. The price level must rise to restore equilibrium; it must rise enough to shift the monetary sector curve upward to a position m_2 such that it will pass through the new overall equilibrium point A_2.

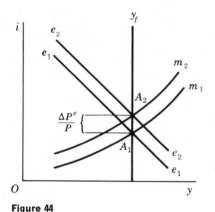

Figure 44   **Figure 45**

Thus the mere *expectation* of inflation causes the price level to rise above what it would be if no inflation were expected. Another way to see this point is to look directly at the monetary sector itself. In Figure 45, the monetary sector is in equilibrium given that income is at the full-employment level, at the initial money rate of interest equal to r. Expected inflation does not alter the real rate at which the expenditure sector reaches full-employment real income. In effect, it affects the monetary sector alone, and thus does not change the equilibrium values of the (real) rate of interest or the other variables in the nonmonetary sectors. Therefore for overall equilibrium the money rate of interest must rise above its previous value r by the full amount of the expected rate of inflation, to $i_1 = r + \Delta P^e/P$. This will occur when the price level rises from P_1 to P_2, shifting the supply curve of money from $(1/P_1)h(i)$ to $(1/P_2)h(i)$; its intersection with $L(i,y_f)$ is shifted from the point A_1 to A_2, raising the money rate of interest by the required amount.

The rise in the price level from P_1 to P_2 restores equilibrium throughout the system in the sense that this was understood in Chapter 2. For equilibrium of expectations we now have the additional condition, however, that the rate of price change per period shall equal the expected rate of price change.

In section 12 of Chapter 2 we found that a change in monetary policy changes the price level in the same proportion as that of the shift in the supply of money, measured at the going rate of interest. (The example considered involved a reduction in the money supply, but the argument applies equally to an increase.) Thus for the system to be in inflationary equilibrium in the present example, the money supply must increase at the same proportionate rate as the public expects the price level to increase. For example, if the monetary authority is increasing the money supply at a rate of 10 percent per period, prices will be rising at 10 percent per period, and if this agrees with the prevailing expectation, whose separate effect on the price level (that is, the increase from P_1 to P_2) has already been realized, the system will be in complete equilibrium.

To show this shift, we let $h_0(i)$ be the nominal supply of money at the starting point for measuring time, $t = 0$, and $h_t(i)$ the nominal supply of money at time t. Expressing the expected rate of inflation as a force rate, we have the equilibrium condition

$$h_t(i) = h_0(i) \exp\left(t\frac{\Delta P^e}{P}\right)$$

$$= h_0(i)e^{(t\,\Delta P^e/P)} \tag{42}$$

as we noted above when revising equation (20).

It is important to understand the two separate causes of a rise in the price level, each fundamentally different from the other. The expectation of inflation per se produces a rise in the price level, a once-for-all rise to be maintained but not repeated. In contrast, the price rise associated with the increase in the quantity of money must proceed continuously to maintain equilibrium. The total price rise after any interval of time has two components, one proportional to the increase in the quantity of money, the other a jump in the price level that will be held but not repeated as long as expectations of further inflation remain unchanged.

This analysis implies that in the transition from an equilibrium with no change in prices, as expected, to an equilibrium in which prices and the quantity of money are increasing at a steady rate, as expected, the overall increase in the price level will be proportionately *greater* than the increase in the quantity of money. Conversely, when the rate of inflation stops or slows down, with a downward adjustment of expectations, the transition will produce a proportionately *smaller* increase in the price level than in the quantity of money.

$$\frac{\Delta P^a}{P} = 0$$

to

$$\frac{\Delta P^a}{P} > 0$$

These results are helpful for avoiding some common errors in the interpretation of actual inflations. First, it is sometimes said that the expectation of inflation by itself can generate an inflation; expecting their cash balances to lose real value, people will try to spend all their cash for real assets, driving all prices up without limit. However, we have seen that the expectation of inflation generates only a single limited rise in the price level; it produces neither a continuing inflation nor a flight from the currency. People are willing to hold some cash balances even at a high expected sacrifice, so their attempt to buy real assets will stop after a certain predictable rise in the price level.

A more subtle argument along these lines is based on self-fulfilling expectations: expectations could be so sensitive to actual changes in the price level as to create an explosive movement through feedback effects. Although possible in principle, this extreme case has never happened in practice, even in the greatest hyperinflation.

Second, observers of an actual severe inflation often argue that since the price level has risen proportionately more than the quantity of money, the rise in the quantity of money cannot have been the "cause" of the inflation. On the contrary, it is argued, since the price rise has been proportionately larger than the increase in the quantity of money, there is a "shortage" of money, and if anything the quantity of money should be increased even more. We have seen, however, that this disproportionate rise in prices is precisely what would be expected in the transition to expectations of inflation. Finding that their cash balances are losing value and will continue to do so, households and firms hasten to spend to reduce them, driving prices up even more. If the monetary authority responds to this situation by increasing the money supply and hence the price level even faster, in due course expectations will adjust to the higher inflation, equilibrium real cash balances will fall, and thus the "shortage" will get worse. We have the paradox that a more rapid rate of increase in the money supply causes a reduction in real cash balances, while a smaller rate of increase causes an increase in real cash balances.

4 AGGREGATE INCOME EFFECTS OF INFLATION AND DEFLATION

Introducing an expectation of change in the price level, as we did in the preceding section in connection with inflation, provides us with an additional theoretical case in the analysis of overall equilibrium. To evaluate it we must first examine real balance effects on the real income of households and on aggregate real income.

Under our assumptions, inflation has no effect on equilibrium real income. It is true that the holder of cash suffers a continuing loss of real income from the loss of real value of that cash, analogous to a tax on the holding on cash balances. He pays this tax by diverting part of his income to enlarging his nominal cash balance, to maintain its desired real value. Somewhere else in the economy there is an offsetting gain, however; the monetary authority and the banks are creating the additional money that each individual is adding to his nominal cash balances, and this money creation is income to someone.

For example, the government may create new money to finance expenditures that would otherwise be financed by taxation. If so, the typical private taxpayer has a smaller regular tax burden to offset the attrition of his cash balances. Alternatively, the commercial banking system may create some or all of the new money that feeds the inflation. Here, the commercial banks' depositors will directly receive the proceeds of the money creation, if the banks pay a competitively determined rate of interest on their deposits; if they do not the banks themselves will receive it, sometimes passing it on to their borrowers by failing to charge competitive interest on their loans.[1] In this case income is transferred from holders of cash balances in general to the banks or their borrowers. In any case aggregate real income is unchanged, and the real equilibrium of the system is undisturbed.

Similar remarks apply to an equilibrium in steady deflation, if it doesn't go too fast. If the system as a whole would otherwise be in equilibrium, the emergence of an expectation of deflation coinciding with the destruction of money at the appropriate rate can also permit a state of equilibrium. To remain strictly analogous to the inflationary case the rate of deflation must be less than the real rate of interest, so that the money rate of interest remains positive. If so, the equilibrium values of the variables in the nonmonetary sectors are unaffected, as in the inflationary case.

---

[1] If the banks charge competitive interest, that is, $r + \Delta P^e/P$, on their loans, their profits will rise by $\Delta P^e/P$ times their loans, which is just the rate of bank money creation. Paying interest on deposits or charging lower interest on loans would transfer part of this extra profit to someone else.

The results change, however, if the rate of deflation is greater than the real rate of interest. Here the formula given in the preceding section for the money rate of interest,

$$i = r + \frac{\Delta P^e}{P} \tag{39}$$

would be negative if r was unchanged. We have ruled out a negative i. Equilibrium will therefore be possible only with a big enough rise in r to permit positive interest on money loans.

If there is a rise in the real rate r, from r_1 to r_2, the equilibrium of the nonmonetary sectors is disturbed, as shown in Figure 46. Expenditure falls to y_2, below full-employment real income. A cumulative deflationary spiral and economic collapse may result.

However, consumption expenditures could come to the rescue. We have seen that when conditions in the monetary sector imply a level of expenditure below full-employment real income, the price level will fall. In the present problem this means that the price level will fall faster than it otherwise would, that is, faster than the rate at which the monetary authority is destroying money. When the public expects faster deflation, it is no longer true that the gain to holders of cash balances from the expected fall in the price level is fully offset by the loss to those who are destroying money: there is a net aggregate gain from the expected increase in real cash balances that results from the excess of the rate of price fall over the rate of destruction of money. The recipients of this expected gain will treat it as any other form of income and will increase their consumption. The accrual of real cash balances is of

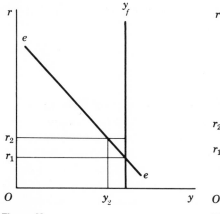

Figure 46

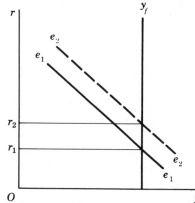

Figure 47

itself an addition to their wealth, and they will want to increase their consumption (reduce their other additions to wealth) by the marginal propensity to consume times this accrual rather than let it all be added to wealth.

If we leave the monetary accrual out of measured real income, for simplicity of presentation, the effect of this increase in consumption is to shift the expenditure sector curve to the right by the product of the multiplier times the directly induced increase in consumption, as shown in Figure 47. If the shift is just large enough, from e_1 to e_2, to move the intersection of the expenditure sector curve with full-employment real (nonmonetary) income to the interest rate r_2, the system will be in overall equilibrium at the rate of deflation that corresponds to r_2.

Of course for each rate of deflation there will be a different real rate, such as r_2, and different shift, such as from e_1 to e_2, and these will not in general match each other at full-employment real income. Overall equilibrium will occur only at a rate of deflation at which they do match, as in Figure 47. Such an equilibrium can always be found, since there is necessarily a limit below which investment cannot fall regardless of the real rate of interest, while there is no limit to the amount of expenditure that can be induced by deflation.

These remarks apply regardless of the real rate of interest, if any, at which the system would be in equilibrium with a stable expected price level. They are especially pertinent, however, to the cases outlined above in which no equilibrium exists for a stable price level: that of the liquidity trap and that of insufficient expenditure at a zero real rate of interest. Each of these cases implies an unlimited tendency for the price level to fall without any destruction of money. By the reasoning just given, overall equilibrium can be found instead at an equilibrium rate of deflation, provided that expectations adjust to it.

5 ORDINARY REAL BALANCE EFFECTS

We have seen that when there is no real balance effect in any of the real equations of the system, the real equilibrium of the system is unaffected by expected inflation. The equilibrium values of the real rate of interest, investment, consumption, income, and so on are all the same as without expected inflation. However, the rise in the money rate of interest with expected inflation reduces the equilibrium value of real cash balances. Therefore the real equilibrium will change if there is a real balance effect in the expenditure sector or in the production-employment sector.

Moreover, the outcome differs according to where the real balance effect is.

If there is a real balance effect on consumption, the fall in equilibrium real balances, due to expected inflation, shifts the expenditure function downward. It now intersects full-employment real income at a lower real interest rate than before, and the equilibrium money rate exceeds the new real rate, not the old, by the expected rate of inflation. Therefore the money rate of interest rises by less than the expected rate of inflation. Figure 48 represents this case. The pre-inflation equilibrium

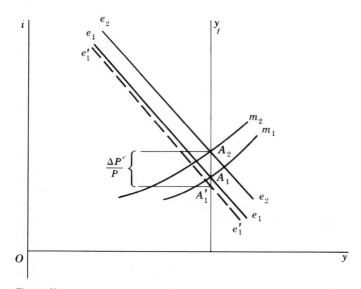

Figure 48

is at the point A_1, where m_1 and e_1 intersect y_f. With the fall in equilibrium real balances associated with expected inflation, e_1 shifts downward to e_1' in terms of the real rate of interest and shifts upward to e_2 in terms of the money rate of interest. The intersection of e_1' with y_f is at A_1', and the expected rate of inflation is the vertical distance between A_2 and A_1'. The decline in real cash balances shifts m_1 upward to m_2, to intersect y_f at the new equilibrium point A_2.

If there is no real balance effect on consumption, but there is one in the production function, the fall in equilibrium real balances lowers full employment real income (where we assume that the direct effect exceeds any opposite indirect effect through employment). In this case, shown in Figure 49, the money rate of interest rises by more than the

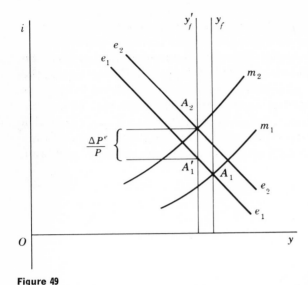

Figure 49

expected rate of inflation. Full-employment real income drops from y_f to y_f', while the expenditure sector curve remains at e_1 in terms of the real rate of interest and rises to e_2 in terms of the money rate of interest. e_2 intersects y_f' at A_2, while e_1 intersects y_f' at A_1'. At this lower real income the money rate of interest must exceed the new real rate by the expected rate of inflation, so that this expected rate is the gap between A_2 and A_1'. A_1' is higher than A_1, so the new money rate of interest is higher than the pre-inflation rate by more than the expected rate of inflation, and the new real rate is higher than the pre-inflation one.

6 MONOPOLY AND INFLATION

In Chapter 3 we found that if legislation, or monopoly power in unions, raised the general wage level in money terms there would be a less than proportionate rise in the price level, a less than proportionate rise in real wages, and a fall in employment. (This analysis assumed no shift in the investment schedule.) There would be inflation only in the form of a once-for-all rise in the price level, not a continuing rise, unless the monetary authority and the wage-setting mechanism worked at cross purposes.

A directly opposite conclusion applies to business monopoly. If universal monopoly should suddenly develop, it might appear that it would raise the price level. However, to draw this conclusion would be to indulge in a fallacy of composition. Although monopoly raises prices for particular products higher than they would be under competition, monopoly need not raise the price level. If full-employment real income, the consumption function, and the investment schedule were all to remain unshifted by the sudden appearance of monopoly, the equilibrium real rate of interest and real cash balances would be unchanged. Therefore the equilibrium price level would not change. Introducing monopoly would lower the marginal value product of labor, and therefore the equilibrium real wage; this fall in real wage would come about through a fall in the money wage. Moreover, the appearance of monopoly would most likely lower the investment schedule, because the marginal value product of capital would also drop; if so, the equilibrium real rate of interest would fall, the equilibrium level of real cash balances would rise, and so the equilibrium price level would *fall*.

Monopoly in product markets combined with a competitive labor market implies as potentially flexible a price level as we would have under competition, except for possible differences in dynamics. If monopolists started to raise the price level, expecting (profitable) declines in output and employment as a result, money wages would fall until equilibrium was restored in the labor market. The fall in money wages would lower the monopolists' marginal-cost curves, making it profitable for them to reduce prices to increase output and employment. This process would continue until full-employment real income was restored. As a result, income would be redistributed in favor of the monopolists, and real wages would decline, but the price level would not increase if the new equilibrium in the labor market implied the old levels of output and employment. As just noted, the price level would fall, not rise, if the monopolists lowered their investment schedule.

In contrast, the appearance of universal monopoly in the labor market would reduce the full-employment level of real income because of conscious choice to that effect by suppliers of labor. When they raise money wages, output is squeezed back by the pinch between costs and demand, so that the reduction in output means a rise in prices, not a fall. The system moves to a new equilibrium at a higher price level and a lower output level.

The appearance of universal monopoly in both product and labor markets is sometimes described as different power groups trying to get more, in total, than the entire national product. But it has the same effects as does monopoly in the labor market: the price level rises and output falls, once-for-all. Our analysis in Chapter 3 showed that this monopoly (or a rise in money wages for any other reason) changes the equilibrium to a new one at a higher price level, but cannot by itself account for a continuing inflation.

When a rise in the price level follows a period of falling or stable prices, the rise sets off loose talk about cost-push, "sellers' inflation," monopolistic price manipulation, and so on. In such cases no one provides any evidence that the amount of monopoly has increased, or that incentives in price-setting and wage-setting have changed in any relevant way. But nevertheless, suppose it is so. The inexorable consequence of such influences, if they succeed by themselves in raising the price level, is that output will fall.

It doesn't happen. In one inflationary upswing after another, output and employment have grown, not fallen. Our monetary analysis has shown that with output holding at a given full-employment level, the price level and the quantity of money increase in the same proportion. Moreover, if the equilibrium money rate of interest does not change, when full-employment output grows the quantity of money must increase to satisfy the resulting increased demand, as well as to match the increase in the price level. For the rise in prices to continue without a rise in unemployment and a decline in output, the quantity of money must rise. (How much it must rise depends on what happens to expectations for the price level.)

In fact, this point is hardly ever disputed. If the monetary authority held monetary growth to what is needed to sustain full-employment output at stable prices, no one argues that both the price level and output would keep rising. However, they sometimes argue that the monetary authority must go along with the price rise, by expanding the money stock, or cause a recession.

We should note that when the money rate of interest has risen because of expected inflation, as happens whenever inflation has continued for some time, getting it back down and adjusting to a new equilibrium may well involve a recession. Indeed, every time a boom ends, even with stable prices during the boom, there is a recession; that follows almost by definition. And an upswing of prices has not as a rule been stopped without also ending the boom and bringing on a recession.

That is painful, so it is tempting to look for another "cause" of the rise in the price level than the growth of the quantity of money. If only the villains who are raising prices or wages would stop it, the inflation could be ended without a recession, so the reasoning often goes. The trouble is that as long as the money supply keeps increasing at an inflationary rate, the "villains" don't stop.

Some of the confusion surrounding these matters is due to our poor understanding of macrodynamics, especially the dynamics of the price level. Prices do sometimes start rising in the midst of unemployment or keep rising after a boom ends and unemployment rises. It is tempting to look for a scapegoat. However, we shall see in Chapter 11 that other explanations are possible, and that the data consistently fit the other explanations better than they do the villain theory. The analysis of the present chapter suggests that we should expect this result.

BIBLIOGRAPHY

Attiyeh, Yossef: "Wage-price Spiral Versus Demand Inflation: United States, 1949–1957" (unpublished Ph.D. dissertation, Chicago, 1959).

Bailey, Martin J.: "The Welfare Cost of Inflationary Finance," *Journal of Political Economy*, vol. 64 (1956), p. 98.

Bronfenbrenner, Martin, and Franklyn D. Halzman: "Survey of Inflation Theory," *The American Economic Review*, vol. 53 (1963), p. 593.

Cagan, Philip: "The Monetary Dynamics of Hyperinflation," in Milton Friedman (ed.): *Studies in the Quantity Theory of Money* (Chicago, University of Chicago Press, 1956), p. 25.

Christenson, C. L.: "Variations in the Inflationary Force of Bargaining," *American Economic Review Supplement*, vol. 44 (1954), p. 347.

Eisner, Robert: "On Growth Models and the Neo-Classical Resurgence," *The Economic Journal*, vol. 68 (December, 1958), pp. 707–721.

Friedman, Milton: "Discussion of the Inflationary Gap," *Essays in Positive Economics* (Chicago, The University of Chicago Press, 1953).

Lewis, H. G.: *Unionism and Relative Wages in the United States* (Chicago, The University of Chicago Press, 1963).

Mundell, Robert A.: "Growth, Stability, and Inflationary Finance," *Journal of Political Economy*, vol. 73 (1965), pp. 97–109.

Phelps, E. S. (ed.): *Microeconomic Foundations of Employment and Inflation Theory* (New York, W. W. Norton & Company, Inc., 1969).

Rees, Albert: "Postwar Wage Determination in the Basic Steel Industry," *American Economic Review*, vol. 41 (1951), p. 389.

Rees, Albert: "Discussion," *American Economic Supplement*, vol. 44 (1954), p. 363.

Samuelson, Paul A., and Robert M. Solow: "Problem of Achieving and Maintaining a Stable Price Level—Analytical Aspects of Anti-Inflation Policy," *American Economic Review Supplement*, vol. 50 (1960), pp. 177–194.

Schultze, Charles L.: "Recent Inflation in the United States," Study #1, Joint Economic Committee (September, 1959).

Slichter, Summer H.: "Do the Wage-Fixing Arrangements in the American Labor Market Have an Inflationary Bias?" *American Economic Review Supplement*, vol. 44 (1954), p. 322.

5

ELEMENTS OF GROWTH THEORY AND MACRODYNAMICS

1 INTRODUCTION

Net investment is nearly always positive, adding to the capital stock; the population grows, and technology improves; so full-employment real income rises steadily. Consumption and investment must rise steadily, to maintain full employment and full resource use. Models of the movement of macroequilibrium over time usually include these features.

To represent these relationships we show the capital stock K in the production function:

$$y = f(N,K) \tag{43}$$

Then if we use an overdot to represent a time derivative, for example

$$\dot{y} = \frac{dy}{dt}$$

we have

$$\dot{y} = f_N \dot{N} + f_K \dot{K} + \dot{f}(N,K)$$

and with competition we have

$$\dot{y} = \frac{w}{p} \dot{N} + rz + \dot{f}(N,K)$$

where $\dot{f}(N,K)$ denotes technological advance (growth not explained by labor force growth and investment). Suppose that investment, the increasing labor force, and technology combine to produce a constant proportionate rate of growth ρ,

$$\dot{y} = \rho y \tag{44}$$

We shall see in the next chapter that a secular rise in income leads to a greater rise in consumption than that caused by an equal temporary upward fluctuation in income: consumption rises to maintain a constant share b^* of the secular rise of income

$$c = b^* y_f \tag{45}$$

To make this relationship hold constantly, consumption must have this same share of growth of income and so must also grow at the rate ρ.

$$\dot{c} = b^* \dot{y} = b^*(\rho y) = \rho(b^* y) = \rho c \tag{46}$$

Investment must then also grow at this rate.

$$\begin{aligned} z &= y - c \\ \dot{z} &= \dot{y} - \dot{c} = \rho y - \rho c \\ &= \rho(y - c) = \rho z \end{aligned} \tag{47}$$

The solutions of equations (44), (46), and (47), showing each variable as a function of time, are

$$\begin{aligned} y_t &= y_0 e^{\rho t} \\ c_t &= c_0 e^{\rho t} \\ z_t &= z_0 e^{\rho t} \end{aligned} \tag{48}$$

where y_0, c_0, and z_0 are initial equilibrium values at $t = 0$.

Although growth is never as perfectly smooth as in equations (48), they give a good approximation of the growth of any economy over long periods and an even better approximation of its potential growth. Thus they provide a norm for the study of economic movement over time.

2 THE GOLDEN AGE AND THE GOLDEN RULE

If it should happen that the capital stock and the labor force both increase at the same rate ρ', where $\rho' < \rho$ if there is technological advance, that is

$$\dot{N} = \rho' N \qquad \dot{K} = z = \rho' K$$

and $K_t/N_t = K_0/N_0 =$ const, it is reasonable to suppose that the equilibrium real rate of interest would remain constant over time. Without technological advance, all economic aggregates would in this case increase at the same rate ρ, a state that some economists call a "golden age," perhaps because all possible technological advance has been exhausted.

Now suppose the rate ρ were higher than the unchanging equilibrium real rate of interest r. In this case the earnings of capital rK would be less than the rate of investment ρK, so that some labor earnings would be used to expand the capital stock. Such high investment is wasteful if it goes on indefinitely.

Consider how such high investment would look from the point of view of a household with an infinite planning horizon. The growth of the labor force in the household at the rate ρ assures that the household's consumption will grow at this same rate if the household consumes all of its labor income. If it consumes less than this amount, investing a constant share such as to keep its wealth growing at the rate $\rho > r$, its consumption at this lower level can also grow only at the rate ρ while it continues this rate of investment. That means that consumption at the lower level, having the same rate of growth, will never catch up to the higher level of consumption. Why consume at the lower rate forever? The household might wish to cross some wealth threshold where it can afford certain things it especially desires, at which point it will invest more slowly. But if there is such a threshold, the household will stop maintaining the assumed growth rate. If there is not, it should stop now, and save less than the income from its capital in order to enjoy some of it.

We can show the same proposition for the economy as a whole. Equations (48) will be assumed to hold, with current income given by

$$y_0 = f(N_0, K_0) = f_N N_0 + f_K K_0 = w N_0 + r K_0$$

assuming, for simplicity, constant returns to scale. Now suppose that the economy can have all the initial capital stock it wants provided it adds to the stock at the proportionate rate ρ. What amount of capital is worth having on this condition? Where

$$c_0 = y_0 - z_0$$

we maximize consumption subject to

$$z_0 = \rho K_0$$

Taking derivatives, we have

$$\frac{dc_0}{dK_0} = \frac{dy_0}{dK_0} - \frac{dz_0}{dK_0}$$
$$= f_K - \rho = r - \rho$$

and for maximum consumption we have

$$\frac{dc_0}{dK_0} = 0 = r - \rho$$

or $r = \rho$. If any more initial capital is accepted, r will drop below ρ, and consumption must go down to maintain the agreed growth rate of capital. It's better not to accept it on these terms, and if the capital stock has in fact risen above this initial level, it is better not to invest all its earnings, letting it grow more slowly than ρ, until or unless the real rate of return $f_K = r$ rises to equal ρ. Doing it this way allows some extra consumption at the beginning and then allows the highest consumption that can be kept growing at the rate ρ. The same logic applies if the labor force grows more slowly than everything else, and if technological advance makes up the difference, keeping r constant and keeping y growing at ρ.

Would an economy or a household ever try to keep capital growing at the golden-age rate if this rate exceeded the real rate of interest? It might, if households do not have infinite planning horizons. Suppose that instead of such planning horizons, where the household sees and plans through successive generations of its descendants, each household sees and plans only to the end of the life cycle of its present heads. The parents expel their children when they come of age and accumulate just enough during their own working years to provide for retirement, leaving no bequest. They sell off their accumulated assets during retirement, to younger people, who are still working and accumulating. With no one to provide for them in their old age, their accumulation is set by their decision on saving for retirement; the economy-wide growth of capital and consumption does not interest them. The amount they choose to accumulate this way could raise the capital stock to the point where r is below ρ, and they could still be in a utility-maximizing equilibrium.

However, if a national social security administration is created, it can set any terms it likes for providing for the old out of the contributions of the young, when it substitutes compulsory accumulation for what was previously voluntary. It would in due course own the entire national capital stock, under our present assumptions. If it pays out as benefits to then-living people only the actuarial value of their past social security taxes, it would give nothing to already retired people and would pay full benefits only to present and future young people who haven't yet paid in anything, when they eventually retire. In this case creating social security does not change the capital stock or its rate of growth; everyone has the same consumption stream he would have had without it. But suppose instead that the social security administration pays more than the actuarial value of past contributions of people who were already partway or entirely through their working careers at the time of its creation. These people can then consume more than they otherwise would. The administration can go on paying such excess benefits until it has reduced the national capital stock to the level at which $r = \rho$, after which it can pay "actuarial" benefits to retired people out of the contributions of the young, using the earnings of the remaining capital stock to maintain its growth (and maintain the productivity of labor). From this point onward everyone would enjoy exactly the same life cycle of consumption he would have had without social security.

It appears that the older people at the time social security begins, who benefit from this plan, get their extra benefits without cost to anyone. Although the depleted capital stock held in the fund would not be enough to cover everyone's retirement, so that the social security fund would not be actuarial, each successive generation in retirement would be provided for by the concurrent contributions of the young. This works just fine, as long as population growth continues, and new generations come along at the required rate to contribute to the retirement of the old.

The household with an infinite planning horizon can operate its own social security system. Each generation can support its elders in their retirement, planning to be supported in turn by its children. They will maintain a capital stock small enough to have a marginal productivity no less than the rate of growth and will save enough to keep it growing at the uniform rate. This amount of saving is the "golden rule" amount; it is the amount it would make sense for each generation to save if its own decision determined the choice of all *preceding* generations. Alternately stated, each generation supports its retired elders at the level at which it would like to be supported in its turn, given existing budget constraints.

For emphasis, we have considered the case in which golden-rule saving maintains a capital stock too small to provide directly for retirement income, so that the young give something to the old on balance. However, there is no reason why the golden-rule capital stock need be this small; it can be large enough for each generation to give a bequest to its heirs. Which is true depends on how fast the marginal productivity of capital declines as a function of the capital-labor ratio, on how much annual retirement income people want to provide for compared to their annual incomes while working, and on the length of retirement compared to their working careers. If under free choice each generation leaves a bequest to its heirs, an informed rational choice will go no further than the golden-rule capital stock, without the help of a social security administration or other social intervention.

3 THE INTEREST RATE AND THE PRICE
LEVEL DURING GROWTH: SUMMARY

The advance of technology, the growth of population, and the growth of the capital stock together suggest the plausible working hypothesis that investment opportunities will also expand, shifting the investment schedule steadily to the right. If the capital stock grows at the same rate as the labor force, in percent, the constant capital-labor ratio would seem to imply that opportunities for new investment also grow at this rate, at an unchanged expected rate of return. If new technology generates new investment opportunities at a constant rate also, it reinforces this point. Roughly this type of growth seems to have been the experience of the United States of the past 100 years; income and investment have multiplied about thirty-fold without much decline in long-term interest rates, and with little sign of slowing down.

When the economy grows this way the investment schedule shifts to the right by the same percentage amount as does full-employment real income, per year. With the simple secular consumption function of equation (45) the expenditure sector curve also has the same percentage shift. These shifts appear in Figure 50, in which the initial period's curves

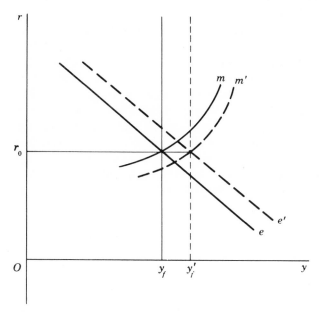

Figure 50

are the solid ones and the later period's curves are the dashed ones. The new expenditure sector curve reaches the new full-employment real income at the same interest rate r_0 as does the old expenditure sector curve the old full-employment real income. The monetary sector curve must shift to the right by the same percentage to maintain full equilibrium, either through monetary expansion or through a decline in the price level.

However, there may be periods of secular decline or secular rise in the equilibrium interest rate, continuing long enough to affect expectations. We shall consider the case of secular decline. When the market adjusts to the expectation of a declining interest rate, short-term interest rates will be higher than long-term rates at any moment, and each will decline over time. Because short-term assets are closer substitutes for money in the typical portfolio than are long-term assets, we suppose that the demand for money depends mainly on short-term rates rather than on long-term rates. In contrast, we suppose that investment depends mainly on long-term rates. Therefore a secular decline in interest rates will create a discrepancy between the rate we should use to represent the monetary sector and the one we should use to represent the expenditure sector. This discrepancy resembles that arising from expected inflation or deflation. It requires a price-level adjustment.

Whether the interest rate declines or remains steady with secular growth, there will be an increased demand for real cash balances. If the monetary authority provides new money to meet this demand, the price level will remain stable; if not, it must decline. If it does decline, when expectations adjust to the decline there will be a discrepancy between the money rate of interest and the real rate, for assets of any given term. This discrepancy also requires a price-level adjustment.

The discrepancies connected with a secular decline in the interest rate and with secular deflation are Mundell effects, named for Robert Mundell, who discovered their primitive forms. If full employment is maintained, they imply no real effects except through real balance effects; but in recession and in other cases involving transitional dynamics, they affect real income and other variables.

4 A SECULAR DECLINE IN INTEREST RATES

If investment opportunities fail to grow in step with the growth of the economy, the equilibrium interest rate will decline. Suppose, for example, that the investment curve and the expenditure sector curve fail to shift at all. In Figure 51, where full-employment income is y_0 initially,

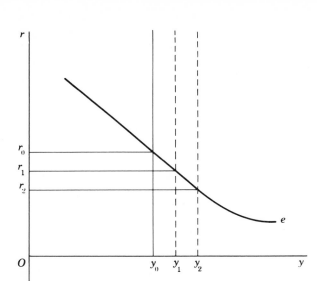

Figure 51

it will be y_1 after one period, y_2 after two periods, and so on. The equilibrium real rate of interest is r_0 initially, will be r_1 after one period, will be r_2 after two periods, and so on. Suppose for simplicity that all types of investment opportunities equally fail to expand. Further, suppose for the moment that money is the only "liquid" asset, that is, that households and firms provide for transactions, for protection against fluctuations in yields, and other like needs by holding cash; they hold short-term assets only for income. This last assumption implies that the long-term rate of interest will be an average of short-term rates—for example, the twenty-year rate will be the discounted average of twenty successive one-year rates, exactly.

The expectation that interest rates will fall will shape the current term structure of interest rates, causing a similar fall from short-term rates through long-term rates. We can see this point through the following argument. Whatever the equilibrium term structure, the yield of each term to maturity will fall over time in step with all the others. The failure of all types of investment opportunities to expand will mean that all types of investments must be stimulated by declines of interest rates for their respective terms, to bring total investment up to the required amount for full employment. Moreover, investors interested only in yield would force rates of different terms to move consistently. Then with short rates expected to fall over time, and with long rates the average of

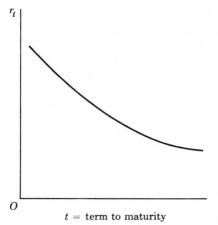

t = term to maturity **Figure 52**

expected short rates, current long rates must be lower than current short rates. Thus the term structure of interest rates in an era of secular decline in interest rates would appear as in Figure 52, declining steadily with the term or expected economic life of the asset.

Relaxing the assumption that money is the only liquid asset moderates the downward slope in the term structure of interest rates that we would otherwise expect, and could reverse it. If short-term assets offer their holders some of the convenience of money, a lower average yield will be acceptable on such assets than on long-term assets. This lower average yield means a lower current yield than would otherwise be the case, and so flattens down the short-term end of the term structure.

However, we are concerned with the difference between a world of unchanging real interest rates and a world of secularly declining interest rates, and so need not be overly concerned with the specific actual shape of the term structure. What the above argument establishes is that the term structure will have more of a tendency to slope down when a secular decline in interest rates is expected than when it is not. The expected secular decline may change a *rising* term structure into a flat one or a *flat* one into a downward-sloping one. In either case the expectation has changed the shape of the term structure in the same direction.

This change in shape affects the link between the monetary sector and the expenditure sector. One term to maturity will best represent investment in real, productive assets, another the choice between holding money and other assets. For example, the average economic life of a physical asset might be twenty years, while liquidity considerations might imply that the demand for money is best represented by a function of the one-year rate of interest. Both investment and the demand for money can be presumed in fact to depend on rates of interest of all terms to maturity, but investment is likely to be sensitive mainly to the longer-term rates, while the demand for money is likely to be sensitive mainly to the shorter-term ones. Therefore a change in the term structure, due to a change from constant expectations to an expectation of secular decline in interest rates, will change the relationship between the two sectors.

Where the demand for money is mainly a function of the short-term rate of interest and investment is mainly a function of the long-term rate, and where the short-term rate is higher than the long-term rate, the effect is like that of the discrepancy between the money rate and the real rate due to inflation. In Figure 53 the expenditure sector curve appears as a

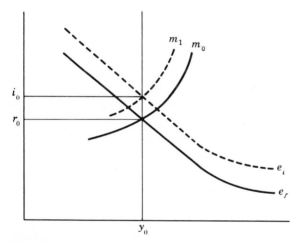

Figure 53

solid line in terms of the long-term rate and as a dashed line e_i in terms of the higher short-term rate. With no expectation of a secular decline in interest rates the two lines would coincide, and the equilibrium rate, both long and short, would be r_0. In that case the equilibrium monetary sector curve would be m_0, expressed in terms of either rate. However, with the short-term rate above the long-term rate, the equilibrium short-term rate will be the higher rate i_0 if the long-term rate stays at r_0. If the monetary sector curve were initially at m_0 in terms of the short-term rate i, it stays there in terms of that variable (and shifts downward in terms of r). A rise in the price level or a reduction in the quantity of money is required to shift the monetary sector curve upward to the point of full equilibrium. In terms of the short-term rate this point is at i_0.

Thus the expectation of declining interest rates, long and short, raises the short rate relative to the long and either drives up the price level or drives down the quantity of money for monetary equilibrium. The lower quantity of real cash balances will be maintained as long as the secular decline in interest rates continues to be expected. Starting from this lower quantity, real cash balances will grow in step with the growth of income, just as it does starting from the higher quantity implied by constant expected future interest rates; but at every point in time it will remain on a lower growth path.

5 THE SECULAR INCREASE IN REAL CASH BALANCES

Figure 50 showed a rightward shift of the monetary sector curve, from the solid line to the dashed one, where the equilibrium rate of interest remains at r_0 during secular growth. To produce this shift, either the price level must fall or the quantity of money must increase. If the monetary authority provides for enough secular growth in the money supply to hold the price level steady, no further analysis is required, for either a constant interest rate or a falling one. (Whether they provide it or not, we assume that the expenditure effects of the growth in real cash balances are already incorporated in the expenditure sector curve.)

Suppose, however, that the monetary authority holds the supply of money constant instead of shifting it to the right. A continuing secular decline of the price level will be required to shift the monetary sector curve to the right, for full-employment equilibrium. When expectations adapt to the secular decline in the price level, money rates of interest, long-term and short-term, will fall below the corresponding real rates by the amount of the expected rate of price fall. Where the required rate of price fall is less than the real rate of interest (for every term), mild deflation will be possible with positive money rates of interest. Where the required rate of price fall exceeds the real rate of interest, full employment will be possible only if a faster deflation generates enough consumption expenditures to push the equilibrium real rate of interest even higher, above the rate of deflation. (The analysis of both types of deflationary equilibrium, showing the shifts in the monetary and expenditure sector curves, appears in Chapter 4.)

6 GROWTH AND UNDER-EMPLOYMENT EQUILIBRIUM

Suppose that during a recession or depression the price level fails to fall enough and that the monetary authority fails to increase the money supply enough for full-employment equilibrium. Then any number of real and price-level effects is possible, depending on how expectations develop. In the simplest case, shown in Figure 54, only full-employment real income shifts, with the growth of population, advancing technology, and whatever net investment there is. Because of recession, the investment schedule remains stagnant, as does the expenditure sector curve. If the price level holds constant (for whatever reason), and the monetary authority also holds the money supply constant, the monetary sector curve also stays where it is. Then the "equilibrium" real and money interest rates remain

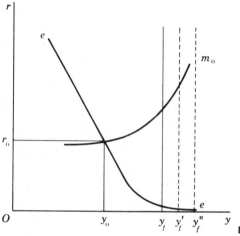

Figure 54

constant at r_0, and real income remains at y_0, as determined by the expenditure and monetary sectors. Unemployment, and the deficit of real income below its potential, grow. The deficit grows also if the price level drifts downward too slowly to raise expenditures as fast as the growth of full-employment real income.

Any of the shifts discussed in the preceding sections would change real income. An expected downtrend in interest rates, which under full employment pushes up the equilibrium price level, would raise equilibrium real income here instead, by shifting downward the monetary sector curve in terms of r. An expected decline in the price level, which under full employment gives an extra downward push to the price level, would lower equilibrium real income here instead, because by assumption the price level fails to fall enough to restore equilibrium (and so cannot fully respond to an extra push).

7 DYNAMICS AND STABILITY

The preceding sections give the main building blocks for an exact theory of economic growth. Because growth has usually come with the passage of time, it is natural to include some of these building blocks in any theory of economic dynamics, that is, of the movement of economic equilibrium over time. However, growth may or may not be a central feature of a dynamic model. Some dynamic models leave growth out entirely; for others, it is merely an extra added distraction. But in some cases, growth is the key to the properties of the dynamic model. We shall set out some of these points in elementary form here; an extended discussion of dynamics appears in Chapter 11.

To illustrate the ways in which growth can affect a dynamic model, consider two extreme cases, one model that is unstable regardless of growth, and one that depends entirely on growth for any hint of instability.

In Chapter 3 we noted that if the marginal propensity to spend from income is greater than 1, the multiplier can be described as either negative or infinite. In this case, the expenditure sector curve slopes upward. Using an informal dynamics of spending-responding like that of Chapter 3, we find that if the interest rate drops below its equilibrium value, spending will rise without limit and so will disrupt the system, without restoring equilibrium. In contrast, if the expenditure sector curve slopes downward, we saw in Chapters 2 and 3 that there are forces that restore equilibrium when there is a small perturbation. Analysis of cases of these kinds is largely independent of considerations of growth, although we may choose to include growth in a time-dependent model that revolves around them.

For comparison, the Harrod growth model (and a similar one by Domar) depends centrally on growth. In section 1 of this chapter, we found that under simple assumptions about the production function and technology, investment must grow exponentially to assure full use of resources. Now suppose further that the production function requires fixed proportions of labor and capital, that there is no technical advance, and that capital grows at the rate ρ while labor grows at the rate ρ'. Then the real income that can be produced by the capital stock grows along the path

$$y_t = y_0 e^{\rho t}$$

whereas the real income that will employ the labor force grows along the path

$$y_t' = y_0 e^{\rho' t}$$

If the labor force grows at a slower rate than the capital stock, that is, if $\rho' < \rho$, capital will sit increasingly idle and the incentive to invest will disappear. (Recall that we have assumed fixed proportions.) Then the economy will collapse into depression. If instead the labor force grows faster than the capital stock, $\rho' > \rho$, capital will be fully employed but there will be growing unemployment of labor. Thus unless the economy stays on the razor's edge, keeping $\rho = \rho'$, there will either be growing unemployment or economic collapse, under the stated assumptions. In models of this sort, growth creates a potential instability.

Any completely unstable model confronts the awkward tendency of real economies to recover from depressions and to keep their booms within reasonable bounds. Thus the builder of such a model usually puts a floor under and a ceiling over its instability, that is, he bounds it. The typical approach uses full-employment real income as the upper bound, and as the lower bound uses some minimum real income based on a rock-bottom investment level that persists in the face of bad business conditions. Figures 55 and 56 illustrate this type of model, using the negative-or-

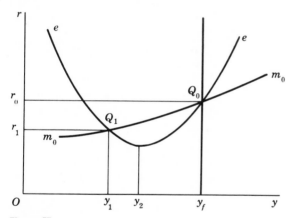

Figure 55

infinite multiplier over a certain range of income. Suppose that at incomes above y_2, business conditions are good enough to induce a marginal propensity to invest greater than the marginal propensity to save. The marginal propensity to spend exceeds 1, the multiplier sequence fails to converge, and the expenditure sector curve slopes upward. However, suppose that at incomes below y_2 the investment schedule is affected so little by changes in income that the marginal propensity to spend is less than 1, and the expenditure sector curve slopes down. Thus this curve slopes down at all incomes below y_2 and rises to the right of this income.

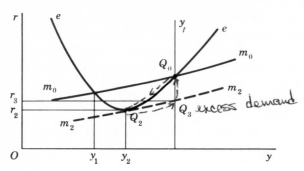

Figure 56

Suppose the economy starts at an initial equilibrium at full employment, with the real interest rate at r_0, and with the monetary sector curve m_0 reaching full-employment real income at this interest rate, passing through Q_0, as does the expenditure sector curve e. If full-employment real income is the upper bound for income, that assures the stability of equilibrium in the upward direction, to the right of Q_0. However, with any displacement of the interest rate above r_0 or of income below y_f, expenditures collapse downward through a multiplier process that moves explosively for a time, because the marginal propensity to spend is greater than 1. During this process the monetary sector curve m_0 holds the interest rate above the corresponding points on the expenditure sector curve, preventing equilibrium at any income above y_1. The collapse ends at the intersection Q_1 between the monetary and expenditure sector curves in Figure 55. This intersection is stable, except for downward pressure on prices and wages.

Now suppose that wages and prices decline, after a delay. In Figure 56, the downward drift of prices and wages shifts the monetary sector curve from its first position m_0 toward m_2 in terms of the real interest rate r. As it passes Q_2 the equilibrium of its intersection with the expenditure sector curve becomes unstable and then disappears, when they no longer intersect. Income drifts upward toward y_2, passes it, and then rushes upward toward y_f. The monetary sector curve now lies entirely below the expenditure sector curve, holding the interest rate below any equilibrium value, assuring expansion. The income-interest-rate combination bumps into the full-employment ceiling at Q_3, at which desired consumption and investment add up to more than the available resources. The pressure of excess demand drives the price level upward, shifting the monetary sector curve back upward to the left, toward its original position m_0. When it gets there the cycle is ready to begin again.

Although the cycle mechanism varies from case to case, and some models include the upward shift of full-employment real income, many models resemble this one in making the cycle depend primarily on the slope parameters of each instant, having no connection with growth as such. The Harrod-Domar approach, in contrast, makes growth a central source of disturbance and assumes a rigid inability of the economy to adapt to its stresses. Neither approach leaves anything to chance. All growth and cycle models of recent years, of this general class, are deterministic. And none is supported by evidence about the causes of instability.

In practice, the growth and fluctuations of real economies are anything but steady, regular, and perfectly predictable. Chance, unpredictable impulses are always there, and often dominate the scene. In Chapter 11, we will consider chance impulses, along with other features of economic dynamics.

BIBLIOGRAPHY

Baumol, William J.: *Economic Dynamics* (New York, The Macmillan Company, 1951).

Cass, David, and Joseph E. Stiglitz: "The Implications of Alternative Saving and Expectations Hypotheses for Choices of Technique and Patterns of Growth," *Journal of Political Economy*, vol. 77 (1969), p. 586.

Domar, Evsey: "Expansion and Employment," *American Economic Review*, vol. 37 (1947), p. 34.

Hahn, T. H., and R. C. O. Matthews: "The Theory of Economic Growth: A Survey," *Economic Journal*, vol. 64 (1964), p. 779.

Harrod, Roy F.: *Toward a Dynamic Economics* (London, Macmillan & Co., Ltd., 1948).

Johnson, Harry G.: "The Neo-classical One-sector Growth Model: A Geometrical Exposition and Extension to a Monetary Economy," *Economica N. S.*, vol. 33 (1966), p. 265.

Koopmans, Tjalling: *On the Concept of Optimal Economic Growth*, Cowles Foundation Discussion Paper No. 163 (New Haven, Conn., Yale University Press, 1963).

Liviatan, Nissan and Levhari: "The Concept of the Golden Rule in the Case of More than One Consumption Good," *The American Economic Review*, vol. 58 (1968), p. 100.

Mundell, Robert A.: "A Fallacy in the Interpretation of Macroeconomic Equilibrium," *The Journal of Political Economy*, vol. 73 (1965), p. 61.

Phelps, E. S.: "The Golden Rule of Accumulation: A Fable for Growthmen," *American Economic Review*, vol. 51 (1961), p. 638.

Phelps, E. S.: "Second Essay on the Golden Rule of Accumulation," *American Economic Review*, vol. 55 (1965), p. 193.

Rose, Hugh: "On the Non-linear Theory of the Employment Cycle," *Review of Economic Studies*, XXXIV (2) (1967), p. 153.

Solow, Robert M.: "A Contribution to the Theory of Economic Growth," *Quarterly Journal of Economics*, vol. 70 (1956), p. 65.

Tobin, James: "Money and Economic Growth," *Econometrica*, vol. 33 (1965), p. 671.

6

THE CONSUMPTION FUNCTION

1 CONSUMPTION AND INCOME

Two features of consumption behavior over time stand out and remain above controversy. First, the proportion of income saved averages about the same percentage of disposable personal income in recent decades as it did in earlier periods going back to the late decades of the nineteenth century. That is, with the *long term* growth of income over the past 100 years the fraction of income consumed appears to have been almost constant, giving a consumption function of the form

$$\frac{C^*}{Y^*} = b^* \qquad \text{or} \qquad C^* = b^* Y^*$$

where the $*$'s denote long-term trend values, and where Y^* denotes personal disposable income. The fraction b^* has averaged about 0.88 in the United States.

Second, short-term fluctuations in income, such as those of business cycles, produce less than proportionate changes in consumption; the marginal propensity to consume is less than b^*. When income is on its long-term trend value, consumption is also, but when income fluctuates away from this value, consumption deviates from its long-term fraction of income. Thus we have a consumption function, for short-term changes, of the form

$$C = b^*Y^* + b(Y - Y^*)$$
$$= (b^* - b)Y^* + bY$$
$$= a + bY$$

where

$$a = (b^* - b)Y^* > 0 \qquad \text{when } b^* > b$$

Various cross-sectional and time-series studies confirm that consumption responds less to short-term fluctuations in income than it does to long-term or permanent changes in income. The value of b typically runs around 0.7 or 0.8 in these studies, and is even lower for households with very unstable incomes, such as farm households. They also show a higher fraction of income saved in high-income households than in low-income households, an effect that mostly disappears when the researcher corrects for temporary changes in income. However, a portion of the higher saving rate remains for high-income households if income is defined to include capital gains.

These phenomena give rise to two basic explanations of consumption behavior, the relative income hypothesis and the permanent income hypothesis. The first asserts that the fraction of income saved rises with the household's relative position in the income distribution, but remains unchanged when all incomes rise with the long-term trend. The second asserts that the fraction of income saved is the same fraction of permanent income (long-term or expected income) for every household, regardless of its position in the income distribution. Either hypothesis could account for the constancy of the fraction of income saved over long periods.

Both theories give similar explanations of short-term variation in consumption over the business cycle. The explanation associated with the relative income hypothesis is that households form habits and expectations based on their best previous year, and so reduce consumption only partially and reluctantly when income drops during a recession. The explanation associated with the permanent income hypothesis is that households discount year-to-year fluctuations in income, adjusting their expected or permanent incomes by only a fraction of each fluctuation, and adjusting their consumption in direct proportion to that. These two explanations are practically indistinguishable.

Where the two hypotheses differ, the data partly support each. Moreover, the two hypotheses merge into one if we drop from the permanent income hypothesis the assumption that every household consumes the same fraction of its permanent income, regardless of its relative income. And both give us the short-run consumption function that we used in ⌐hapter 2.

Certain conspicuous differences in households average out over the whole economy. The typical young household saves and invests heavily in household durables; the typical old household whose head is still in the labor force saves and invests mainly in income-bearing assets to provide for retirement. Households of intermediate ages save less, especially while the children are in college. These differences have no effect on aggregate saving for the whole economy because the relative age distribution of households changes only slightly over long periods; old households disappear, new ones are formed, and the ones in between get older, leaving the distribution about the same. Moreover, lifetime consumption patterns change only gradually, if at all.

Aggregate saving, because of these constancies, depends mainly on how much the typical household adds to its inherited wealth over its lifetime. In the aggregate, each generation transfers more wealth to the next generation than it received from the previous one. The different relative income groups may save and transfer different proportions of their lifetime earnings this way, but if each of these different groups continues its past habits and if the distribution of income and wealth remains unchanged, aggregate savings will remain an unchanged fraction of income.

2 CONSUMPTION AND THE RATE OF INTEREST

Whether a rise in the rate of interest can be expected to increase or decrease saving has long been an open question. Almost all writers who have discussed the question have alleged that either result is possible. A fairly complete view of the problem, in its full ambiguity, may be seen in Marshall's statement on the subject:[1]

> Suppose, for instance, that villagers have to get timber for building their cottages from the forests; the more distant these are, the smaller will be the return of future comfort got by each day's work in fetching the wood, the less will be their future gain from the wealth accumulated probably by each day's work: and this smallness of the return of future pleasure, to be got at a given present sacrifice, will tend to prevent them from increasing the size of their cottages; and will perhaps diminish on the whole the

[1] Alfred Marshall, *Principles of Economics*, 8th ed., Macmillan, London, 1938, pp. 234–235. See also pp. 533–534.

amount of labour they spend in getting timber. But this rule is not without exception. For, if custom has made them familiar with cottages of only one fashion, the further they are from the woods, and the smaller the usance to be got from the produce of one day's work, the more days' work will they give. . . . Again, as Sargant has pointed out, if a man has decided to go on working and saving till he has provided a certain income for his old age, or for his family after his death, he will find that he has to save more if the rate of interest is low than if it is high.

This statement of Marshall's clearly illustrates the confusion of most discussion of this topic, because it fails to say what other things remain constant when the rate of interest varies. In particular, Marshall says nothing about holding income or wealth constant. Indeed, his examples, and most others used in this connection, clearly let real income and wealth change along with the rate of interest. Distinct variables that affect saving behavior become confounded.

Just as a consumer's reaction to a change in his current opportunities, through changes in relative prices and in real income, can be separated into an income effect and a substitution effect,[1] his reaction to a change in his future opportunities relative to his present opportunities can be separated into a wealth effect and a substitution effect. The decision problem he faces is similar in both cases, and the analysis of his behavior can and should also be similar. Therefore we analyze and apply the wealth and substitution effects separately.

The simplest case is that in which changes in the rate of interest are temporary deviations from equilibrium, while real resources and wealth remain unchanged. If households know their true long-run wealth positions, the effect of the change, apart from a redistribution of wealth, will consist of a pure substitution effect.

The "substitution effect" here is the effect on consumption of a change in the relative prices of current and future goods, where each household's long-run overall wealth position is unchanged. The choice between current and future goods has the same properties as the choice between two current goods; in both cases the household will take more of the good that has become cheaper. That is, the substitution effect between current commodities is negative; the sign of the change in the consumption of a good is opposite to the sign of the change in its relative price. By the same token, the substitution effect between current and future commodities is negative; the sign of the change in current consumption is opposite to the sign of the change in the rate of interest (since a

[1] See J. R. Hicks, *Value and Capital*, Oxford University Press, New York, 1950, pp. 26–37 and 307–311.

rise in rate of interest makes current goods more expensive relative to future goods). Hence the response of saving to arbitrary changes in the rate of interest, where the wealth position of the economy is unchanged, must be positive. This conclusion holds with the same certainty as the conclusion that the demand curve for a particular current commodity must slope downward if real income is held constant along the curve.[1]

In contrast, when a change in the rate of interest is associated with a change in the wealth position of the economy, as with an unexpected and substantial technological advance, the response of aggregate saving will be the combined result of a substitution effect and a wealth effect. The theoretical apparatus for analyzing this case must accordingly be more elaborate, because these two effects can work against each other.

3 CONSTANT REAL RESOURCES

To understand the effects of arbitrary changes in the rate of interest we must clarify the notion of constancy of real resources or wealth. Consider an economy with a given technology and with known and definite possibilities for current and future investment. At any given time this economy has a limited set of opportunities to produce alternative present and future streams of consumption goods, all viewed together from the present. People's present and future economic plans in the aggregate, including their plans for saving, for retirement, and for bequest, will be limited by these same possibilities. Real resources, or wealth, remains unchanged when the rate of interest changes if these long-run possibilities remain unchanged.

For example, suppose that the rate of interest suddenly rises, for whatever reason, without any change in physical capital, land, or labor or in their present or prospective productivities. If a householder experienced no offsetting changes, he could go on consuming the same total quantity of current goods and yet have more goods at some future time because of the increased earnings of his savings. This cannot be true of everyone at once, however, because there is no new productivity or wealth to provide an increase in future consumption. Offsetting effects on their opportunities must limit households in the aggregate (and perhaps everyone individually) so that they can barely carry out their old plans, notwithstanding the rise in the rate of interest. They can obtain more future goods only by a sacrifice of current consumption, and a *change* in

---

[1] *Ibid.* See also Friedman, "The Marshallian Demand Curve," *Journal of Political Economy*, vol. 57, pp. 463–495, 1949.

saving will produce no more in the aggregate than it would have previously (although to each household it would appear to do so).

Apart from distributional considerations, each householder typically will find that although the possibility of carrying out his old plans is unaffected by the change of the interest rate, the apparent results for alternative plans have changed. If he was previously just satisfied with his plans, he now has an inducement to reduce his current consumption; future goods have become cheaper relative to current goods.

Since his subjective marginal rate of substitution between present and future goods was previously just equal to the price ratio implied by the old rate of interest,[1] the new higher rate of interest enables him to obtain additional future goods at a lower cost in terms of current goods than he would be willing to pay. Each householder typically will consume less, therefore, and aggregate saving will increase. Similarly, if the rate of interest were to fall without any change in real resources, aggregate saving would decrease.

This argument, applied to households taken separately, depends solely on the assumptions of rationality and continuity of tastes. Applied to saving in the aggregate, the argument also depends either on the assumption that the distribution of wealth does not change or on the assumption that it does not matter if it does. (These assumptions underlie almost any discussion of aggregate economic behavior.) This conclusion applies to a wide variety of cases of variation in the interest rate, especially to all chance variation or acts of policy that have nothing to do with technological change.

This conclusion is independent of any notion of the "elasticity of demand for future goods." As has already been indicated, without explicit constancy of real resources, it would appear that a rise in the rate of interest would enable the saver to have more future goods for the same expenditure on them, that is, with the same saving. Whether he would in fact save more would then appear to depend on whether his price elasticity of demand for future goods was greater than unity. This notion is implicit in the passage from Marshall quoted above and has been repeated by several writers. However, it is a mistake to apply it to arbitrary changes in the interest rate. If no technological change or other such change has occurred, additional future goods can be obtained only by an additional sacrifice of current consumption. Hence the only aspect of the elasticity of demand for future goods that is relevant to

---

[1] For an elaboration of this point, see, e.g., John F. Due and Robert W. Clower, *Intermediate Economic Analysis*, 4th ed., Richard D. Irwin, Inc., Homewood, Ill., 1961, pp. 73–85.

this problem is its sign; and this sign, like the sign of the elasticity of constant-real-income demand for every other good, is negative. In other words, the interest elasticity of savings, for constant real resources, is positive.

4 WEALTH EFFECTS AND THEIR DISTRIBUTION

It could happen that each householder will find his long-run wealth position unaffected by arbitrary changes in the rate of interest. Consider, for example, an economy consisting of (1) a collection of greater-family households of constant age composition and with an infinite time horizon, as described above in Chapter 5, and (2) a collection of riskless enterprises financed entirely by perpetual bonds. The households expect to have unchanged tastes into the indefinite future and plan their consumption into the indefinite future. The prospective consumption of yet unborn members of the household figures within the same preference structure as that of its present members. The enterprises plan their investment, if any, into the indefinite future according to the present and expected rates of interest. Further, suppose this economy has reached the stationary state, given the marginal productivity of existing capital.

In this stationary economy, the only economic decision that anyone needs to make is what to do when there is an arbitrary variation in the rate of interest. Suppose, for example, that a new bond tax applies to all present and prospective bond holdings, the proceeds of which are paid out to households in fixed sums equal to their new tax liabilities. This tax-expenditure structure, however, is set so that changes in the assets of any consumer unit will not affect the lump sum it receives from the proceeds of the tax.

Since every household gets back a lump fixed sum equal to the tax it will pay if it does not change its assets, each household can continue with its old plans if it prefers to. However, it now faces a different rate of interest net of taxes. Whereas, its marginal subjective rate of substitution between current and future goods was previously equal to the price ratio implied by the rate of interest, it will now find that future goods have become relatively unattractive. It will therefore try to sell some assets so as to increase current consumption at the expense of future consumption. That is, in this situation, every consumer unit will plan to save less than previously; viz., it will now plan to dissave. This will be true of every consumer unit because there are no wealth effects for any of them and hence no differential wealth effects among them.

In the more complex world we live in there are undoubtedly differential wealth effects of interest-rate changes. By and large, moreover, people do not plan into the indefinite future but plan for their own lifetimes and leave it to their children and grandchildren to plan theirs in turn, after a certain age. Net saving and investment continue and the economy grows. Firms plan their growth and study their prospects only for a limited time into the future. A tax-expenditure structure that avoided all differential wealth effects, as in the model just considered, would be difficult to devise. If one followed the rule of taxing all assets and paying out lump fixed sums in proportion to present assets, young persons with plans to go on saving would not be compensated for the tax on the additional claims they expect to acquire, and old people with plans to dissave would be overcompensated for future taxes on assets they expect to sell. Hence to prevent all wealth effects, the lump-sum payments would have to reflect both present and future asset holdings rather than merely present asset holdings. In principle this could be done: the wealth effects for everyone together must sum to zero, since the tax-expenditure plan does not alter the underlying productive potential of the economy. Of course, it need not be true that people's *responses* to uncompensated effects on their long-run wealth positions will sum to zero, and this introduces an element of uncertainty into our analysis (as it does into almost any aggregate analysis).

5   CHANGES IN THE PRODUCTIVITY OF CAPITAL

Consider again the passage from Marshall quoted at the beginning of this chapter. In Marshall's first example, concerning the villagers and the timber for their cottages, the change in circumstances changed the real production potential of the economy, since the forests were supposed to have become more distant from the village. This change simultaneously reduces the level of consumption that people can expect to enjoy in the long run and reduces the productivity of incremental saving. It presents us with two distinct effects on behavior to analyze: the effect of the change in wealth, and the effect of a change in the rate of interest.

As already shown, a change in the rate of interest changes saving in the same direction. However, a change in underlying production potential adds a new influence. If an increase in production potential should cause saving to rise, for the same rate of interest, the curve showing saving as a function of the rate of interest (for given real resources, and income) will shift to the right. If the increase causes saving to fall, the saving curve will shift to the left. Knowledge of the direction and size

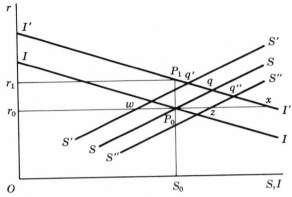

Figure 57 (Source: Martin J. Bailey, "Saving and the Rate of Interest," *Journal of Political Economy,* vol. 65, p. 279, 1957. Reprinted by permission of the University of Chicago Press; copyright 1957 by the University of Chicago.)

of this shift, along with knowledge of the slope of the saving curve itself and of the new investment function, are required to predict the new level of saving and the new equilibrium rate of interest in the overall model of the economy.

For example, in Figure 57 the saving and investment functions for the initial real income and resources are shown as SS and II, respectively, intersecting at P_0, where the equilibrium interest rate and amount of saving and investment are r_0 and S_0, respectively. If the shift in the saving curve caused by the rise in real income is positive, say P_0z, so that the new saving curve is $S''S''$, and if the new investment function is $I'I'$, the new equilibrium point will be q''. If instead the saving curve shifts leftward by wP_0, to $S'S'$, the new equilibrium point will be q'. If the new equilibrium point is in the range P_1x on the new investment function, both saving and the rate of interest will have increased relative to the old position; if it falls outside this range, one or the other will have decreased. Clearly, at least one must increase whenever the investment curve shifts upward. The sign of the shift in the saving function is sufficient to determine which of them must increase. If the shift is negative, the equilibrium rate of interest must increase, and saving may also increase. If the shift is positive, saving must increase, and the rate of interest may also increase.

In summary, we find that for arbitrary deviations of the interest rate from equilibrium each saving function shown in Figure 57, for full-employment real income, has a positive slope. Translated into the regular form of the national income model, this result means that in the consumption function of the form

$$c = a + b_1 y + b_2 r$$

the coefficient b_2 is negative. When the rate of interest goes up, for given income, production function, and so on, consumption goes down and saving goes up. This influence adds a second interest-rate term to the equation of the expenditure sector, as noted in Chapter 3, and so increases the effect of the interest rate on equilibrium income in this sector:

$$y = \frac{a + g_0 + (b_2 + g_1)r}{1 - b_1}$$

where both b_2 and g_1 are negative, reinforcing each other.

We further find that when the investment curve or the production function shifts upward, we should consider a possible shift in the consumption function also. The change in current income produced by a shift in the production function already enters into the consumption function and does not shift it. (However, it does shift the saving curve in Figure 57.) The improved future possibilities can shift the consumption function upward, depending on household expectations and reactions. The future improvement that is already assured with existing resources and with previous plans for future capital accumulation serves to increase permanent income, and so will shift the consumption function upward if the permanent income hypothesis is partly or wholly true. However, the relative income hypothesis in its pure form predicts no such shift; it makes current consumption a function of current relative income and of past experience only.

Even with the permanent income hypothesis we must add the assumption that households know about and react to the improvement in future possibilities, which they observe in the form of improvements in current asset prices or yields. Although it is reasonable to suppose that they will react, shifting the consumption function upward, whatever shift there is can be less than or greater than the increase in current income, leaving the effect on saving uncertain. If we assume perfect foresight, the outcome hinges on whether future incomes will increase by a larger proportion than does current income. If current and future incomes all increase in the same proportion, permanent income increases by this same proportion also, and the proportion of income saved will remain unchanged. The same proportion saved out of a larger current income means larger current saving (a rightward shift of the saving curve in Figure 57), so that saving will necessarily increase. To produce the opposite result, future incomes must increase so much more than current incomes as to shift the saving curve back to the left of where it was before the increase in the productivity of investment, far enough to offset the increase in the equilibrium rate of interest.

We return to Marshall's example of the villagers who use timber from distant forests. If income and wealth per household are expected to remain constant indefinitely, housing will be a constant fraction of income, and a decline in the productivity of housing investment (because of greater distance to the forests) will reduce future incomes by the same proportion as it does current income. In this case, the combination of the permanent income hypothesis (or the relative income hypothesis) and the pure substitution effect of the change assures a decline in saving.

However, if the villagers expect to accumulate capital and grow wealthier over time, and if their income elasticity of demand for housing is greater than 1, the services of housing make up a larger fraction of future income than they do of current income. In this case, a decline in the productivity of housing investment lowers future income more than it does current income, and so lowers permanent income relative to current income. If the permanent income hypothesis is true, consumption will become a smaller fraction of current income, and in this case it could decline more in absolute amount than does current income, so that saving increases. These are the only assumptions that can lead to Marshall's paradox, in which saving increases when the rate of interest falls. In particular, if the relative income hypothesis is strictly true, it cannot happen.

6 LAND PRICES, SAVING, AND PORTFOLIOS AT RATES OF INTEREST NEAR ZERO

Now consider how household saving might react to very low rates of interest. For this problem, we must use a special version of the real rate of interest. It is not enough to have some rate of interest that is correlated with the general level of rates of interest. Instead we must consider the yield on a permanent asset such as the site value of a piece of land. (In the United Kingdom the rate on consols, a nonredeemable bond having a fixed money interest payment in perpetuity, is the money counterpart to the yield on site values.) This rate is simply the ratio of expected annual net rent to the price of the site. Although the relative advantage of a site can change, it does not depreciate. Therefore the expected flow of rent for the intrinsic merits of a site is perpetual; no matter how high prevailing prices of sites are they still offer positive net yields to their owners. As the prices of sites rise, the rate of interest implied by the ratio of their yields to their prices falls toward zero, but is positive.

Consider, for example, a choice urban site whose expected annual rent is $1 per square foot for cleared ground. In this case, a rate of interest of 5 percent per year implies a price of $20 per square foot for the site, an order of price sometimes observed now. Should the rate of interest fall to 1 percent, the price of the site would be $100 per square foot; to 0.00001 percent, $10 million per square foot; . . . ; to 0.000,000,000,004 percent, $25 trillion per square foot, and so on. This last price is equal to the current rate of national output of the United States for a fifty-year period, the approximate life expectancy of a man twenty-five years old. The lucky young man who owned such an urban site could sell 1 square foot and buy the entire present national output of the United States for several decades, at a subsequent loss to his heirs of a dollar a year in income. It is hard to doubt that someone would be tempted by the time these prices were reached, or perhaps even sooner, to consume out of capital—to dissave—enough to overwhelm other households' saving and eliminate aggregate net saving.

This argument falls short of logical necessity. Nothing in economic principle proves the actual existence of any site values based on permanent expected net rents; nor, if they do exist, does rational behavior require that anyone will sell land and consume capital at any price of land, no matter how high. We do in fact encounter site values based on superior location of a permanent character, however, and some households have been known to spend out of capital. It is reasonable to conclude that at some low positive rate of interest consumption would increase to as much as the economy can produce.

However, it is evident that before this argument becomes operative the total value of sites would rise astronomically, and therefore the fraction they represent of total wealth would rise nearly to 1. If indeed the equilibrium rate of interest were so low as to raise site values to the order of magnitude of billions or trillions of dollars per square foot, all other physical wealth would be relatively negligible, worth only a few square feet of land at such prices. There is no reason to doubt that the system can adapt to this imbalance, but if it had to adapt suddenly there would be problems for monetary policy, to be discussed below.

7 REAL CASH BALANCES AND CONSUMPTION

A change in real cash balances resulting from a change in the price level might affect consumption expenditures directly; this idea is usually credited to Pigou. He proposed it as a means of assuring equilibrium in a competitive system.[1]

> As money wage-rates fall money income must fall also and go on falling. Employment, and so real income, being maintained, this entails that prices fall and go on falling; which is another way of saying that the stock of money, as valued in terms of real income, correspondingly rises. But the extent to which the representative man desires to make savings otherwise than for the sake of their future income yield depends in part on the size, in terms of real income, of his existing possessions. As this increases, the amount that he so desires to save out of any assigned real income diminishes and ultimately vanishes; so that we are back in the situation . . . where a negative rate of interest is impossible.

Note that Pigou's statement does not say simply that people will consume more because they are wealthier, when a fall in the price level increases real balances; he says that the increase in their possessions satisfies certain of their motives for saving *from a given real income.*

If Pigou's proposition is correct, its contribution to full-employment equilibrium depends on the further assumption that the change in consumption produced by the increased real cash balances exceeds the change in real income that would be directly produced by the increased real cash balances. Discussions of this general problem have always proceeded on the implicit assumption that the change in real income is zero, which would imply that any increase in consumption at all is helpful. A large enough increase in real cash balances might then induce enough consumption to bring aggregate demand up to the full-employment level, since the full-employment level of effective demand and of income is a fixed goal.

However, we saw in Chapter 3 that real income, properly measured, is directly a function of the quantity of real cash balances. That people are willing to hold these balances at positive rates of interest on alternative assets implies that the cash balances have positive productivity or yield direct satisfaction. If they have a positive marginal physical productivity, real income as ordinarily measured will increase, when real cash balances increase, without any increase in other productive services. If they yield direct satisfaction, a correct measure of income would include this. For any given level of productive-service inputs, therefore, an increase in real cash balances will increase real income and thus increase the gap that effective demand has to fill.

Further comment may be needed on the case in which real cash

---

[1] A. C. Pigou, "The Classical Stationary State," *Economic Journal*," vol. 53, p. 349, 1943. But see also G. Haberler, *Prosperity and Depression*, 3d ed., League of Nations, Geneva, 1941, pp. 389 and 499.

balances yield direct satisfaction. It might seem that even if correctly measured real income would include this, there could still be expected an increase in expenditures on goods and services as a result. However, the direct satisfaction yielded by real cash balances is itself a form of consumption. There is therefore no reason, on income grounds alone, to expect an increase in the consumption of *other* things when willingly held real cash balances increase.

The proposition that emerges from the above discussion is the following: the effect of changes in willingly held real cash balances on consumption will contribute to the existence and stability of equilibrium if and only if the change in consumption is greater than the income produced by the corresponding increments to real cash balances. That is, the marginal propensity to consume out of the imputed or actual product of increments to real cash balances must be greater than 1, if the Pigou effect is to make a positive contribution to stability.

8 THE RATIO OF NONHUMAN WEALTH TO INCOME AS A FACTOR IN CONSUMPTION BEHAVIOR

Although Pigou's own statement can be reconciled with our analysis, its implications as just stated can easily be overlooked. These and other implications are more readily apparent in the statement that consumption, besides depending on permanent income, depends directly on the ratio of nonhuman wealth to income. When real cash balances increase, both real income and the ratio of nonhuman wealth to income increase. Consequently, the marginal propensity to consume out of these changes in income may be higher than the marginal propensity to consume out of those changes in income where the ratio of nonhuman wealth to income does not change.

Suppose that the government sent every tax-paying household a $1,000 government bond, newly issued, and financed it by a corresponding increase in each household's income tax liability. Such a change would have no direct effect on the market value of already existing wealth; total nonhuman wealth would accordingly increase by the amount of the new bonds. Personal disposable income would not change, because the interest on the bonds would offset each citizen's increased income tax. The Pigou effect implies that consumption would increase over what it otherwise would be.

That the ratio of nonhuman wealth to income should be a factor in the consumption decision is equivalent to saying that the source of a permanent-income stream, and not merely its amount, helps to determine consumption. The main difference between nonhuman wealth and labor is that the former can be sold at its present capitalized value, whereas the latter generally cannot. A possible reason why a household might consume more where it receives a bond without any change in its disposable income is that a salable asset is a superior reserve against contingencies, for example, against unforeseen medical expenses. A household without salable assets has to meet expensive contingencies by borrowing against future earning power; this will generally involve higher interest costs than the loss of yield on sold assets (or than the interest on loans secured by collateral) and may be distasteful to the borrower. Therefore the increase in nominal wealth could make the household feel better off despite the constancy of its income.

However, the higher interest cost on unsecured loans generally reflects real costs to the lender. To the extent that higher transaction costs are involved in personal loans, the prospective lower borrowing cost to the potential borrower who receives a marketable asset is matched by resources released from the personal-loan industry; any increase in the consumption of the former as a result is matched by an increase in production by the latter. To the extent that personal loans have a higher risk of default, because further unforeseen contingencies might make it impossible for the borrower to repay, the risk premium charged by the lender for this matches a benefit to the borrower in the form of the possibility of default. When the prospective borrower receives a marketable asset (as in the government-bond example just given), and he uses it to meet a contingency, he will be left with no further reserve to meet a subsequent contingency; when he has borrowed against personal earning power, the possibility of default constitutes such a reserve. Consequently the conversion of human wealth to nonhuman wealth, without any change in income, need not make the household feel better off.

A possible distaste for unsecured borrowing, regardless of the interest cost, could conceivably make the household feel better off whenever the probability of such borrowing was reduced. This could lead to greater consumption, which would constitute a positive Pigou effect. While this is possible, however, it is hard to believe that it is entirely unconnected with and distinct from the extra cost of unsecured borrowing, or from the unpleasant connotations of the situations requiring such borrowing. To the extent that it merely reflects these other considerations, it is fully covered by the analysis just given. To the extent that it is independent of these considerations, it would be the basis for a genuine Pigou effect. Were this the only basis, it would be difficult indeed to take the Pigou effect seriously as a significant economic phenomenon; and regardless of that, it is only a possible basis, not an assured one.

9   THE REACTION TO A WINDFALL OF CAPITAL

Before concluding this discussion of the Pigou effect, consider another reason for it. This reason is that people might consume some fraction of windfall capital gains (in excess of the income subsequently yielded by such capital gains if saved). If a person received a gain of labor income that did not involve a corresponding increase in the expected incomes of his children, it is possible that he would consume at least part of the gain itself, over and above the interest it earns when saved, in his own lifetime and not add it entirely to his ultimate estate. If a person received a gain of labor income that did involve a corresponding increase in the expected incomes of his children, it is possible that he would consume not only the entire increase but would reduce the estate that he had planned to leave. Thus, also, if a person received a windfall capital gain, he might consume part of the extra capital itself and not give it all to his children.

All this is possible, but there is nothing in the fragmentary evidence available to suggest that people do behave in this way. Each succeeding generation has had more total wealth than the last, and each succeeding generation has nevertheless passed on yet more total wealth to its heirs. The gains in wealth in all forms that have been received have not only not been consumed; they have been augmented. Similarly, as one moves cross-sectionally up the income distribution, one finds no tendency to greater consumption of capital, nor is there compelling evidence of a tendency to consume any part of the pure windfall element of capital gains (as distinct from the part of so-called capital gains that are really ordinary income).

In sum, our arguments suggest that the Pigou effect is a frail reed on which to rest the supposed tendency to equilibrium of a competitive system. The effect can be either positive or zero, and if positive may stop short of restoring equilibrium, regardless of how much real cash balances increase.

10   SUMMARY

That consumption increases with current income is established beyond any reasonable doubt. However, there is little direct evidence on the influence of the rate of interest and real cash balances. For the time being we must rely entirely on analysis, inference, and untested hypotheses concerning the influence of both variables. The theory bearing on the role of the rate of interest is relatively the more satisfactory. If in our consumption function we allow separately for the effects of any change in current or long-run expected income, the rise in the rate of interest alone reduces consumption. This conclusion is as certain as the proposition that a demand curve, adjusted to hold real income constant along it, must slope down. The only doubt about it arises in connection with changes in the income distribution.

The state of the theory of the effects of real cash balances is less satisfactory, in that no firm conclusion emerges. The proposition that the real quantity of cash balances, or the ratio of wealth to income, is a variable in the consumption function has a weak logical foundation, in spite of its superficial appeal. It might be true, but there is no strong presumption in its favor. It is certainly of little relevance to the issue of whether or not equilibrium always exists at a positive rate of interest, even though most discussion of the Pigou effect has involved that issue.

BIBLIOGRAPHY

Bailey, Martin J.: "Saving and the Rate of Interest," *Journal of Political Economy*, vol. 65 (1957), p. 279.

Clower, R. W., and M. Bruce Johnson: "Income, Wealth, and the Theory of Consumption," in J. N. Wolfe (ed.): *Value, Capital and Growth* (Chicago, Aldine Publishing Co., 1968).

Duesenberry, James S.: "Income-Consumption Relation and Their Implications," in Lloyd Metzler et al.: *Income, Employment and Public Policy* (New York, W. W. Norton & Company, Inc., 1948).

Farrell, M. J.: "The New Theories of the Consumption Function," *Economic Journal*, vol. 69 (December, 1959), pp. 678–696.

Ferber, Robert: *A Study of Aggregate Consumption Functions*, National Bureau of Economic Research, Technical Paper 8 (New York, 1953).

Fisher, Irving: *The Theory of Interest* (New York, Augustus M. Kelley Publishers, 1930).

Friedman, Milton: "The Marshallian Demand Curve," *Journal of Political Economy*, vol. 57 (1949), p. 463.

Friedman, Milton: *A Theory of the Consumption Function* (Princeton, Princeton University Press, 1957).

Haberler, Gottfried: "The Pigou Effect Once More," *Journal of Political Economy*, vol. 60 (1956), p. 240.

Hicks, J. R.: *Value and Capital* (New York, Oxford University Press, 1950), pp. 26–37; 307–311.

Modigliani, Franco, and Richard Brumberg: "Utility Analysis and the Consumption Function," in Kenneth Kurihara (ed.): *Post Keynesian Economics* (New Brunswick, N.J., Rutgers University Press, 1954), chap. 15.

Patinkin, Don: "Price Flexibility and Full Employment," in American Economic Association: *Readings in Monetary Theory* (New York, McGraw-Hill Book Company, 1951), chap. 13.

Pigou, A. C.: "The Classical Stationary State," *Economic Journal*, vol. 53 (1943), p. 343.

7
THE
MONETARY
SECTOR

1 THE DEMAND FOR CASH BALANCES AND INCOME

The relationship of the quantity of money to income has much in common with that of consumption expenditures to income, despite superficial differences. The desired quantity of real cash balances is in part related to the volume of transactions, which in turn is closely connected with current income. It is also related to wealth or expected income, however, because it depends on how large a fraction of their wealth people feel they can afford to hold in cash. As wealth increases and long-term expected income, or permanent income, increases with it, we should expect the relationship between cash balances and current measured income to change. Thus from a long-run point of view we should expect the demand for money to be a function of both current income and permanent income, or of current income and wealth.

On the whole, this expectation is borne out by research on the relationship between money and income. In the long run, money is found in most countries to rise more than proportionately to income, suggesting an income elasticity of demand greater than unity when long-term average income rises. In the short run, however, the quantity of money fluctuates less than proportionately to current income. Thus cash balances demanded resemble consumption, although the resemblance is partly due to the upward-sloping *supply* curve of money, and only partly due to its small short-run elasticity of demand with respect to income.

2 THE DEMAND FOR CASH BALANCES AND THE INTEREST RATE

The demand curve for cash balances presents some of the same difficulties of measurement as does the investment schedule, in relation to the rate of interest. (See Chapter 8, below.) In both cases agreement is almost universal that the function slopes down. In both cases, measurement of the slope has been difficult because of the interaction among variables in the system, and because as a general rule variation in the rate of interest (especially the long-term rate) has been small compared to other variables.

However, occasional instances of very high rates of inflation have permitted reliable observation of the effect of the cost of holding cash balances on the real quantity held. As we noted in Chapter 4, the money rate rises over the real rate of interest by the amount of the expected rate of inflation. This rise means variation in the money rate of interest independent of the real rate, the variable in the investment function. Free market rates of interest are usually unreported in inflation, but the expected rate of inflation can be estimated and used as an independent variable to trace the demand curve for cash balances. Empirical studies of inflations ranging through rates from 10 percent per year to more than 100 percent per day confirm the expected effect on the demand for cash balances. The very large changes in the rate of inflation in these studies swamped other factors and brought out the demand curve for money sharply in observed data. An example appears in Figure 58, showing a scatter diagram and regression line for real cash balances as a function of expected rates of inflation in the Austrian hyperinflation of 1921–1922.

Although rates of inflation of 10 percent per year and up, when they are sustained for many years, permit observation of the demand curve for cash balances, as a general rule the results are clear-cut only for much higher rates. In European hyperinflations, real cash balances typically varied erratically, relative to a standard calculation of expectations, until the rate of inflation approached 50 percent per month. At low rates of inflation, such as those experienced in the United States in this century, the dynamic lags of the system and the interactions render interpretation difficult, with occasional anomalous movements in the price level and in real cash balances. But no one has yet offered an alternative theory of the

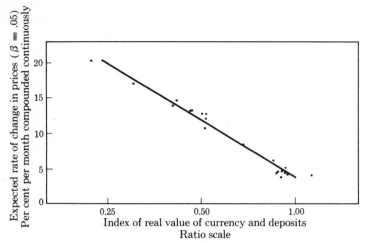

Figure 58 Real cash balances and expected inflation in the Austrian hyper-inflation, 1921–1922. (Source: Philip Cagan, "The Monetary Dynamics of Hyper-inflation," in *Studies in the Quantity Theory of Money*, edited by Milton Friedman. Reprinted by permission of the University of Chicago Press; copyright 1956 by the University of Chicago.)

demand for cash balances that would explain such movements systematically.

3 RISK AND PORTFOLIO ANALYSIS

To understand the monetary sector better, we turn to some elements of portfolio analysis. This will help us see the logic of the downward-sloping demand curve for money, and also that of the upward-sloping supply curve of money.

A portfolio holder can reduce the risks connected with variability in the relative values of different assets by diversification. Consider a portfolio made up of two assets with present prices p_1 and p_2. The owner of this portfolio will decide how much of each of the assets to hold on the basis of their prospective prices and their comparative risks. He would like to minimize risk and maximize the expected future value of his portfolio but usually cannot do both simultaneously; the maximum expected future value will usually occur at an asset distribution with a greater than minimum risk, and a minimum risk will usually occur at an asset distribution with less than maximum expected future value. Thus he must compromise between these two considerations. If the amount of the first asset he decides to hold is a_1, the amount of the second asset a_2 will be determined by the constraint that the total value of both add up to his present wealth V.

$$V = a_1 p_1 + a_2 p_2$$

where both a_1 and a_2 are positive or zero. Since at the moment of decision V is given and fixed, a_1 and a_2 can only be varied in such a way as to hold V constant; that is,

$$dV = p_1 \, da_1 + p_2 \, da_2 = 0$$

which is to say,

$$\frac{da_1}{da_2} = -\frac{p_2}{p_1} \tag{49}$$

The value of this portfolio at some future date will be

$$V' = a_1 p_1' + a_2 p_2'$$

where p_1' and p_2' are the prices at that time (including interest and dividends). If the portfolio owner knew these prices in advance, he could maximize V' by buying exclusively that asset that would rise most in relative price. Using a Lagrange multiplier, we have

$$V' = a_1 p_1' + a_2 p_2' - \lambda(a_1 p_1 + a_2 p_2 - V)$$
$$\frac{\partial V'}{\partial a_1} = p_1' - \lambda p_1 = 0$$

or

$$\frac{p_1'}{p_1} = \lambda$$

if $p_1'/p_1 > p_2'/p_2$, then $p_2'/p_2 < \lambda$, and he maximizes V' by setting a_2 at zero, its lowest possible value. (For simplicity, we disregard short sales.)

Inasmuch as the portfolio owner doesn't know the future prices of these assets, he must use instead his expectations, say $\bar{p}_1$ and $\bar{p}_2$. If no other consideration intervened, he would hold exclusively that asset with the highest expected relative rise in price. However, the higher-yielding asset may also have the greater risk; it could turn out in fact to yield less than does the asset with the lesser expected yield.

Suppose that the risk connected with the future value of the portfolio can be represented by the variance of the probability distribution of future values. This variance is the expectation

$$\begin{aligned}
\sigma_v{}^2 = E(V' - \bar{V})^2 &= E[a_1(p_1' - \bar{p}_1) + a_2(p_2' - \bar{p}_2)]^2 \\
&= a_1{}^2 E(p_1' - \bar{p}_1)^2 + 2a_1 a_2 E(p_1' - \bar{p}_1)(p_2' - \bar{p}_2) \\
&\quad + a_2{}^2 E(p_2' - \bar{p}_2)^2 \tag{50}
\end{aligned}$$

where $\bar{V}$ is the expected value of V'.

$$\bar{V} = E(V') = a_1 E(p_1') + a_2 E(p_2') = a_1 \bar{p}_1 + a_2 \bar{p}_2$$

Now consider in turn two distinct cases. In the first case the future prices of the two assets are highly correlated; in the second case they are uncorrelated. The first case represents the choice between money and bonds, where the maturity value of the bonds is fixed in money terms. If inflation or depression changes the general price level, the real value of a given holding of money changes in the same proportion as does the same-sized holding of bonds. However, bonds fluctuate in price, before maturity, with fluctuations in the interest rate; and they carry some default risk. Thus although the real value of bonds is highly correlated with that of money, the correlation is imperfect, and their risk is greater than that of money. The second case represents the choice between money or bonds, on the one hand, and stocks or real assets, on the other. The prices of stocks and real assets rise with the general price level, though with less than perfect reliability. Changes in their real values are comparatively uncorrelated with changes in the real value of money and bonds.

For the first case, we denominate the bonds in the same units as money, the numeraire.

$$p_2 = p_1 = p_1' = \bar{p}_1 = 1$$

We suppose that the future price of the bond has a random element ϵ

$$p_2' = p_1' + \epsilon = 1 + \epsilon$$

and

$$\bar{p}_2 = 1 + \bar{\epsilon}$$

Then

$$V = a_1 + a_2$$
$$V' = a_1 + a_2(1 + \epsilon)$$

and

$$\bar{V} = a_1 + a_2(1 + \bar{\epsilon})$$

If bonds have a positive expected money yield, that is,

$$\bar{\epsilon} > 0$$

$\bar{V}$ would be maximized by holding all bonds and no money.

However, risk is least with all money and no bonds. Equation (50) for this case becomes

$$\sigma_v^2 = a_2^2 \sigma_\epsilon^2$$

which can be made equal to zero by setting $a_2 = 0$. Therefore portfolio holders who dislike risk will be induced to hold bonds only if bonds offer a positive expected yield.

For the second case, we assume that the real value of money has a positive risk, denoted by $\sigma_{p_1}{}^2$, that the prices are relative (not money) prices, and that the probability distributions of future values of the two assets are independent. We have from (50)

$$\sigma_v{}^2 = a_1{}^2\sigma_{p_1}{}^2 + a_2{}^2\sigma_{p_2}{}^2 \tag{51}$$

Now consider how the risk associated with the portfolio is affected by increasing the amount held of the second asset and correspondingly reducing the amount of the first. We have from (51) and then (49)

$$\frac{\partial \sigma_v{}^2}{\partial a_2} = 2a_1 \frac{da_1}{da_2}\sigma_{p_1}{}^2 + 2a_2\sigma_{p_2}{}^2$$

$$= -2\left(a_1 \frac{p_2}{p_1}\sigma_{p_1}{}^2 - a_2\sigma_{p_2}{}^2\right) \tag{52}$$

In particular, suppose as before that the second asset is the more profitable, riskier one, and the question is whether to hold any of it at all. When none of it is held, the risk effect of introducing it is obtained from (52) by setting $a_2 = 0$, which gives

$$\left[\frac{\partial \sigma_v{}^2}{\partial a_2}\right]_{a_2=0} = -2a_1 \frac{p_2}{p_1}\sigma_{p_1}{}^2 < 0 \tag{53}$$

Since a_1, p_1, p_2, and $\sigma_{p_1}{}^2$ are all positive, (53) is necessarily negative *no matter how great the riskiness of the second asset.* That is, introduction of a risky, profitable asset into the portfolio both raises its overall profitability and up to a point lowers its overall riskiness; it is therefore necessarily worthwhile to add some amount of this asset to the portfolio. This proposition is valid even if the two assets are merely equally profitable, since in that case risk is lowered by diversifying (adding some of the riskier asset) without any loss of profits. It is valid also when there are many assets, since in that case the "second asset" can be a composite of all assets held other than the one we are directly considering, without effect on the analysis.

The result for bonds implies that no portfolio owner who dislikes risk will hold any bonds at a zero yield. In contrast, the result for other assets (stocks and real assets) implies that *every* portfolio owner who dislikes risk will hold some of these assets even at zero yields, assuming only that their real value has a zero or negative correlation with that of money. (In practice, the correlation has been negative in the past: stock prices have changed more than proportionately to changes in the general price level.) The conventional belief that all portfolios would shift entirely to money if all yields were zero is wrong, being based exclusively on the case of bonds. Portfolio owners who dislike risk would hold no bonds at zero yields, but *would* hold stocks and real assets. As a corollary, it follows that if the quantity of real cash balances were increased sufficiently, a point would be reached at which the public would be willing to hold existing private wealth without any risk premium, that is, without any excess of yield over the pure risk-free rate of interest. The only qualification on this conclusion is that its validity depends on the existence of some risk associated with the future real value of money.

4 LIQUIDITY TRAP?

The preceding analysis implies that the monetary sector cannot prevent the interest rate from falling far enough for full-employment equilibrium. In the preceding chapter, we found that consumption would rise far enough to assure full employment at long-term rates of interest near zero, regardless of short-term expectations. (We reach a similar finding on investment in Chapter 8, below.) We now find that there is some quantity of real cash balances large enough to drive the interest rate on every asset other than bonds to zero.

Keynes and other writers argued that the long-term interest rate might be held at or above some positive value by expectations of a later rise in the long-term rate. We have noted that bonds and other assets fixed in money terms may have minimum interest rates, but these present no problem for economic equilibrium: the monetary authority can buy them all or leave their interest rates where they are. It is the yield on real assets that matters for investment, and the argument of the preceding section implies that this yield can be zero when bond yields are positive.

An infinitely extensive demand for real cash balances at a positive interest rate is therefore impossible. An infinitely elastic demand curve for cash balances means that people are willing to hold additional real cash at the same rate of return on alternative assets no matter how much real cash they already hold. No matter how far the price level has fallen with given nominal cash balances and no matter how few alternative assets they hold, households prefer cash. This means, for example, that even if the price level falls so far that any household could buy all the world's marketable wealth with one of the small denomination coins in its possession, everyone will refuse to buy, presumably waiting because of fear of a capital loss should the price fall still further.

Such a proposition is out of the question, of course. No one has seriously suggested that matters could go that far. That a horizontal section (or almost horizontal section) of demand curves for cash balances might be sufficiently extensive to interfere with a stabilizing monetary policy is possible, but that is a different issue. Thus the liquidity trap is not an absolute bar to equilibrium.

In a competitive economy with perfectly flexible prices, there is some price-level low enough to assure full-employment equilibrium, with given nominal cash balances. Or, with flexible and stabilizing monetary policy, there is some nominal quantity of money large enough to assure full-employment equilibrium at any given price level.

However, as noted, there may be practical problems about reaching full employment. In the first place, few economists seriously suggest that price-level flexibility is either practical or desirable as the means to assure full employment. Habits and expectations, which help determine prices, adapt too slowly to bring full employment quickly—experience has proved that point. Moreover, when a variety of painless policy options appear to assure prompt equilibrium without transitional unemployment, and without fluctuations in the price level, these commend themselves for consideration.

On the face of it, a stabilizing monetary policy would appear to be enough to assure full employment, because an increase in the quantity of money can drive the interest rate down as close to zero as needed. However, if the needed rate should be very close to zero, the monetary authority might have to buy land in large quantities. Land would become the dominant real asset at very low rates, and portfolio balance would require cash balances in comparable, astronomical quantities. Considerations of portfolio risk imply that people could be induced to hold land at these prices, in preference to other assets, only if the quantity of real cash balances were of at least the same order of magnitude as the value of all land. If the quantity of cash were great enough, the risk of holding land would be balanced by the risk of holding cash, and monetary (portfolio) equilibrium would be possible.

A quantity of real cash balances immensely larger than the quantity of nonland assets could come into being in three ways. First, it would occur if the price level fell to the appropriate near-infinitesimal fraction of its present level. Second, the necessary money could be put into circulation, without a fall in the price level, if taxes were less than expenditures for a long enough time, the deficit being financed by money creation; the time delay could be made brief if the government printed the right amount of money at once and gave it away. Third, the monetary authority could exchange newly created money for land; it would have to buy land, because no other asset would exist in sufficient quantities to satisfy the assumed need for money creation. This third alternative is well outside the scope of monetary policy as it is usually interpreted and would more nearly resemble fiscal policy. Few would take seriously the first alternative, price flexibility, as a practical possibility. Consequently, if rates of interest extremely close to zero should be necessary for overall equilibrium, the only practicable way to get enough money into circulation to achieve portfolio equilibrium at an unchanged price level would be through some variant of fiscal policy.

5   THE SUPPLY OF MONEY

The portfolio analysis of the preceding sections applies equally to business firms and to banks. Like households, they economize cash more carefully at high yields on alternative assets than at low yields. In the case of banks, the cash that matters for portfolio analysis is excess reserves. The banking system as a whole in the United States can increase deposits without receiving increased Federal Reserve credit only by reducing their excess reserves. At high interest yields, in periods of "tight money," they do reduce their excess reserves compared to periods of low interest yields.

Thus the normal reaction of banks to changes in interest rates, along the same lines as the reactions of households and business firms, implies an upward-sloping supply curve of money, where "money" includes bank deposits. The Federal Reserve System could offset this normal reaction by reducing Federal Reserve credit when interest rates go up; however, they don't reduce credit, they increase it. Acting like any other bank, the Federal Reserve System usually allows member bank borrowing to rise when interest rates rise. Also, when the U.S. Treasury feels embarrassed by increased interest rates, the Federal Reserve typically buys portions of the Treasury's new issues. These practices reinforce the normal reactions of the banks.

Although the point is not well-established, the rate of interest and the quantity of money tend generally to drift upward and downward together during most phases of recession and recovery. Federal Reserve Board policy statements and descriptions of events support this impression. For example, consider the following quotation from a statement by the Chairman of the Federal Reserve Board of Governors in March, 1961:[1]

> Almost a year ago, in the *earlier part of 1960*, the Federal Reserve System began to lean against the incipient down-wind of what has come increasingly to be classified as the fourth *cyclical decline* of the post-war era.

[1] Statement of William McC. Martin, Jr., Chairman of the Board of Governors of the Federal Reserve System, before the Joint Economic Committee, March 7, 1961.

Already, as the winter faded, and with it the inflationary psychology that had characterized the economic situation carrying over from 1959, bank reserve positions—which govern the ability of the banking system to expand loans—had been made less dependent on borrowed funds.

Then, with the spring in progress, the Federal Reserve moved further: first, to promote still greater ease in bank reserve positions; and next, beginning in May, to provide additional reserves to induce a moderate expansion in bank credit and the money supply. . . .

Nevertheless, the money supply showed a stubborn downtrend until mid-1960. . . .

The most significant thing about the Federal Reserve's operations in 1960 is not that they were extraordinary but, instead, that they were typical of Federal Reserve operations under the flexible monetary policy that has been in effect now for a full decade.

That policy, as I have capsuled it before in the shortest and simplest description I have been able to devise, is one of leaning against the winds of inflation and deflation alike—with equal vigor. . . .

Now here let me note something about the decline in interest rates that took place in 1960. During the first eight months market rates on Treasury bills and intermediate term issues fell much more sharply than on bonds, as is usual in a period of decline. . . . (italics supplied)

The italicized parts of the quotation give the sequence of events, while the remainder makes clear that this sequence is regarded as normal Federal Reserve policy under the stated conditions. There are many other statements, and sequences of events, in a similar vein.

However, this is not a complete description of Federal Reserve policy. Sharp shifts in the supply of money, resulting from deliberate policy actions, appear from time to time. The impression is given that when an obvious decline in production and employment passes a certain point, a sharp shift to easier money can be expected and that the opposite shift can be expected once recovery has proceeded beyond a certain point.

Over long periods, the policy in peacetime appears to be one of allowing the quantity of money to increase approximately in proportion, or slightly more than in proportion, to the long-run growth in real output. Given the demand function for money this has been consistent with a very slight rise in the price level over long periods, apart from the inflations during and directly following wars.

BIBLIOGRAPHY

Bronfenbrenner, Martin, and Thomas Mayer: "Liquidity Functions in the American Economy," *Econometrica*, vol. 28 (1960), p. 810.

Cagan, Philip: "The Monetary Dynamics of Hyperinflation," in Milton Friedman
    (ed.): *Studies in the Quantity Theory of Money* (Chicago, University of Chicago
    Press, 1956), p. 25.
Duncan, Acheson J.: "'Free Money' of Large Manufacturing Corporations and the
    Rate of Interest," *Econometrica*, vol. 14 (1946), p. 251.
Friedman, M.: "Money, II, Quantity Theory," *International Encyclopedia of the
    Social Sciences* (1968).
Friedman, Milton: "The Demand for Money: Some Theoretical and Empirical
    Results," *American Economic Review Supplement*, vol. 49 (May, 1959), pp.
    525–528.
Kalecki, M.: "The Short-term Rate of Interest and the Velocity of Cash Circulation,"
    Review of Economics and Statistics, vol. 23 (1941), p. 97.
Kisselgoff, Avram: "Liquidity Preference of Large Manufacturing Corporations,"
    Econometrica, vol. 13 (1945), p. 334. "Reply," *Econometrica*, vol. 14 (1946),
    p. 254.
Latané, H. A.: "Cash Balances and the Interest Rate—A Pragmatic Approach,"
    Review of Economics and Statistics, vol. 36 (1954), p. 456.
Meltzer, Allan H.: "The Demand for Money: The Evidence from the Time Series,"
    The Journal of Political Economy, vol. 71 (June, 1963), pp. 219–246.
Meltzer, Allan H.: "Money, Intermediation, and Growth," *Journal of Economic
    Literature*, vol. 7 (1969), p. 27.
Patinkin, Don: "Financial Intermediaries and the Logical Structure of Monetary
    Theory," *The American Economic Review*, vol. 51 (March, 1961), pp. 95–116.
Robertson, D. H.: "Some Notes on the Theory of Interest," in *Money, Trade and
    Economic Growth*, in honor of J. H. Williams; reprinted in *Utility and All That*
    (New York, The Macmillan Company, 1952).
Samuelson, Paul A., and Robert M. Solow: "Analytical Aspects of Anti-inflation Pol-
    icy," *The American Economic Review*, vol. 50 (May, 1960), pp. 177–194.
Selden, Richard T.: "Monetary Velocity in the U.S.," in Milton Friedman (ed.):
    Studies in the Quantity Theory of Money (Chicago, University of Chicago Press,
    1956), p. 179.
Tobin, James: "Liquidity Preference and Monetary Policy," *Review of Economics
    and Statistics*, vol. 29 (1947), p. 124.

8

PRODUCTION, EMPLOYMENT, AND INVESTMENT

1 THE PRODUCTION FUNCTION: INTRODUCTION

In our models, we have presented the relationship between inputs and outputs almost exclusively in terms of the labor input. For short-term fluctuations in output, this is a reasonable simplification: output and labor employment are highly correlated. From a long-run point of view, this is a much less reasonable simplification, however; for long-run analysis and for many other problems, variations in capital and other inputs must also be taken into account, as we did in Chapter 5.

A striking feature of research results in the field of production is the wide variety of cases in which a single relatively simple form of function has fitted the data. This form is the Cobb-Douglas function, suggested by Charles W. Cobb and Paul H. Douglas in 1928[1]; in terms of the two factors labor and capital, the function is

$$y = \gamma N^\alpha K^\beta \qquad (54)$$

[1] Charles W. Cobb and Paul H. Douglas, "A Theory of Production," *American Economic Review Supplement*, vol. 18, pp. 139–165, March, 1928.

where y is the product, N and K are the quantities of labor and capital inputs, respectively, and γ, α, and β are constants.

With this production function, the marginal physical product of an input, say labor, is

$$\frac{\partial y}{\partial N} = \gamma \alpha N^{\alpha-1} K^{\beta} = \frac{\alpha}{N} \gamma N^{\alpha} K^{\beta} = \alpha \frac{y}{N} \tag{55}$$

If the wage w is equal to labor's marginal product, the total wage bill measured in units of the product will be

$$Nw = N \frac{\partial y}{\partial N} = \alpha y \tag{56}$$

That is, the fraction of the product going to labor will be α, labor's exponent in the production function. The corresponding proposition is true of capital.

Although it has worked well in most applications, the issue is not yet settled whether the Cobb-Douglas function, which has a unitary elasticity of substitution between factors, is a satisfactory representation of the aggregate production function. A variety of studies using both cross-sectional and time-series data have tried to measure the elasticity of substitution between labor and capital, with confusing results. Cross-sectional studies typically measure this elasticity at about 1 and higher, whereas time-series studies typically find it to be less than 0.5. Moreover, the results vary erratically with minor changes in the data and in the specification of the estimating equations. Research aimed at clearing up these problems is still proceeding actively.

In this connection, an alternative production function has served as a vehicle for empirical study. It is the constant-elasticity-of-substitution (CES) production function, first proposed by Arrow and others.[1] The function has the form

$$y = \gamma[\delta K^{-\rho} + (1 - \delta)N^{-\rho}]^{-\frac{\lambda}{\rho}} \tag{57}$$

where γ, δ, λ, and ρ are constants, and where the elasticity of substitution σ works out as

$$\sigma = \frac{1}{1 + \rho}$$

When $\sigma = 1$, $\rho = 0$, and the function becomes the Cobb-Douglas function. When $\lambda = 1$, it has constant returns to scale.

[1] Arrow, K., H. Chenery, B. Minhas, and R. Solow, "Capital-Labor Substitution and Economic Efficiency," *Review of Economics & Statistics*, pp. 225–250, August, 1961.

2 THE DEMAND FOR LABOR AND CAPITAL

To construct the national income models of Chapters 2 and 3, we took the capital stock as fixed and assumed the existence of an investment schedule without deriving it from the demand for capital stock. The production function, with capital stock as an explicit factor of production, gives us the basis for such a derivation. If this function is

$$y = f(N,K) \tag{58}$$

and if there is perfect competition in product and factor markets, the wage and interest rate in full equilibrium would be

$$
\begin{aligned}
w &= f_N(N,K) \\
r &= f_K(N,K)
\end{aligned} \tag{59}
$$

Equations (59) can be solved to show the demands for labor and capital stock as a function of the real wage and the interest rate. For capital, the appropriate variables are the expected average real wage during the whole economic life of new capital and the expected interest rate during the period the capital is being created. This latter period is short compared to the economic life of the capital, so that the current long-term interest rate should serve well in a demand function. However, the current real wage is unlikely to represent expected future real wages adequately, and these determine the expected yield of investment.

To represented expected investment yields, the most successful research has used a variable to represent expected output. In ordinary demand analysis for a consumer good or service, the prices of complements and substitutes prove to be useful variables, and the same should be true of the demand for factors of production; however, it has not worked out that way in practice. Output, profits, and real wages as seen by the firm tend to be highly correlated, so that any of them might prove to be a useful variable.

To illustrate the suggested demand analysis, consider again the Cobb-Douglas production function.

$$y = \gamma N^\alpha K^\beta \tag{54}$$

For given capital stock, we derive the demand for labor from

$$\frac{\partial y}{\partial N} = w = \gamma \alpha N^{\alpha-1} K^\beta \tag{55}$$

which gives

$$N = \left(\frac{\alpha\gamma}{w}\right)^{1/1-\alpha} K^{\beta/1-\alpha} \tag{60}$$

as a particular form of the demand curve for labor used in Chapters 2 and 3. Then similarly for capital we have

$$\frac{\partial y}{\partial K} = r = \beta\gamma N^\alpha K^{\beta-1}$$

$$\qquad\qquad = \beta\gamma^{1/1-\alpha}\left(\frac{\alpha}{w}\right)^{\alpha/1-\alpha} K^{(\alpha+\beta-1)/(1-\alpha)} \qquad\qquad (61)$$

which can be inverted to give desired capital stock as a function of the real wage and the interest rate. Alternatively we can write

$$\frac{\partial y}{\partial K} = r = \frac{\beta y}{K} \qquad\qquad\qquad (62)$$

and

$$K = \frac{\beta y^*}{r}$$

where y^* is the expected output level for which business firms plan their capital equipment. A similar derivation for CES or other production functions would also show desired capital stock as a function of expected output and the interest rate. (With constant returns to scale, we can get similar results by assuming downward-sloping demand curves for output.) This provides us with a basis for analyzing investment, to which we will return in section 4.

Equation (60), the demand function for labor, has an elasticity of $-1/(1-\alpha)$. When our knowledge of the aggregate production function improves, we can estimate this demand more reliably. But more fundamentally, we know from the theory of the firm that the elasticity of substitution between distinct factors must always be negative (or at most zero) in competitive equilibrium, and so the demand for each factor must slope down, like the demand for a commodity. Empirical work on production functions has conclusively shown that the elasticity of substitution differs significantly from zero with the right sign, even though its exact values remain in doubt. Thus the sign of the slope of the demand curve for labor is known both from theory and evidence and is free of controversy.

That substitution between capital and labor is possible and profitable over a wide range is confirmed by comparing production methods in different countries. For example, textile firms using the same equipment in Japan as their American counterparts use several workers to tend each machine, whereas in the United States one worker tends several machines. The large difference in labor costs compared to capital costs in the two countries is the explanation. One can find many examples of a similar nature; and systematic international comparisons of capital-labor ratios form a part of the empirical research that confirms the expected sign of the elasticity of substitution.

3 THE SUPPLY OF LABOR

It has long been a matter of speculation whether the quantity supplied of labor decreases or increases when the real wage increases. The evidence of history suggests strongly that it decreases: there has been a definite trend toward shorter working weeks with the passage of time and the growth of real income. At the same time, the size of the labor force as a fraction of total population has remained roughly stable; young people enter the labor force at a later age and older people retire at an earlier age than before, but these withdrawals have been approximately offset by increased participation of women, over that period for which data are available.

From a short-run point of view, the bulk of the nonseasonal variability in labor force participation is due to married women entering and leaving paid employment. (There is a strong seasonal variation connected with summertime employment of high school and college students.) Variation of these kinds is too small to play a major role in short-term variations of income. In the short term, changes in the demand for labor due to changes in general business conditions are the main source of variations in employment.

What we can deduce a priori about the supply of labor parallels our deductions about consumption and the demand for money, based as they all are on household decisions. However, in this case analysis fails to establish the sign of the slope. Leisure for the working member of the household is a good, like current consumption and like the convenience of cash balances. Therefore we expect that as real income increases, other things equal, leisure will increase at the expense of participation in the labor force. However, other things change systematically with real income, the most important of these other things being real wages. A rise in real wages increases both real income and the sacrifice of real income required for extra leisure. That is, it contains both an income effect and a substitution effect. The two effects work in opposite directions, so that a priori reasoning fails to establish the slope of the supply curve of labor.

As is true in the case of the effect of the rate of interest on saving, if we could separate a pure substitution effect we could be sure of its sign. Unlike the case of the rate of interest and saving, however, we can't be sure that the income effects on labor supply cancel out with arbitrary and short-run variation of real wages. An arbitrary increase in the real wage raises labor income at the expense of capital income; for households that supply labor, these effects do not cancel, because these households have less capital than do those that rely primarily on income from capital. Thus the labor supply itself will be influenced by an income effect.

4 THE INVESTMENT FUNCTION—INTRODUCTION

In Chapter 2, we assumed that the level of investment is a downward-sloping function of the rate of interest,

$$I = G_0 + G_1 i \tag{11}$$

with $G_1 < 0$. We reasoned that businessmen decide how much to invest by ranking the expected profitabilities of different projects and then undertaking those most profitable ones for which funds are "available" or those yielding a net profit after allowing for the cost of funds. In Chapter 3, we introduced income as a variable in the investment function, noting that variations in income imply variations in expected sales and output. Also, we introduced the real wage rate because of its role in the expected profitability of investment. Our analysis in section 2 suggests that these relationships should flow from the theory of the profit-maximizing firm. We found there a demand for capital stock as a function of the interest rate and expected output, as illustrated by the Cobb-Douglas case.

$$K^d = \frac{\beta y^*}{r} \tag{62}$$

Equation (62) gives us a demand for physical capital as a productive input, but it does not give us an investment schedule. To convert it to an investment schedule involves the speed of adjustment of the capital stock to its desired level. Moreover, this speed of adjustment can be complicated: it could change at one speed in response to changes in expected output and at another to changes in factor input prices. A change in expected output with no change in input prices means that firms will expand or contract without changing technology. Thus they will buy more or buy less of the same equipment for replacement and expansion and will not change the equipment they already have. In contrast, when relative input prices change firms will change the way they combine inputs and may change the types of machines they buy.

When the rate of interest changes, the full user cost $d + r$ of particular equipment changes proportionately more when depreciation d is small than when it is large; capital with low depreciation rates ("long-lived" capital) is affected relatively more. Therefore, at lower interest rates each firm will tend to find that the new capital that looks most profitable has lower average depreciation rates than does the capital it already has. However, the capital it already has will generally remain profitable and so will not be replaced immediately. Later on, when old capital wears out, it will be replaced with longer-lived equipment if the interest rate is still low.

This reasoning implies a two-stage adjustment of the capital stock when the interest rate changes. First, the number of machines will change to the new desired level; second, old machines will be replaced with different ones when they wear out. The first stage resembles the adjustment of capital stock to a change in expected output, while the second takes longer. This phenomenon is called the "putty-clay" concept of investment. It applies only where the type of equipment changes with changes in factor prices; if the most efficient opportunity merely involves changing the number of men per machine, without changing the type of equipment, the concept does not apply. To the extent that it does apply it means that interest-rate effects on desired capital stock will be spread out over a longer period than will the effects of a change in expected output. Therefore the interest-rate effects will be smaller in any given period than they otherwise would be and will be harder to measure.

Many of the above assertions have been borne out empirically. Investment functions fitted to time series and cross-sectional data have consistently done better with variables that represent expected output than they have with interest rates, except for residential housing and public utilities, where both types of variable do well. This latter result is to be expected, because as we noted above the interest rate is more important in the user cost of relatively long-lived capital. For plant and equipment investment, few studies have succeeded in measuring an interest-rate effect, and the issue is still in doubt.

Some studies at first showed an effect of current and lagged profits on investment, supposedly reflecting imperfections in the capital market; but the weight of evidence now shows these results to be spurious. An important source of confusion has been the interaction between investment and other economic variables. Investment fluctuates more vigorously than does any of the other main variables of the system and seems to cause most major economic fluctuations. During these fluctuations, when total expenditures, output, and employment fall, profits of business firms also fall; when the former variables recover, profits do also. Meanwhile the interest rate follows a course of its own, reflecting shifts in both the monetary and expenditure sectors. Therefore investment correlates better with profits than it does with the rate of interest. Since in practice the expectations and perceived opportunities of different business firms tend to be highly correlated with each other and with general business conditions, the same relationship holds for individual business firms. It holds also for investment in one year and profits of the previous year, since good years and bad years both tend to go in runs of several years at a time. It would be a mistake to interpret these relationships as showing conclusively that profits, either representing the availability of funds or the expected profitability of investment, are the principal determinant of investment. Rather, the interpretation should at least in part be just the reverse.

Another problem, one of semantics rather than substance, hinges on the failure to distinguish between a potentially important variable that has failed to vary much and a variable that has no effect when it does vary. Questionnaires addressed to businessmen, asking them the factors that determine their investment decisions, typically fail to make this distinction, merely asking the respondents to list factors in order of their "importance." If some other driving factor, such as opportunities or expectations, has varied relatively much more than has the rate of interest, the latter will naturally not be considered important. This says little, however, about how sensitive investment decisions would be to given changes in the rate of interest, other things equal; that is, it says little about the slope of the investment function.

5 INVESTMENT TO ADJUST THE CAPITAL STOCK

To illustrate the adjustment approach, suppose that from a long-run point of view businessmen determine their stocks of plant, equipment, and other capital as a function of current income and the interest rate. Consider again the Cobb-Douglas case, which gave us the demand equation (62). Putting it in logarithmic form, we have

$$\ln K^d = \ln \beta + \ln y^* - \ln r \tag{63}$$

Now consider what (63) implies for investment. Investment increases the capital stock toward the desired level; how rapidly business firms attain this desired level, given the costs involved, determines the volume of investment. Suppose that the speed of adjustment of business firms can be represented by a fraction δ by which they make up in one period the difference between the desired and actual capital stocks, in logarithms. To a first approximation, investment per period as a fraction of the existing capital stock will then be

$$\frac{z}{K} = \delta \ln K^d - \ln K = \delta \ln \beta + \delta \ln y^* + \delta \ln r - \delta \ln K \qquad (64)$$

The presence of $\ln K$ in (64) has important implications. What the capital stock is at the beginning of a period depends on past values of income and on the extent to which business firms have adjusted to their desired levels of capital stock in the past. As past values of expected production have depended on past values of income, past incomes as well as current income implicitly enter into this equation. Therefore, in this equation, investment depends on the movement of income and not merely on its level.

We illustrate this point with a simple case. Suppose that the adjustment of desired to actual capital stock is always complete in the current period, that is, $\delta = 1$ in (64). In this case it simplifies into the form

$$\frac{z}{K_t} = \ln \beta + \ln y_t^* + \ln r_t - \ln K_t \qquad (65)$$

where the subscript t has been attached to expected income, the interest rate, and the capital stock to indicate that they refer to the current period. Suppose also that expected income equals current income (output), $y_t^* = y_t$. Since adjustment was also complete in the previous period, we have

$$\ln K_t = \ln K_{t-1}^d = \ln \beta + \ln y_{t-1} - \ln r_{t-1} \qquad (66)$$

Substituting (66) into (65), we have

$$\frac{z}{K_t} = \ln \beta + \ln y_t - \ln r_t - \ln \beta - \ln y_{t-1} + \ln r_{t-1}$$

$$= \ln \frac{y_t}{y_{t-1}} - \ln \frac{r_t}{r_{t-1}} \qquad (67)$$

In this expression investment depends simply on the change in income and the change in the rate of interest from the previous period.

Equation (67) implies that if both income and the rate of interest remain constant, investment will be zero; the desired capital stock is the same as the existing capital stock, so that there is no net investment. If income has grown along a certain trend line, investment will be constant at some positive level as long as income continues to grow by the same amount each period, if the rate of interest remains constant. If the growth of income slows down, investment will suffer an absolute decline even though income is still growing; if the growth of income speeds up, investment will rise. This relationship implies great sensitivity of investment to changes in the rate of growth of income. This phenomenon is known as the *accelerator effect.* The more general expression (64) has the same implications, to a lesser degree. The adjustment of the capital stock to its desired level may take more than one period (the usual period for this analysis is a year); if so, fluctuations in investment are less volatile. This form of investment function is called the *flexible accelerator.*

Also, we have already seen that fluctuations in the investment schedule are damped by movements in the rate of interest because of reactions through the monetary sector. Finally, changes in income are partly discounted by business firms and do not lead to equal changes in expected output. Nevertheless, this analysis helps to explain the volatility of investment. Any change in expected production implies a large change in the desired capital stock (except when unemployed resources are readily available), and any significant change in the desired capital stock implies a massive flow of investment. Except where damping factors offset them, changes are magnified at each step in the multiplier-accelerator sequence.

Empirical work on investment, as noted above, broadly confirms this approach to investment behavior. Current output and other indicators of future profitability of a firm's investment, such as the value of its shares in the stock market, have the predicted relationship to investment after a lag. These indicators lead the peak consequent flow of investment by three or four quarters, and the investment flow continues at declining rates thereafter.

However, except in housing, public utilities, and the like, interest-rate effects have eluded attempts at direct measurement. In part, this may be due to the predominant role of other effects and the limited range of variation of interest rates over the periods studied in recent empirical work. It also may be due to longer lags in the effect of the interest rate, for plant and equipment investment. But as we noted in the discussion in section 2 of the demand for labor, it is enough for this purpose that the elasticity of substitution between labor and capital is known to have the expected sign. Most research on this elasticity confirms the expected long-term adjustment of capital to relative factor prices. Because we do not know the lag structure of the reaction of investment to changes in the rate of interest, we do not know the precise implications for investment of the elasticity of substitution; but it does confirm that the investment function has the expected slope.

6 INVESTMENT AT LOW RATES OF INTEREST

Since the development of Keynesian economics, there has been a sharp division of opinion on whether investment would rise considerably at very low rates of interest. Professor Knight and a few others took the view that virtually unlimited investment opportunities exist with positive rates of return; many other economists have accepted the view that investment would fail to increase significantly in response to any fall in the rate of interest, no matter how close to zero it fell.[1] This is purely an issue of fact, and given the widespread doubt that exists concerning investment opportunities when expectations are at depression lows, the burden of proof is on the proponent of unlimited opportunities to show where they are. In addition, if it can convincingly be shown that investment opportunities are ample, it must further be shown that a sufficient number of investors would find it advantageous to proceed at once rather than to delay starting the investments until later, regardless of short-run expectations. We shall consider this latter point first.

In typical recessions and depressions, business expectations for the short run are that sales and output are likely to remain low and perhaps fall lower for a time, before they get better. For this reason, many investment projects are delayed that would proceed immediately if short-run expectations were better. At the same time, the rate of interest when there is declining income and employment tends to fall below what it is when expectations are better. When business later improves, the equilibrium rate of interest will rise, and business firms must weigh the cost of installing capital that will not be employed for a time against the higher probable costs of borrowing or of securing new equity capital when expectations and business conditions improve. This consideration will weigh differently according to the durability or capital intensity of the investment. A more durable piece of equipment, or, more generally, one involved in a relatively capital-intensive process, is more affected by borrowing costs than a less durable one because interest or net capital yield is a larger share of value added, as noted earlier. For capital that depreciates or turns over rapidly (inventories, for example), interest costs are relatively unimportant. Consequently, the prospect that interest costs will rise later when business improves will have a greater effect on the optimal timing of very durable or capital-intensive types of investment than on that of less durable types, and will dictate

---

[1] See, for example, the following exchange: Nicholas Kaldor, "The Recent Controversy on the Theory of Capital," *Econometrica*, vol. 5, p. 201, 1937 and "On the Theory of Capital: A Rejoinder to Professor Knight," *ibid.*, vol. 6, p. 163, 1938; Frank H. Knight, "On the Theory of Capital: In Reply to Mr. Kaldor," *ibid.*, p. 63.

an earlier start on the more durable kinds than on the less durable kinds, for given expectations of when business is likely to improve.

Further, investment in things that do not depreciate when they are not used will be more sensitive than other investment to prospective rises in capital costs, because for it the cost of investing early, before the capital will actually be employed, is only the interest cost and does not include depreciation. For example, suppose a machine lasts ten years when actually used but lasts indefinitely when not used, and suppose that investors are acting on the assumption that a machine purchased now will remain idle for ten years. If it is expected that with the improvement in business the rate of interest will rise to q percent, it will be worthwhile to purchase the machine now if the rate of interest falls below $\frac{1}{2}q$ percent (approximately); in that case the total interest cost over the twenty-year expected life of the machine will be less than it would be if the money were borrowed and the machine purchased just before its ten years of active life. At the other extreme, if the machine has only a ten-year life regardless whether it is used or not, say because the machine rusts, it will not be worthwhile to buy it now no matter how low the rate of interest falls. Where the rate of depreciation is positive but small when the machine is not used, so that the machine would still have most of its useful life after ten years, it will be worthwhile to buy the machine now if the interest rate falls below some lower fraction of q percent than $\frac{1}{2}$.

The type of investment that might be undertaken when expectations are poor will therefore be a capital-intensive investment whose rate of depreciation is especially low when it is idle. There is, of course, no logical necessity for businessmen to expect that business will ever improve in the future or to expect that the interest rate will rise. We are now considering what is probable or plausible, however, and need therefore only note that after every recession and depression in the past business has gotten better and interest rates have risen. As a practical matter, it is safe to assume that businessmen expect this. If this is true, and if some types of capital last long enough when not used to have some value left after a long depression there will be some ratio of the current long-term rate of interest to the expected postdepression long-term rate of interest low enough to make it worthwhile to invest immediately in these types of capital.

If a machine's durability can be increased by using more durable materials and more careful workmanship, the increased investment in the resulting more expensive machine has a positive yield if the life of the machine is increased by a greater proportion than the proportion of increase in cost, for given prices and running costs. For example, suppose the machine as currently made is worthless after ten years of use, suppose that its lifetime can be increased to thirty years while doubling its cost, and suppose that it depreciates in value by a constant amount each year. For each dollar of original cost of the less durable machine, the more durable one will initially cost two dollars and will have a depreciated value of $1⅓ after ten years, when the less durable one is valueless. The extra dollar of investment now obtains an extra $1⅓ after ten years, giving an annual rate of return of 3 percent compounded. In the most extreme case, in which the more expensive machine lasts forever, the extra dollar of investment now obtains an extra two dollars—the whole cost of the machine—after ten years, giving an annual rate of return of 7.2 percent. However, if the machine's lifetime is only doubled by doubling the initial cost, each extra dollar of cost obtains only an extra dollar of value after ten years, giving a zero rate of return.

Most manufacturing equipment in the United States is made of metals of comparatively low durability such as cast iron and carbon steel. Substitution of stainless and high-hardness steels for these would lengthen the expected life of such equipment by a multiple of the order of ten to fifty times or more, while raising the cost by a factor of from five to ten times. (The details of these estimates are presented in Appendix A to this chapter.) If we take an intermediate figure of a cost multiple of seven for achieving this degree of increase in durability, a changeover of all current gross investment in producers' durable equipment to machines of the more durable kind would multiply gross investment in this equipment by seven.

However, it is unreasonable to suppose that all current gross investment in producers' durable equipment could be induced to switch over to the more durable machines, at any positive though low rate of interest. For some the rough calculation made in Appendix A would be inappropriate because of atypical conditions of wear and tear and atypical costs of increasing durability. For some, the risk of adverse price movements because of probable technical advance (that is, obsolescence) would reduce below zero the prospective rate of return to increased durability. Suppose then on these grounds we reduce our estimate of this prospect to cover only one-quarter of gross investment in producers' durable equipment. In this case gross investment would be multiplied by 2½ times ($7 \times \frac{1}{4} + 1 \times \frac{3}{4} = 2\frac{1}{2}$). This ratio would continue to apply as both gross investment and the total economy grew. When all machines in the affected quarter of the capital stock had been replaced by the more durable ones, replacement demand would fall to zero for a time and gross investment for this sector would fall by about half. As a result, gross investment would thereafter be about 1⅝ as much as it would have been had the less durable machines been installed throughout, until replacement demand commenced again. Thus the average effect on gross investment in producers' durable equipment over a long future period would be approximately to double it. If, in a period of bad expectations, the more durable type of machines were the only kind that would be installed, this durable investment alone would on the average amount to about the full-employment rate of equipment investment.

A second type of investment whose approximate yield is fairly easy to figure is land reclamation and improvement. The long-run productivity, net of the costs of utilization and of maintenance of fertility, of hilly land could be increased by flattening and grading; mountainous land good at most for grazing could be leveled and made arable, and marshy lands, lake bottoms, and the fringes of the ocean could be filled to make arable land. Although such investments rarely have a high enough productivity to be worthwhile at current rates of interest, they almost certainly have some positive yield.

In some instances, such as filling along the coast of the Gulf of Mexico and topping the fill with dredgings from the Mississippi River silt deposits, land of productivity comparable to the highest now existing could be created. A more detailed evaluation of yield is therefore unnecessary.

The first 50 miles or so out from the 1,500-mile United States coast of the Gulf of Mexico, the depth of the water reaches some 200 feet, with an average depth of around 100 feet. The average cost of filling at these depths would run over $450,000 per acre at present prices, the main element of the cost being transportation of the stone and earth fill over long distances. The total cost of filling the 48 million acres in the 50- by 1,500-mile strip would therefore be of the order of $19,600 billion. This investment by itself represents the full-employment investment of the United States economy for a period of about fifty years: full-employment investment in the decade of the 1960s averaged about $100 billion per year, and this figure will grow at around $3\frac{1}{2}$ percent per year. An opportunity of a similar magnitude exists along the Atlantic Coast, and if these are used up there is the possibility of going into deeper water. Investment of the same general order of magnitude would be involved in the leveling of mountains in those areas with sufficient rainfall to assure positive productivity of the leveled land. Leveling in the Great Plains also represents an opportunity of the same order of magnitude; the area is larger, but the cost per acre would be smaller.

All these investments together assure a huge backlog of investment opportunities at low rates of yield on equity investment. Even if expectations were so bad that gross investment of the current types fell to zero, and even if business were not expected to improve for ten or twenty years, there would be some positive rate of interest low enough to make these investments worthwhile, given their durability.

BIBLIOGRAPHY

Abramovitz, Moses: "Economic Growth in the United States," *The American Economic Review*, vol. 52 (September, 1962), pp. 762–782.

Abramovitz, Moses: "Resource and Output Trends in the U.S. since 1870," *American Economic Review Supplement*, vol. 46 (1956), p. 5.

Brown, Murray (ed.): *The Theory and Empirical Analysis of Production* (New York, National Bureau of Economic Research, 1967).

Clark, John Maurice: "Business Acceleration and the Law of Demand: A Technical Factor in Economic Cycles," *Readings in Business Cycle Theory*, ed. American Economic Association (Homewood, Illinois, Richard D. Irwin, Inc., 1951). Or in *Journal of Political Economy*, vol. 25 (March, 1917), pp. 217–235.

Cobb, Charles W., and Paul H. Douglas: "A Theory of Production," *American Economic Review Supplement*, vol. 18 (March, 1928), p. 139.

Dennison, Edward F.: "The Unimportance of the Embodied Question," *The American Economic Review*, vol. 54 (March, 1964), pp. 90–94.

Diamond, James J.: "Further Development of a Distributed Lag Investment Function," delivered at the Summer 1961 Meeting of the Econometric Society, Stillwater, Okla.

Domar, Evsey: "Expansion and Employment," *The American Economic Review*, vol. 37 (March, 1947), pp. 34–35.

Eisner, R.: "A Distributed Lag Investment Function," *Econometrica*, vol. 28 (1960), p. 1.

Eisner, Robert, and M. I. Nadiri: "Investment Behavior and Neo-Classical Theory," *The Review of Economics and Statistics*, vol. 50 (1968), p. 369.

Fabricant, Solomon: *Basic Facts on Productivity Change*, National Bureau of Economic Research, Occasional Paper 63 (New York, 1958), pp. 10–22.

Grunfeld, Yehuda: "The Determinants of Corporate Investment," in A. C. Harberger (ed.): *The Demand for Durable Goods* (Chicago, The University of Chicago Press, 1960).

Haavelmo, T.: "The Probability Approach in Economics," *Econometrica*, vol. 12 (1944), Supplement.

Jorgenson, D. W.: "The Theory of Investment Behavior," in R. Ferber (ed.): *Determinants of Investment Behavior* (New York, National Bureau of Economic Research, 1967).

Jorgenson, D. W.: "Anticipations and Investment Behaviour," *The Brookings Quarterly Econometric Model of the United States* (Chicago, Rand McNally and Company, 1965).

Jorgenson, D. W., and Z. Griliches: "The Explanation of Productivity Change," *The Review of Economic Studies*, vol. 34 (1963), p. 249.

Kaldor, Nicholas: "On the Theory of Capital: A Rejoinder to Professor Knight," *Econometrica*, vol. 6 (1938), p. 163.

Kaldor, Nicholas: "The Recent Controversy on the Theory of Capital," *Econometrica*, vol. 5 (1937), p. 201.

Knight, Frank H.: "On the Theory of Capital: In Reply to Mr. Kaldor," *Econometrica*, vol. 6 (1938), p. 63.

Koopmans, T. C.: "Identification Problems in Economic Model Construction," *Econometrica*, vol. 17 (1949), p. 125.

Koopmans, T. C.: "Statistical Estimation of Simultaneous Equation Relations," *Journal of the American Statistical Association*, vol. 40 (1945), p. 448.

Kuh, Edwin: "Theory and Institutions in the Study of Investment Behavior," *The American Economic Review*, vol. 53 (May, 1963), pp. 260–268.

Mincer, Jacob: "Labor Force Participation of Married Women," in *Aspects of Labor Economics* (Proceedings of the 1961 Conference of Labor Economics, National Bureau of Economic Research, Inc.).

Muth, R. F.: "The Demand for Non-farm Housing," in A. C. Harberger (ed.): *The Demand for Durable Goods* (Chicago, The University of Chicago Press, 1960).

Phelps, E.: "Money-Wage Dynamics and Labor-Market Equilibrium," *Journal of Political Economy*, vol. 76 (1968).

Samuelson, Paul A.: "Interactions Between the Multiplier Analysis and the Principle of Acceleration," *Readings in Business Cycle Theory*, ed. American Economic Association (Homewood, Illinois, Richard D. Irwin, Inc., 1951). Or in *Review of Economic Statistics*, vol. 21 (May, 1939), pp. 75–78.

Solow, R. M.: "A Contribution to the Theory of Economic Growth," *Quarterly Journal of Economics*, vol. 70 (February, 1956), pp. 65–94.

Solow, R. M.: "Some Recent Developments in the Theory of Production," in M. Brown (ed.): *The Theory and Empirical Analysis of Production* (New York, National Bureau of Economic Research, Inc., 1967).

Solow, R. M.: "Technical Change and the Aggregate Production Function," *Review of Economics and Statistics*, vol. 39 (1957), p. 312.

A APPENDIX
EQUIPMENT
DURABILITY

1 NOTE ON THE ECONOMICS OF DURABILITY

It was noted in the text that additional durability yields a positive profit only if the proportionate increase in durability is greater than the proportionate increase in cost. If the proportions were merely equal, a series of the short-lived machines with combined lives equal to the life of the durable machine would have the same total cost as it would. The costs of the series of machines would be deferred for all of them after the first one; and if buying the durable machine doesn't save some of these costs (other costs equal), the firm gains nothing by doing so. Looked at this way, the investment in durability has a zero yield when the two proportions are equal, and this approach and conclusion agree with the discussion in the text based on the depreciated value of the durable machine at the time the short-lived one would wear out.

The ratio of the proportionate increase in durability to the proportionate increase in cost is a crude but useful parameter for comparing different investments in durability. It can be shown that for any given value of this ratio the shorter the life of the short-lived machine the more profitable is the investment in durability. For example, suppose a machine costing $10,000 that lasts ten years can be replaced by another machine costing $20,000 that lasts forty years, and that each machine will produce an operating surplus of $1,500 per year before depreciation, throughout its life. Then the investment yield on the first machine is 8 percent and on the second is 7 percent. Now for comparison suppose a machine costing $1,440 that lasts one year can be replaced by a machine costing $2,880 that lasts four years, and that each machine will produce an operating surplus of $1,500 per year before depreciation throughout its life. The investment yield on the first machine is 8 percent and on the second is 43 percent. (All yields are force-rates of interest.) In both examples the cost ratio is 2, the durability ratio is 4, the annual operating surplus is $1,500, and the yield on the less durable machine is 8 percent. Shortening the durability of each machine (that is, subjecting it to more rigorous use) while holding the yield for the less durable machine and the cost ratio of the two machines constant increases the yield of the more durable machine.

Hence, in practice we should expect to see materials with given relative durability characteristics introduced first into those uses where depreciation is most rapid, provided the relative durability of these materials does not drop off in such uses. Suppose that the relative durability of the more durable materials is at least as great in the less strenuous, longer-life uses as it is in the more strenuous ones. *Then, we can be sure that investment in the more durable material has a positive yield if it is profitably employed in the more strenuous uses.* Its positive yield in the most strenuous use, the first use into which the material is likely to be introduced, establishes that the durability ratio d exceeds the cost ratio c; this implies that the yield of investment in durability is positive for every longer-lived use in which d/c is as great as it is in the use observed.

If we can find some currently profitable use of an expensive durable material in short-lived equipment, we need only establish that its contribution to relative durability is at least as great in longer-lived uses. That assures that the substitution yields a positive rate of profit in all such uses, assuming that the effect of durability on maintenance costs behaves normally. This reasoning makes it unnecessary to study detailed engineering data to determine profitability in each case; we need only consider the change in the durability advantage as we proceed to the uses involving slower depreciation.

However, uncertainty about future relative prices looms more important as we proceed to the uses involving slower depreciation. The longer a machine is expected to last, the longer the period in which it will be affected by changes in relative prices. Those changes in relative prices that can go in either direction, such as those connected with shifts in demand, involve additional risk for more durable equipment without involving any reduction in the mathematical expectation of profit. However, those changes in relative prices that result from technical advance are likely only to lower the value of the machine. A machine becomes obsolescent when the introduction of more efficient machinery lowers the price of the good it produces relative to the prices of other productive services. When this happens the economic value of a machine can fall to zero long before it would have if relative prices had remained constant. This consideration undoubtedly renders the expected yield negative in some cases where it would be positive at current relative prices and thus makes it unattractive to invest in extra durability at any positive interest rate, no matter how low. Most machinery will be affected to a greater or lesser degree by this risk, though some types of machinery obviously suffer from it more than others.

The foregoing analysis has assumed equal maintenance costs for both types of machines, which is usually not the case. It is reasonable to expect that maintenance costs will fall in a manner roughly comparable to the fall in depreciation costs. If all parts of a new machine have increased durability in the same proportion, relative to the corresponding parts of the old machine, their higher unit cost of replacement at correspondingly longer-spaced intervals will average out less than the old on an annual basis in the same way as depreciation. The costs of labor and other services connected with the maintenance activity will also be less on an annual basis than with the less durable machine. The same aggregate total of such services will be needed over the entire lifetime of the more durable machine as for the less durable one, since the same sequence of replacement and other maintenance activities would simply be stretched out over a longer lifetime. This implies a reduction in the annual cost of these services in exact proportion to the increase in the life of the machine.

Whatever the saving in annual maintenance costs for the more durable machine, its important feature is that it begins to be realized within the life span of the less durable machine. By contrast, the gain from durability per se is realized only after the less durable machine would be scrapped. The greater the ratio of the lifetime of the more durable machine to that of the less durable one, the greater the saving will be during the life span of the less durable one. This will be more true if most maintenance is concentrated in the latter part of the life of the machine, as is typically the case. Consequently this is a partial offset to the obsolescence consideration. In some cases, it will be the dominant factor in the profitability of the more durable alternative.

2   SOME ASPECTS OF DURABILITY

Although many physical characteristics are relevant to the durability of machinery, in proportions varying with the nature of the function the machinery performs, certain forces tending to limit the life of the machinery are nearly always present and are overcome in the same general ways. The most important causes of physical depreciation are abrasion, deformation, fatigue, and corrosion. The ability of materials to resist each of these kinds of wear tends to be correlated with their ability to resist the others, though an infinite variety of properties is available in different materials. We shall concentrate on some of the key properties of steel, the principal material in most machinery, and in particular on corrosion.

Corrosion and rusting rates vary as a function of the environment of the material, and the advantages of one material over another vary widely with the environment. As a general rule, the resistance of steel to corrosion varies directly with its chromium content; nickel and other alloying elements also increase resistance. The relative advantage of the high-chromium steels, measured in relative corrosion rates, tends as a general rule to decline with increasing corrosiveness of the environment. In ordinary atmosphere a very high-chromium steel lasts almost indefinitely—far more than a hundred times as long as ordinary carbon steel; in more highly corrosive environments such as those found in oil refineries and chemical plants, the high-chromium steel's life is sometimes as little as four times as great as that of carbon steel, itself very short.

As it happens, the increase of chromium content in steel into the "stainless" range, with suitable changes in the alloying elements and with suitable treatment of the steel, increases simultaneously the ability of the steel to resist all kinds of wear and depreciation. By increasing the chromium and other alloy content, the hardness, fatigue strength, tensile strength, toughness, and resistance to corrosion can all be increased, although for any given steel (and among different ones), some of these properties can be increased at the expense of others. Durability in almost any use can therefore be increased by shifting from the low-alloy and carbon steels, the ones predominantly used now, to stainless-type steels. The critical factor here is strength, particularly resistance to fatigue, given the superiority of these steels with respect to corrosion.

3   PRESENT USES OF STAINLESS STEELS AS EVIDENCE OF A POSITIVE YIELD TO DURABILITY

We noted in the discussion of corrosion that the less corrosive the environment, the greater is the relative lifetime of stainless steels with respect to it. The relative advantage, in terms of proportionate extension of life, of stainless steels is greater with less strenuous conditions of the types causing other kinds of failure as well. In section 1, we noted that if the fall in relative advantage with increasing strenuousness of use is not too rapid, the most strenuous uses will be the most profitable ones for the more durable material. Moreover when there is such a fall, that they are used now in some very strenuous use assures that their use in less strenuous uses would yield some positive profit at current prices.

At present stainless steel is used in many places where corrosion rates are high, for example, in the chemicals industry; this type of use is its most important at the present time. In automobile engines, it is used for exhaust valves and valve seats, where corrosive forces and high-temperature stresses are high. It is used in high-pressure, high-temperature dies and in other metal-working tools, where great strength, resistance to abrasion, and endurance are required. Hence it follows that it would have a positive, though possibly low, profitability in less strenuous, less corrosive uses, wherever the threat of obsolescence of the newest machinery types is not serious enough to nullify the gains from durability.

Among the types of industry where old types of equipment are still in use and where obsolescence is relatively unimportant are transportation and public utilities, food processing, the clothing industry, and others. Industries where obsolescence is clearly very important are the automobile industry, other consumer durables, electronics, farm equipment, and mining. Then there are mixed or doubtful industries. The chemicals industry, the steel industry, and the machine tools industry already use highly durable equipment in the places where it is most profitable. Not all the equipment of these industries is in heavy-duty uses, however, and some that is not could probably be made more durable with profit. Here the probability of obsolescence will vary greatly by type of equipment. Similar remarks concerning obsolescence also apply to textiles and light manufacturing generally; some obsolesce and some do not. Without detailed study of all these industries, the guess as to what fraction of investment could profitably be made much more durable, e.g., by changing over to the use of stainless steels from low-alloy steels, is bound to be arbitrary. The guess of one-quarter used in the text is not intended to be either highly conservative or the opposite, but merely a fair one that will serve to illustrate the magnitudes likely to be involved.

B APPENDIX

COSTS OF
LAND RECLAMATION
BY FILLING BODIES
OF WATER

The cost of stone, gravel, and earth fill ranges from 50 cents to $1 per cubic yard, plus transportation cost where distances are involved. A cubic yard of these materials weighs around 2 tons; the cost of transportation over land is about 1 cent per ton-mile, over water about one-fourth this amount. Earth and stone in large quantities for filling offshore in the Gulf of Mexico would not be available in the immediate area but would have to be brought a substantial distance. It is safe to say that it would have to travel an average distance of at least 100 miles by land and 100 by water, which implies a transportation cost of $2.50 per cubic yard. This plus the materials cost totals $3 to $3.50; the figure given in the text is based on $3.

The number of cubic yards in a space a mile square and 100 feet deep is 103,253,333; at $3 per yard, this implies a cost per square mile of reclaimed land of $309,760,000, or $484,000 per acre; the figure used in the text was $450,000.

9
THE IMPACT
OF
GOVERNMENT

1 INTRODUCTION

Throughout our analysis we have disregarded the government, treating its activities as part of consumption and investment. In effect, we have considered the government to be a combined household and business firm, like those in the private sector of the economy, and regulating its actions as they do. Whether this procedure is strictly correct depends on how households and business firms react to the government: in a world of accurate knowledge and foresight, it is correct.

Government expenditures on consumption goods and services add to the welfare of private households. Government expenditures on investment goods will yield their future product in one way or another to private households also. Under full employment, either type of expenditures reduces the total real resources currently available to households for private consumption and addition to wealth. If these facts are recognized and weighed accurately by households, then the government can, without error, be consolidated into the private sector.

This point has been overlooked by most authors, who have cast the government in a separate role, in effect as if private households ignored the goods and services supplied by government. As the truth may lie somewhere between the extremes of perfect knowledge and ignorance, we shall now consider the effects of government expenditures and of their financing from both points of view.

2 A CONTINUOUSLY BALANCED BUDGET

Suppose that government always finances its expenditures x by tax receipts t, without ever incurring either deficit or surplus in its accounts, so that $t = x$. If households disregard government expenditures entirely in making their decisions about current consumption and addition to wealth, they will look only at disposable incomes after taxes, not including government services. Accordingly, we have for the consumption function (in its simplest form)

$$c = a + b(y - t) = a + b(y - x) \tag{68}$$

where t is real tax collections, x is real government expenditures, and c now includes only private consumption, not government consumption. Total real national income, with government reported separately, is

$$y = c + z + x \tag{69}$$

Substituting (68) into (69) and collecting terms, we have

$$y = \frac{a + z + x(1 - b)}{1 - b} \tag{70}$$

where investment is assumed to be independent of income. If there is a shift Δz in private investment, we subtract the old from the new values in equation (70) and obtain

$$\Delta y = \frac{1}{1 - b} \Delta z = k \, \Delta z$$

Thus we have the same multiplier as before.

If, in contrast, there is a shift Δx in government expenditure, proceeding similarly we obtain

$$\Delta y = \frac{1}{1 - b} \Delta x(1 - b) = \Delta x$$

In this case, the multiplier is 1: the increased government expenditure adds itself, and nothing more, to aggregate expenditures. This result is due to the term $-bx$ in equation (68), which represents the taxation that finances the additional expenditure; the consumer reaction to this taxation reduces the overall effect below what it is for other expenditure changes, exactly canceling out the excess of the multiplier over unity.

However, if households value government expenditures as income, as they would meals supplied without charge at their jobs or other such income in kind, and similarly count in their consumption the consumption component of government expenditures, the consumption function will be

$$c + x_c = a + b(y - t + x) = a + by \tag{71}$$

Since the budget is balanced and the government expenditures count as income, the effect of taxation as such disappears; thus this consumption function is the same as the one originally considered, except that the government component of consumption x_c is now stated separately. The function (71) may also be written

$$c = a - x_c + by \tag{72}$$

Substituting (72) into (69) and collecting terms, we obtain

$$y = \frac{1}{1 - b} (a - x_c + z + x)$$

$$= \frac{1}{1 - b} (a + z + x_I) \tag{73}$$

where $x_I = x - x_c$ is the investment component of government expenditures.

Here the effect of a shift in private expenditures is the same as before. However, the effect of a shift in government consumption expenditures is now zero, since x_c does not appear anywhere in (73); the effect of a shift in government investment is now the full multiplier effect.

$$\Delta y = \frac{1}{1 - b} \Delta x_I = k \, \Delta x_I \tag{74}$$

An increase in government consumption will be matched by an *equal* decrease in private consumption, leaving no net increase in expenditure. An increase in government investment will be viewed and reacted to by consumers as an increase in income, in and of itself, even though it is financed by taxes. (The depressing effect of the taxes is fully offset by the receipt of income by the people who produce the additional government investment.)

The results for the case where households regard government consumption and investment as having full value are exactly those obtained originally when the government was considered as consolidated into the consumption and investment functions. The zero multiplier for a shift in government consumption, though it may appear paradoxical, fits into the original analysis because it shifts the *composition* of total consumption without carrying with it a shift in the total itself that consumers desire to have at any given level of income. We can view the private offset to the consumption supplied by the government as having two components: those who are taxed to finance it reduce their consumption by the fraction b of the taxes, the regular reaction to any change in income, and those who are the recipients or beneficiaries reduce private consumption by the fraction $1 - b$ of this consumption, the regular fraction saved out of any income received. The sum of the two fractions is 1, that is, $b + 1 - b = 1$, giving a total reduction in private consumption just equal to the consumption goods supplied by the government. We would have a similar result for government investment if it preempted an opportunity for private investment for the same object (e.g., public power); here the multiplier would also be zero.

3 TOTAL TAX RECEIPTS HELD CONSTANT

Suppose that instead of maintaining a balanced budget the government holds total tax receipts at a fixed level. If households disregard both government expenditures and government debt in making their consumption decisions, we have instead of equation (70) the expenditure sector function

$$y = \frac{1}{1 - b} (a + z + x - bt) \tag{75}$$

Here, as before, the multiplier for shifts in private expenditures is the original k; in addition, since t is a constant, the multiplier for any change in government expenditures is also the original k

$$\Delta y = \frac{1}{1 - b} \Delta x = k \, \Delta x \tag{76}$$

In contrast, if households value government expenditures as income, and government consumption as part of their consumption, but count as a reduction of their private incomes only taxes actually paid (that is, they disregard government deficits), the consumption function is as written in the first equality in (71). The expenditure sector now becomes

$$y = \frac{1}{1 - b} (a + bx - bt + z + x_I)$$

$$= \frac{1}{1 - b} [a + bx_c - bt + z + (1 + b)x_I] \tag{77}$$

where in the second equality we have separated x into its components x_c and x_I and collected the terms in x_I. Following the usual procedure, we find that the effect of a shift in government consumption is

$$\Delta y = \frac{b}{1-b} \Delta x_c = \left(\frac{1}{1-b} - 1\right) \Delta x_c = (k-1) \Delta x_c \qquad (78)$$

That is, the multiplier for this case is $k - 1$. The effect of a shift in government investment is

$$\Delta y = \frac{1+b}{1-b} \Delta x_I = \left(\frac{1}{1-b} + \frac{b}{1-b}\right) \Delta x_I$$
$$= (k + k - 1) \Delta x_I = (2k - 1) \Delta x_I \qquad (79)$$

The multiplier for this case is $2k - 1$. This relatively large multiplier is due to the desire to spend now (not to save entirely) some of the income implicit in the value of the government investment. Such spending adds to the respending of the income received by the productive services that supply the investment.

Besides valuing government expenditures as income, households may regard deficit financing as equivalent to taxation. The issue of a bond by the government to finance expenditures leads to future interest payments and possible ultimate repayment of principal. That is, it implies future taxes that would not be necessary if the expenditures were financed by current taxation. If a typical household were to save the entire amount that was made available to it by a switch from current taxation to deficit financing, the interest on the saving would meet the future tax charges to pay interest on the government bonds; the amount saved would be available to meet possible future taxes imposed to repay the principal of the government bonds. If the household has a definite consumption plan for the future, and if it knows the future tax effects of the shift from current taxation to deficit financing, then it will save all the disposable income it gets from the switch from current taxes to a bond issue. That is, the household will consume exactly the same amount, whichever form of financing is used.

For example, suppose that a city government undertakes a large new expenditure, such as the paving of its streets, that can be financed either by a special levy on property owners or by a bond issue. In the latter case, a known addition to property taxes will finance interest and repayment on the bonds. Suppose further that the typical household holds some amount of bonds in addition to its house, to provide for the retirement income of the heads of the household and for an estate for their heirs. If the city decides on the special levy, the household will sell part of its bonds to pay it; if the city issues bonds and levies a new property tax to service them, the household will expect to pay the (small) extra property tax over a long period rather than the (large) once-for-all special levy. It will come to the same thing from the household's point of view, however; the property tax increment will be just equal to the earnings of the bonds that the household would have sold to pay the special levy.[1] If the household is not confused or misinformed, it will make the same decision in either case on how to allocate its remaining resources among current consumption, retirement income, and estate. Hence the effect on consumption of tax and bond financing is the same, under these assumptions.

This result is clearer if we note that at the time of the expenditure the sale of bonds by households (to outsiders, presumably) in the case of a special levy is exactly equal to the sale of bonds by the city in the case of bond financing. The loss of interest income in the first case is equal to the cost of interest payments in the second. Moreover, the sale of the household's bonds to pay a special levy is matched by a rise in the sale value of the house because of lower future property taxes. There is therefore no reason for the household to react differently to the two cases; the only difference will be the form in which it holds its wealth. This perfect substitution between private and community assets and liabilities, as seen by the household, is plausible because of the known distribution of taxation under normal city government: a home-owning household knows how it will be affected by additional property taxes levied to service a bond issue.

When the choice between taxes and deficit financing is made at a higher level of government, especially at the Federal level, the situation is less clear because the distribution of future Federal taxes is uncertain. Nevertheless there is a strong presumption that future tax liabilities have some influence on consumption behavior. Consider the problem in relation to another type of example. Suppose the taxpayer is faced with the alternatives of a certain-sized tax to be paid once only, say 10 percent

---

[1] This assertion is not strictly accurate for two reasons. First, the servicing of municipal bonds typically includes amortization at a scheduled rate, so that total servicing exceeds the interest. Without serious loss of generality, however, we can assume that no amortization is planned; if the argument of the text is valid for this case, it is valid also for any schedule of amortization. Second, the rate of interest on the household's assets (and liabilities) is different from the rate on the city's bonds, unless the household holds only those bonds as assets. The difference in rates reflects differences in risk and in tax treatment, however, which to a first order of approximation makes the typical household indifferent between a sale of its own assets, with one yield, and a sale of bonds by the city, with another.

of one month's income, and a 10 percent income tax that will continue indefinitely month after month. If the tax is only temporary, the taxpayer can pay by drawing on past savings and will very likely make up the loss gradually over a period of several months or more. If the tax is permanent, he cannot handle the first month's tax in this way, because in subsequent months he has additional tax to pay at that time; he will have to make a permanent adjustment to about a 10 percent lower living standard immediately, paying most of this month's tax out of this month's consumption. Surely there can be no doubt that the taxpayer will behave differently, with regard to this month's consumption, in the two cases; he will take account of future tax liabilities. It follows that when the government increases his future tax liabilities, e.g., by deficit financing, it will affect his consumption immediately to whatever extent he foresees them. Exactly accurate foresight in this respect is an extreme case, as is the case of no foresight at all; we can be confident that the true multipliers will lie between the ones we obtain for these extremes.

If future tax liabilities implicit in deficit financing are accurately foreseen, the level at which total tax receipts are set is immaterial; the behavior of the community will be exactly the same as if the budget were continuously balanced. The government can be consolidated with the private sector; additional government investment has a multiplier effect equal to k, while additional government consumption replaces private consumption and has a multiplier effect of zero. Our results here are the same as for the corresponding part of section 2.

4 TAX REVENUES FLUCTUATE WITH INCOME

In practice, the government budget is not continuously balanced nor are tax receipts held constant; instead, tax revenues tend to rise when income rises and to fall when income falls. A simple way in which this might happen, which illustrates the principles involved, is that total tax receipts are a linear function of income,

$$t = t_1 + t_2 y \tag{80}$$

where t_1 and t_2 are constants. Since changes in tax revenues never absorb the entire change in income, we assume $0 < t_2 < 1$.

In this case, if households disregard government expenditures in making their private consumption decisions, the consumption function is

$$c = a + b(y - t_1 - t_2 y) = a - bt_1 + b(1 - t_2)y \tag{81}$$

and the expenditure sector function is

$$y = \frac{1}{1 - b(1 - t_2)} (a - bt_1 + z + x) \tag{82}$$

Following the usual procedure, we find that the effect of a shift in private investment is now

$$\Delta y = \frac{1}{1 - b(1 - t_2)} \Delta z = k^* \, \Delta z \tag{83}$$

Since t_2 is a fraction, $b(1 - t_2) < b$, and hence $k^* < k$. The new multiplier k^* is smaller than the original multiplier because the government takes a slice of additional taxation out of each increment to income, and consumers base their additional consumption only on what is left. The multiplier in this case for shifts in government expenditure is the same as for shifts in private expenditures.

$$\Delta y = k^* \, \Delta x \tag{84}$$

If households value government expenditures as income and government consumption as consumption, but disregard government deficits, the consumption function becomes

$$c + x_c = a - bt_1 + b(1 - t_2)y + bx \tag{85}$$

and the expenditure sector function is

$$y = \frac{1}{1 - b(1 - t_2)} [a - bt_1 + bx_c + z + (1 + b)x_I] \tag{86}$$

The multiplier for shifts in private expenditure is k^*, as given by (83). However, the multiplier effect for shifts in government consumption becomes

$$\Delta y = \frac{b}{1 - b(1 - t_2)} \Delta x_c = bk^* \, \Delta x_c \tag{87}$$

while that for government investment is

$$\Delta y = \frac{1 + b}{1 - b(1 - t_2)} \Delta x_I = (1 + b)k^* \, \Delta x_c \tag{88}$$

If households value government expenditures as income, government consumption as consumption, and government deficits as equivalent to taxes, the actual total of tax revenues is irrelevant, and the analysis of the latter half of section 2 is again applicable. Equations (71) through (74) continue to hold; the multiplier is zero for government expenditures on consumption and is k for government expenditures on investment.

5 SUMMARY OF MULTIPLIERS

The results of this chapter appear in Table 1. Each row in the table corresponds to a different tax policy, while each group of columns corresponds to a different assumption about the reactions of household consumption to shifts in government expenditure and to changes in the government budget deficit. The entry in each space in the table gives the ratio of the ultimate change in income to the shift in expenditure indicated at the head of its column, that is, the multiplier, for the set of assumptions applying to its row and column.

Note that the entries in column (1.2), the multipliers for a shift in government expenditures when households disregard everything about the government except the taxes it currently collects, are always between the corresponding multipliers in columns (2.2) and (2.3). Columns (2.2) and (2.3) give the multipliers for shifts in government expenditures when households react to government expenditures but not to deficits. In fact, in every row the entry in column (1.2) is a weighted average of the latter two multipliers, where the weight for the one in column (2.2) is b and the weight for the one in column (2.3) is $1 - b$. Thus, if the government were to shift its expenditures with a fraction b of consumption and a fraction $1 - b$ of investment, households would act as though they disregarded government expenditures entirely; this is true regardless of the type of financing used (where households disregard deficits). The reason is that the indicated composition of the shift in government expenditures is just that mix of consumption and investment that households privately would adopt; hence they would not react to it in determining private consumption.

Note also that all three rows are the same in the group of columns (3). This naturally follows from the assumption that households react to deficits in the same way as to taxes; a given shift in expenditure will therefore have the same effect regardless of the nature of the financing of the government budget.

6 VARIATIONS IN TAXES

The analysis of government multipliers implies that if households disregard future tax liabilities connected with outstanding government

Table 1 Multipliers under various assumptions about household behavior and tax receipts

Assumptions about behavior of households

	(1) Households disregard both government expenditures and government deficits		(2) Households include government expenditures in income and government consumption in consumption, but disregard government deficits			(3) Households include government expenditures in income and government consumption in consumption, and regard deficits as equivalent to taxation		
	Types of expenditure shifts							
Assumptions about tax receipts	*Private expenditure* Δz or Δa (1.1)	*Government expenditure* Δx (1.2)	*Private expenditure* Δz or Δa (2.1)	*Government consumption* Δx_c (2.2)	*Government investment* Δx_I (2.3)	*Private expenditure* Δz or Δa (3.1)	*Government consumption* Δx_c (3.2)	*Government investment* Δx_I (3.3)
(a) Continuously balanced budget $t = x$	$\dfrac{1}{1-b}$ $(=k)$	1	$\dfrac{1}{1-b}$ $(=k)$	0	$\dfrac{1}{1-b}$ $(=k)$	$\dfrac{1}{1-b}$ $(=k)$	0	$\dfrac{1}{1-b}$ $(=k)$
(b) Fixed total tax receipts ($t = $ const)	$\dfrac{1}{1-b}$ $(=k)$	$\dfrac{1}{1-b}$ $(=k)$	$\dfrac{1}{1-b}$ $(=k)$	$\dfrac{b}{1-b}$ $(=k-1)$	$\dfrac{1+b}{1-b}$ $(=2k-1)$	$\dfrac{1}{1-b}$ $(=k)$	0	$\dfrac{1}{1-b}$ $(=k)$
(c) Tax receipts fluctuate with income $t = t_1 + t_2 y$	$\dfrac{1}{1-b(1-t_2)}$ $(=k^*)$	$\dfrac{1}{1-b(1-t_2)}$ $(=k^*)$	$\dfrac{1}{1-b(1-t_2)}$ $(=k^*)$	$\dfrac{b}{1-b(1-t_2)}$ $(=bk^*)$	$\dfrac{1+b}{1-b(1-t_2)}$ $[=(1+b)k^*]$	$\dfrac{1}{1-b}$ $(=k)$	0	$\dfrac{1}{1-b}$ $(=k)$

bonds, a tax cut will have a multiplier effect. This can be seen most easily by comparing the first and second rows of the column for government expenditures in part (1) of Table 1. If both expenditures and tax revenues are increased by the same amount, the multiplier is 1, whereas if expenditures are increased and tax revenues held constant, the multiplier is k. The difference between these two results, $k - 1$, tells us what the effect would be of cutting taxes back from the higher level to the original level. Thus the multiplier effect of a tax cut is $k - 1$ with the assumed household behavior.

However, if households fully anticipate future tax liabilities, a tax cut financed by increased government debt will have no multiplier effect whatever: the reduction in taxes is just offset by prospective future taxes in connection with the future servicing of the additional debt. This can be seen by comparing the first two rows of either government expenditure column of part (3) of Table 1; as the multiplier is the same whether an increase in expenditures is financed by taxes or by increased debt, the switch from one method of finance to the other has no multiplier effect.

Whether or not households adjust to future tax liabilities in determining their consumption, a tax cut financed by money creation will be regarded by them as an addition to income; the issuance of money does not imply future interest payments to be financed by taxes. (For present purposes it is sufficient to consider the outcome when the price level remains constant.) The multiplier will therefore be the same in this case as in the case where households disregard deficit financing, that is, $k - 1$. Allowing for the possibility of increased transfer payments (negative taxes), private expenditures can be increased to an unlimited extent by this means.

In particular, the government can induce a big enough increase in private expenditures to permit a high enough equilibrium interest rate for normal monetary policy. An increase in government expenditures, especially investment expenditures, would also suffice, via the relevant multiplier from the preceding section.

7 OPEN-MARKET OPERATIONS AND MONEY CREATION

The discussion of the preceding two sections has an important bearing on the monetary sector. We have noted a possible effect on taxpayers of changes in their expected tax liabilities, in connection with changes in the outstanding government debt. We can imagine changes in the quantity of money occurring in two distinct ways: the government can drop money from airplanes or confiscate some part of outstanding cash balances (as is typically done in a "currency reform"), on the one hand, or it can exchange money for government interest-bearing obligations, on the other. The second method alters the nonmoney assets and liabilities of the private sector, while the first does not. If the typical household does not give equal weight to a change in its holdings of government bonds and to the corresponding opposite change in its future tax liabilities, the net effect on the household's view of its financial position will differ for the two methods of changing the quantity of money.

Indeed, such an asymmetry of household calculation implies a modification of the monetary sector, if there are government bonds outstanding, with either manner of change in the money supply. We argued previously that the demand for real cash balances should be unaffected by a change in the price level, so that the demand function can be written

$$m = L(i,y) \tag{19}$$

This implies that a change in the quantity of money results in an equiproportionate change in the equilibrium price level, other things equal. A change in the price level will change the real value of the outstanding stock of government bonds, however, and will therefore change the real nonmoney wealth the private sector believes itself to hold, if households have the asymmetry of outlook just indicated. This change in nonmoney wealth must in general be expected to cause a change in the quantity demanded of real cash balances. For example, it is possible that people who feel less wealthy than before, with unchanged incomes, will choose to economize more on real cash balances. A contrary argument is also possible, namely, that they will feel less "liquid," that is, less able to meet financial contingencies, because of the reduction in real wealth, and will therefore choose to offset this partly by holding more of their remaining wealth in the relatively liquid form of cash. In either case, equation (19) is disturbed; a new variable must be introduced, the real quantity of government debt.

$$m = L\left(i,y, \frac{B_g}{P}\right) \tag{89}$$

where B_g is the total of government debt.

With this alteration in the monetary sector, it will generally not be true that a change in the quantity of money will change the equilibrium price level in the same proportion; further, the amount by which the price level changes will depend on the manner in which the quantity of money is increased. An open-market operation directly changes B_g

because the monetary authority is exchanging bonds for money and then has the effect of changing B_g/P further in the same direction because of the resultant change in the price level. A direct gift or confiscation of money involves the second effect but not the first and so will have a different ultimate effect on the price level. Each different change in B_g/P implies, in general, a different change in the equilibrium price level, through its role in (89).

These results apply when there is some asymmetry in household reactions to government. When household behavior permits full consolidation of the government sector with the private sector, the simpler form of equation (19) rather than (89) applies.

Moreover, when households anticipate all future taxes, an open-market operation by the monetary authority has the same multiplier effect as does a deficit financed by money creation. Both add to the money supply, and both substitute this addition for bonds that would otherwise be held by private households and firms. Thus both cancel the future tax liability implied by these bonds. For this case of household behavior, the multiplier is $k - 1$ for every change in the money supply, whatever causes the change. (Changes in investment produce an additional multiplier effect of k.) Thus for this case the only relevant policies are expenditure policy and policy for the money supply. It contrasts sharply with the case in which households disregard future taxes, in which the mix between taxes and deficit affects expenditures, and in which monetary policy has no multiplier effect.

BIBLIOGRAPHY

Baumol, W. J., and M. H. Peston: "More on the Multiplier Effects of a Balanced Budget," *American Economical Review*, vol. 45 (1955), pp. 140–148.

Bishop, Robert L.: "Alternative Expansionist Fiscal Policies: A Diagrammatic Analysis," part 3, chap. 5 in Lloyd Metzler et al.: *Income Employment and Public Policy* (New York, W. W. Norton & Company, Inc., 1948).

Gurley, John G.: "Fiscal Policies for Full Employment: A Diagrammatic Analysis," *Journal of Political Economy*, vol. 60 (1952), pp. 525–533.

Haavelmo, T.: "Multiplier Effects of a Balanced Budget," *Econometrica*, vol. 13 (1945), pp. 311–318.

Haberler, Gottfried: "Multiplier Effects of a Balanced Budget: Some Monetary Implications of Mr. Haavelmo's Paper," *Econometrica*, vol. 14 (1946), p. 148f.

Musgrave, Richard A.: *The Theory of Public Finance: A Study in Public Economy* (New York, McGraw-Hill Book Company, 1959).

Rolph, Earl R., and George F. Break: *Public Finance* (New York, The Ronald Press Company, 1961).

Samuelson, Paul: "Simple Mathematics of Income Determination," in *Income, Employment and Public Policy, Essays in Honor of Alvin H. Hansen* (New York, W. W. Norton & Company, Inc., 1948).

10
POLICIES
FOR ECONOMIC
STABILIZATION

1 INTRODUCTION

By virtue of their great bulk in most national economies, governments cannot avoid playing an important role in economic stabilization. Indeed, it is now universally taken for granted that a national government should deliberately contribute to stability of income and employment at satisfactory high levels, or at least should avoid aggravating whatever instability there may be. There is less agreement about exactly what and how much the national government should do, as a brief review of the development of modern views of this subject shows. This chapter also shows the application of our analysis of previous chapters and of the concept of efficient resource allocation to this problem.

The two main ways the government influences economic stability are through monetary policy and fiscal policy. The former consists of policies directly affecting the supply curve of money, such as the open-market policy and the direct-lending policy of the central bank; the latter consists primarily of policies determining the total expenditures and total tax collections of the government.

2 MONETARY AND FISCAL POLICY: THE SETTING

Monetary and fiscal policies in the past few decades present a contrast. Fiscal policy has evolved steadily from the primitive "balance the budget" outlook. Economists have regularly contributed to its evolution and have seen their views reflected in proposals and decisions of the U.S. Congress and of the executive branch. In contrast, monetary policy has evolved but little, from an equally primitive beginning. Moreover, neither the authorities nor economists have used the theories of micro- and macroeconomics to enrich their understanding of the role of monetary policy, as a rule. Little of the discussion of monetary policy, unlike fiscal policy, uses any systematic theory or model of the role of money and government in the economy such as the approach we take here to both subjects.

MONETARY POLICY

The Federal Reserve Act of 1913 described itself as "An act to provide for the establishment of Federal reserve banks, to furnish an elastic currency, to afford means of rediscounting commercial paper, to establish a more effective supervision of banking in the United States, and for other purposes." The text of the Act authorized that "any Federal reserve bank may discount notes, drafts, and bills of exchange arising out of actual commercial transactions; that is, notes, drafts, and bills of exchange issued or drawn for agricultural, industrial, or commercial purposes . . . but . . . shall not include notes, drafts, or bills covering merely investments . . . or trading in stocks, bonds, or other investment securities, except bonds and notes of the Government of the United States." At the time of the formal establishment of the System, the Comptroller of the Currency stated that

> It supplies a circulating medium absolutely safe, which will command its face value in all parts of the country, and which is sufficiently elastic to meet readily the periodical demands for additional currency, incident to the movement of crops, also responding promptly to increased industrial or commercial activity, while retiring from use automatically when the legitimate demands for it have ceased. Under the operation of this law such financial and commercial crises, or 'panics,' as this country experienced in 1873, in 1893, and again in 1907, with their attendant misfortunes and prostrations, seem to be mathematically impossible. . . . it furnishes a discount system by which every well-managed member bank may have the opportunity of converting into money by rediscounting . . . all commercial paper having not more than three months to run . . . to enable banks to meet the demands which may arise from unexpected runs, or in financial crises, or other extraordinary demands. . . . by making

it possible for any well-managed bank to convert its assets readily into cash to meet unexpected contingencies or runs, the necessity for large reserves heretofore required ceases.

These provisions of the Act and opinions of its effects reflected the known problems it was designed to correct. The history of the United States before the First World War had been repeatedly punctuated with depressions and recessions that almost always included banking panics, whose severity often made matters worse. Often the boom before the panic and recession had included speculation in securities, which was blamed for the later trouble. Prevailing opinion just before the war blamed the laissez-faire approach to banking and the lack of a central bank for these problems, and this opinion led to the creation of the Federal Reserve System.

The hopes for the Federal Reserve System in the early years of its existence stood on two ideas of its role in preserving overall economic stability, one relating to recessions and one to inflations. First, it would prevent wholesale banking failures and protect the integrity of the monetary and credit system by serving as a banker of last resort: when banks were in trouble, they could turn to the Federal Reserve Banks for rescue. Second, it would avoid dangerous credit expansion, which might lead to a speculative boom and a subsequent collapse, by extending credit only for bills of exchange arising out of actual commercial transactions. If the Federal Reserve System extended credit only for the purchase of goods actually in existence, so the theory went, the System could never support dangerous speculation or unsound expansion. This view is known as the *real bills doctrine.*

The real bills doctrine had two major defects. First, by emphasizing the quality and not the quantity of the credit base, it overlooked the main possible source of inflationary monetary expansion. If it issued too much credit, the Federal Reserve System would finance an inflation by assisting businessmen bidding against each other, in effect, for the same real goods. Second, it overlooked credit expansion based on U.S. Treasury obligations, which the Federal Reserve System dealt in freely and which existed in large quantities even then.

Both these defects showed their effects immediately, during the inflation that started during the First World War and continued through 1920. The U.S. Treasury sold securities to the Federal Reserve System in exchange for newly created money, to hold down their interest cost, during wartime deficit financing. The attendant business boom led the commercial banks to rediscount freely with the System and to expand credit. This latter source of new money was even more important than the first: by 1920, member banks had borrowed more than their reserves, even though they satisfied the apparent restrictions on the purposes of the borrowings. This heavy borrowing shocked the Federal Reserve Board. As a result, the Governors started to speak of the quantity of Federal Reserve credit as a policy variable. Then later in the 1920s they formulated the doctrine that responsible bankers don't like to remain continuously in debt to the central bank; that is, the Governors put member banks on notice that the System would not permit them to do so. Thereafter the Governors clearly understood that the quantity of money and credit would not automatically be kept in bounds by following the dictates of the real bills doctrine. The new doctrine implied in fact that monetary policy had moved from primarily automatic to almost wholly discretionary control by the Central Bank.

The System's official self-description puts the change as follows:

> For the first two decades of the System's existence, Federal Reserve Bank authority to extend credit was confined to advances collateraled by obligations of the United States and to discounts of or advances on so-called 'eligible paper.' Eligible paper includes commercial paper representing loans of limited maturities to meet the current needs of commerce, industry or agriculture but excludes loans made for investment or speculative purposes. It was thought by the System's founders that this limitation of Federal Reserve lending authority would act as an automatic brake on overexpansion of bank credit and money. Experience showed that such restrictions on the types of paper eligible for discount did not in fact prevent an overexpansion of bank credit and money in periods of business boom when eligible paper was plentiful. . . . In coping with emergency banking developments, member banks properly feel free to rely on full use of Federal Reserve lending facilities to meet unusual cash drains which they may experience. Under normal banking conditions, however, member banks generally are reluctant to borrow from a Federal Reserve Bank, or to stay long in debt. Special circumstances may at times weaken this reluctance, but it nonetheless persists as a force affecting member bank borrowing. . . . In general, it is a well-established rule of prudence for member bank operations that, under normal conditions, borrowing from the Federal Reserve Banks should be to replenish reserves when, in meeting temporary banking needs, they have fallen below current legal requirements. Accordingly, when member banks are obliged to borrow, they feel under pressure to restrict their lending or to adjust their investment positions in order to pay off such indebtedness as soon as possible.
>
> The policy of the Federal Reserve with respect to member bank borrowing expresses itself . . . in granting or discouraging loans.

In their annual report for 1926, the Board had put it more bluntly:

> Though there are circumstances that may explain and justify continuous borrowing by a member bank over a considerable period of time, particu-

larly if the need for borrowing arises from general economic conditions in the borrowing bank's locality, the funds of the Federal reserve banks are primarily intended to be used in meeting the temporary requirements of members, and continuous borrowing by a member bank as a general practice would not be consistent with the intent of the Federal Reserve Act.

The hope that the System would serve as a banker of last resort, preventing monetary crises with cumulative runs on the banks, also proved too optimistic. Events in 1914, when the System was being formed, proved prophetic, although they were not understood at the time. Following the crisis of 1907, Congress had passed the Aldrich-Vreeland Act of May 30, 1908, permitting the issue of emergency currency, through "national currency associations," without the customary backing of gold; that is, it permitted the printing and issue of a limited amount of new money for five years. Although no new money had been issued with this authority, the Federal Reserve Act of 1913 extended it for a further year. Before the outbreak of World War I, heavy gold outflows began and threatened to create a banking crisis, but the emergency currency provisions prevented it. At that time, the Federal Reserve System was just being formed, and the observers of the day overlooked the lessons of the episode. Being on the gold standard limited the Federal Reserve System's powers to issue credit, in a banking crisis or at any other time. It could not simultaneously observe the rules of the gold standard and prevent a monetary contraction by issuing credit to the banks, if gold flowed out of the country.

This problem came home to roost in the depression of 1929–1933. The collapse of the speculative boom on the stock market led to a recession, which worsened, after occasional signs of recovery, when banking failures accompanied a general monetary contraction. Then, in August, 1931, began the collapse of the international gold standard, spreading from one country to another, and leading to a massive outflow of gold from the United States. The public began withdrawing currency in large quantities from the banks. The Federal Reserve System allowed bank reserves to contract, and banks began to fail wholesale. By March, 1933, the banking system had collapsed and virtually all banks were closed. The Federal Reserve System had failed in what many had believed was its main function.

Congress responded to the crisis by going off the gold standard and by creating the Federal Deposit Insurance Corporation (FDIC). The Corporation takes over banks that fail and keeps them open, generally assuring depositors of the immediate availability of their deposits at full value. Although the FDIC has reserves equal to scarcely more than 1 percent of insured deposits, the confidence it creates has helped to prevent any monetary crisis in the nearly four decades since its creation. Moreover, just as Congress acted promptly to moderate the monetary contraction and banking crisis of 1932–1933, one may suppose it would act promptly again if events threatened to overwhelm the FDIC. (These and other cases suggest that, for all its obvious defects and delays, the Congress is at least as good an instrument of monetary policy as is the Federal Reserve System it created. As a sequel, in the 1960s Congress responded to a new gold outflow by authorizing the suspension of the remaining requirement for gold backing of Federal Reserve liabilities.)

There remained the unresolved problem of possible inflation through monetary expansion by Federal Reserve purchase or rediscount of federal government bonds, notes, and bills. As noted earlier, it had happened during World War I, when the inflation was further fed by unrestrained borrowing by the banks from the System. It happened again during and after World War II, when the Treasury again preferred monetary expansion to a high interest rate on bonds issued to finance the wartime deficit. Although the deficit financing ended with the end of the war, at the Treasury's insistence the System continued to hold down the interest rate on government bonds through 1950. At the time, business, the public, the authorities, and most economists feared the return of depression and unemployment, so that the postwar inflation was less serious than it otherwise might have been. It ended with a recession in 1949, in spite of a rate of interest on government bonds of less than $2\frac{1}{2}$ percent, which now seems absurd. In the spring of 1950 recovery began, and it received a strong boost in the summer with the outbreak of the Korean War. Now, instead of depression, the public and business feared the return of wartime controls and shortages; the price level shot up, and money and credit grew rapidly.

By this time, the Federal Reserve System fully understood the inflationary potential of its policy of holding down the interest rate on government bonds, and it asked for a change in the policy. In due course, the System had its way, reaching an "accord" with the Treasury announced in March, 1951. Interest rates on government bonds drifted upward toward 3 percent thereafter, and the System sharply curtailed its purchases of government bonds. In its annual report for 1951, the Board of Governors said, "Federal Reserve net purchases . . . totaled 1380 million dollars in the first four months of the year, declined to 250 million in May and June and to less than 20 million in the last half of 1951." Shifting from continuous support to hold down interest rates, the System bought government bonds only occasionally to limit day-to-day movements in these rates. The extraordinary thing about this change in policy was that it happened in the middle of a war. Due to this and to the limited resource demands of the war, the price level stopped rising after February, 1951, and remained stable for several years.

These episodes illustrate the trial and error, ad hoc development of monetary policy since the establishment of the Federal Reserve System. The crises have led to policy changes and to the creation of new monetary institutions, but no positive doctrine or theory of monetary management has emerged.

FISCAL POLICY

Fiscal policy contrasts sharply with this record, even though it too has had its trial and error elements. In the 1920s the guidelines of fiscal virtue were to keep the budget balanced and small. In the early 1930s, the federal government started emergency public works and relief expenditures but continued to set these guidelines as its goal. President Roosevelt expressed the accepted views of the times in his request of March 10, 1933 to the Congress for the passage of the Economy Act of 1933:

> For three long years the Federal Government has been on the road toward bankruptcy. . . . For the fiscal year 1934, . . . the deficit will probably exceed $1,000,000,000 unless immediate action is taken. Thus we shall have piled up an accumulated deficit of $5,000,000,000. With the utmost seriousness I point out to the Congress the profound effect of this fact upon our national economy. It has contributed to the recent collapse of our banking structure. It has accentuated the stagnation of the economic life of our people. It has added to the ranks of the unemployed. . . . Upon the unimpaired credit of the United States Government rest the safety of deposits, the security of insurance policies, the activity of industrial enterprises, the value of our agricultural products and the availability of employment. . . . National recovery depends upon it. Too often in recent history liberal governments have been wrecked on rocks of loose fiscal policy.

So saying, he proposed and Congress agreed to reduce veterans' benefits, and to reduce salaries of federal employees by 15 percent, along with other minor economies.

However, the President showed some understanding of the fiscal impact on the private sector of the economy, in terms which, though not entirely new at the time, had a modern ring. In a comment on his June 16, 1933 request for public works expenditures under Title II of the National Industrial Recovery Act, he said "(1) it would employ a vast number of idle men and women in useful work; (2) it would create a substantial resumption of enterprise which was an essential element in the fight for recovery; (3) it would act as a means of priming the pump of business by distributing purchasing power throughout the land." Nevertheless, a balanced budget was still a near-term objective. In his budget message of January 3, 1934, he said,

> The excess of expenditures over receipts during this fiscal year amounts to over 7 billion dollars. . . . We should plan to have a definitely balanced budget for the third year of recovery and from that time on seek a continuing reduction of the national debt. The excess of expenditures over revenues . . . has been rendered necessary to bring the country to a sound condition after the unexampled crisis which we encountered last spring. It is a large amount, but the immeasurable benefits justify the cost.

In March, 1934, he vetoed the appropriation bill because congressional appropriations exceeded the executive request by $228 million without increasing taxes. His messages through calendar 1938 continued both ideas, that of the expansionary effects of government spending and that of the desirability of balancing the budget.

In the late 1930s, Keynesian macroeconomics took hold among economists, and it became respectable to view fiscal policy as a positive instrument for recovery. It appears that the new theory influenced the President's budget message of January 5, 1939:

> The necessity of increasing Federal expenditures a year ago to check a recession is a well-known fact. Any decision to decrease those expenditures now that recovery has just started would constitute a new policy which ought not to be adopted without full understanding of what may be the result. . . . I believe I am expressing the thought of the most far-sighted students of our economic system in saying that it would be unwise either to curtail expenditures sharply or to impose drastic new taxes at this stage of recovery. . . . Sound progress toward a budget that is formally balanced is not to be made by heavily slashing expenditures or drastically increasing taxes. On the contrary, it is to be sought by employing every effective device we may have at our command for promoting a steady recovery, which means steady progress toward the goal of full utilization of our resources.

The long depression in the United States economy contributed to the ascendancy of Keynesian ideas among most economists, who also widely feared a relapse into depression after World War II. As noted earlier, this fear pervaded the business community and the government as well. Many felt that large-scale public works and other drastic fiscal measures would be required to carry the country over the postwar transition without serious unemployment. This atmosphere helps explain why most industrial countries pursued inflationary policies for several years after the war. It also explains the adoption in the United States of the Employment Act of 1946.

The Employment Act of 1946 begins with the following declaration:

The Congress declares that it is the continuing policy and responsibility of the Federal Government to use all practicable means consistent with its needs and obligations and other essential considerations of national policy, with the assistance and cooperation of industry, agriculture, labor, and State and local governments, to coordinate and utilize all its plans, functions, and resources for the purpose of creating and maintaining, in a manner calculated to foster and promote free competitive enterprise and the general welfare, conditions under which there will be afforded useful employment opportunities, including self-employment, for those able, willing, and seeking to work, and to promote maximum employment, production, and purchasing power.

To implement this policy, the act required annual economic reports by the President to the Congress, created the Council of Economic Advisers to advise the President and "to develop and recommend to the President national economic policies to foster and promote free competitive enterprise, to avoid economic fluctuations or to diminish the effects thereof, and to maintain employment, production, and purchasing power," and created the Joint Economic Committee of the House and Senate to study these matters. In ten years, the accepted role of the federal government had changed dramatically.

At that time, the predominant view among economists was that aggressive fiscal policy, including changes in expenditures, was a desirable and necessary part of the arsenal of weapons to be used against any serious recession. A small minority dissented, saying that neither monetary nor fiscal policy should be deliberately manipulated to stabilize the economy: the natural fluctuation in budget deficit and surplus due to the movement of tax revenues with changes in national income should be the principal influence toward stability, they said. Nevertheless, there were many points of virtually universal agreement. Almost all economists accepted the constructive contribution of automatic stabilizers and opposed any attempt to keep the budget constantly balanced regardless of the condition of the economy. Few thought it practical to use discretionary variations constantly to iron out small variations in economic activity. And virtually all agreed that discretionary measures would be necessary if there were another major depression. Most saw the difficulty of forecasting and of obtaining prompt action by the Congress and by other authorities.

In the late 1940s, the idea also became current of using formulas enacted by Congress that would authorize executive use of stabilizing changes in taxes and expenditures when price, production, and employment indexes moved outside stated tolerances. This idea is called *formula flexibility* in fiscal policy.

The consensus of views changed gradually as the United States economy went through a series of mild recessions without falling into deep depression or stagnation. The earlier fears receded, and the practical problems of discretionary expenditure policy received more notice. As recently as the 1958 recession, the overwhelming majority of economists writing letters to the *New York Times* and other metropolitan newspapers favored public works to overcome it; and virtually all favored special enactment of a tax cut. However, these opinions hit the street within a month or so of the bottom of the recession, and had their proposals been enacted it would have been during the upswing, with the full effects delayed until around the subsequent high point of the economy. (As it happened, another recession came immediately in 1960–1961, so that the expansionary effects of the proposed policies would have been beneficial then. However, these economists, including the present author, thought they were fighting the 1958 recession, not the one of 1960–1961!) This episode encouraged a more cautious view thereafter.

Meanwhile official policy on budget management moved toward the prevailing views among economists. During this period, the President spoke out against the outmoded view that the budget must be balanced every year, saying or implying that deficits during recessions could be balanced by later surpluses during booms. The Treasury accepted this view and subscribed to the proposition that automatic fluctuations of the budget helped stabilize the economy, but official policy rejected most deliberate, discretionary manipulation of expenditures and tax rates for this purpose. However, Congress had willingly voted emergency public works and relief expenditures during the depression of the 1930s and would assuredly do so again in a major depression. Moreover, in the recessions of 1958 and 1961 Congress enacted temporary extensions of unemployment insurance for persons who had exhausted their regular unemployment benefits. (This type of special relief would be a form of formula flexibility if it became the law or custom always to extend it when unemployment passed some high level. It also has the automatic feature of being cut off when the unemployed find jobs, so that it would not destabilize by adding fuel to a boom, even if enacted too late to help overcome a recession.)

Noting that congressional action takes time, in 1962 the Council of Economic Advisers recommended and the President proposed that the President have the authority to change income tax rates within specified limits to help stabilize the economy. Moreover, in the 1960s it became routine to seek special tax legislation with a view to its effects on total economic activity and inflation. Congress has generally passed this special tax legislation, when proposed, but rejected the idea of delegating its power over tax rates to the President.

In summary, economists and the government have come a long way from the view that the government budget should always be balanced, if necessary by cutting expenditures and raising tax rates in a recession, and now accept the idea of using budgetary policy to help stabilize the economy. In principle, they also accept the same role for monetary policy, but there is not the same body of accepted doctrine and analysis of monetary policy that there is of fiscal policy.

3 OPTIMAL BEHAVIOR OF THE SUPPLY OF MONEY WHEN EXPENDITURES FLUCTUATE

Consider again the first national income model, developed in Chapter 2, and summarized in Figure 59. As before, the combined equations of the expenditure sector are represented by the curve $e_0 e_0$, the combined equations of the monetary sector by the curve mm, and the combined equations of the production-employment sector by the vertical line y_f. In the initial position of overall equilibrium, the real and money rate of interest both equal r_0 and real income equals y_f.

Now suppose that the initial position in Figure 59 is the typical one, around which short-run fluctuations take place. Suppose also that from a short-run standpoint the monetary sector and the production-employment sector are stable, that is, that all short-run disturbances originate in the

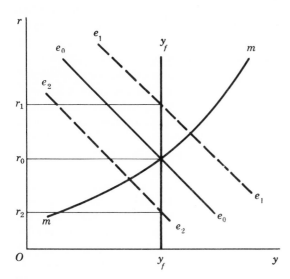

Figure 59

expenditure sector. For example, we might suppose that the sole source of instability of the economy is in the instability of the investment schedule. In this case, short-term fluctuations will start as shifts of the expenditure sector curve above and below its average position, as shown by the shift upward of e_0e_0 to e_1e_1 and downward to e_2e_2 in Figure 59.

The analysis of Chapter 2 showed that such shifts imply shifts in the same direction of the equilibrium price level, if the supply curve of money stays fixed. When the expenditure sector curve shifts upward to e_1e_1, the new equilibrium rate of interest will be r_1; the monetary sector will be in equilibrium at this higher rate of interest only when a sufficient rise in the price level shifts the monetary sector curve upward to the left to intersect full-employment real income at r_1. The price rise reduces real cash balances to the smaller amount the public wishes to hold, at full-employment real income, at the higher rate of interest r_1. Similarly, when the expenditure sector curve shifts downward to e_2e_2, the new equilibrium rate of interest will be r_2. The monetary sector will be in equilibrium at this lower rate of interest only when a fall in the price level shifts the monetary sector curve downward to the right to intersect full-employment real income at r_2. The price fall increases real cash balances, symmetrical with the reduction just indicated for the opposite shift.

Now if the price level could be counted on in practice to move swiftly and smoothly to its new equilibrium level with every shift in the expenditure sector curve, there would be little problem of economic stability. Employment and output would be at their full-employment levels almost continuously; the fluctuations in the price level would merely be an inconvenience. In practice, however, the price level fails to move swiftly and smoothly from one equilibrium to another. Even when it moves upward, a price level change in the United States economy is a slow and painful process; thus employment and output fluctuate substantially with fluctuations in the expenditure curve. When it shifts upward, temporary "shortages" develop because prices are not adjusted upward rapidly enough to clear all markets; when it shifts downward, "unsold supplies" and unemployment develop, for a similar reason. For this reason, and because fluctuations in the price level are also an inconvenience, a policy that will stabilize output and employment at high levels, without price fluctuations, is desirable.

One stabilizing policy suggests itself because of our model of the monetary sector. When the equilibrium money rate of interest rises from i_0 to i_1, equilibrium in the monetary sector is restored only when the quantity of real cash balances falls from m_0 to m_1 in Figure 60. Therefore, the supply curve of real cash balances $[(1/P)h(i)]_0$ must shift to the left to the new position $[(1/P)h(i)]_1$. This shift can come either through a rise

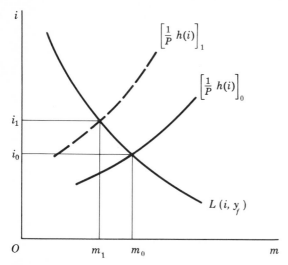

Figure 60

in the price level or through a deliberate shift to the left of the function $h(i)$, that is, through a reduction in the quantity of money supplied at each interest rate. By avoiding a change in the price level, this reduction avoids shortages and inconvenience. Similarly, a deliberate policy of increasing the supply of money when the expenditure sector curve shifts downward avoids a fall in the price level, with the attendant unemployment and accumulation of unsold goods. If the government can consistently execute such policies in step with shifts in the expenditure sector curve, it should do so.

The right policy would increase the supply of money when the expenditure sector curve shifts downward and decrease it when it shifts upward. The ideal size of the change in the money supply would be one just large enough, in each case, to push the rate of interest to its new equilibrium level with no change in the price level. To succeed perfectly, the authorities would have to know the change in the equilibrium rate of interest. But even if they don't know it exactly, the monetary authority might know whether the rate should rise or fall. In particular, when output, employment, and the market rate of interest all start to decline, an increase in the supply of money, pushing the market rate of interest downward still further, is required. Similarly, when output, the price level, and the market rate of interest start to rise at relatively full employment, a decrease in the supply of money, pushing the market rate of interest upward still further, is required.

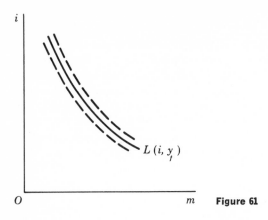

Figure 61

Indeed, if all disturbances arose solely from the expenditure sector, the authorities could approximate an ideal policy without any knowledge of what change was required in the rate of interest. In Figure 61, every point of equilibrium is on the same demand schedule for real cash balances: that for full-employment real income. If the supply of money always shifts to prevent any change in the price level, output, or employment, the resultant supply curve of money *coincides* with the demand curve for money at full employment and at the going price level. With a tendency for the equilibrium rate of interest to rise, due to rising expenditures, the authorities would reduce the quantity of money supplied by the difference in the amount demanded due to the rise in the interest rate. They would increase it with declining expenditures.

When expenditures tend to increase above the full-employment level, the demand curve for real cash balances may temporarily shift upward also, as shown in Figure 61. Similarly, when expenditures tend to fall below the full-employment level, the demand curve for real cash balances temporarily shifts downward. With a demand function for real cash balances that is otherwise stable, the authorities need only keep the relationship between the market rate of interest and the quantity of money within as close a range as possible around this curve. When the demand curve for cash balances shifts upward toward the upper dashed curve in Figure 61, the authorities would reduce the supply of money until this sector reached a point near the original demand curve because of the damping effect on expenditures of the rise in the rate of interest. A similar and opposite policy would serve for downward shifts in expenditures. All that is required is knowledge of the demand curve for money at full-employment real income; nothing need be known, directly, about the determinants of the equilibrium rate of interest.

Unfortunately for this easy prescription, however, not all disturbances arise in the expenditure sector, nor in this sector and the production-employment sector combined. The demand function for real cash balances can shift autonomously, and the supply can shift because of disturbances in the banking system. These imply a more complicated policy. The simple prescription just given works only when it is known that the demand function for real cash balances has not changed. Otherwise exact knowledge of required changes in the rate of interest is necessary for a successful stabilizing monetary policy.

4   OPTIMAL BEHAVIOR OF THE SUPPLY OF MONEY IN RESPONSE TO MONETARY DISTURBANCES AND SUMMARY

Disturbances in the monetary sector, other than those stemming directly from mistakes by the authorities, can consist either of shifts in the public's demand for real cash balances or of shifts in the behavior of the banking system. The latter type of shift affects the supply curve of money. In either case, we saw in Chapter 2 that as a first approximation such shifts have no effect on the variables of the real sectors of the economy. In the ultimate equilibrium, real cash balances will change, if the public's demand for them has shifted, or will be unchanged, if the disturbance has affected only the supply of money. In either case, the price level will change unless the monetary authority prevents it. As no real variable is affected, including the rate of interest, the monetary authority can prevent any real effect of the disturbance by holding the rate of interest unchanged at its equilibrium value.

If the disturbance consists of a shift in the demand curve for real cash balances, the appropriate action for the monetary authority is to change the quantity of money in exact proportion to this shift, at the equilibrium rate of interest. If the disturbance arises in the banking sector, e.g., if the banks change their desired excess reserves, the authorities should change central bank credit by this desired amount, so as to hold deposits constant. Similarly, if the disturbance consists of a change in the public's desired ratio of currency to deposits, which causes a change in bank reserves, the appropriate action for the monetary authority is to offset most of the change in reserves so as to hold the total of currency plus deposits constant. They control reserves (central bank credit) by open-market operations.

The appropriate policy of the monetary authorities in response to disturbances in the monetary sector, holding the market rate of interest constant, can be represented by a horizontal supply curve of money. It

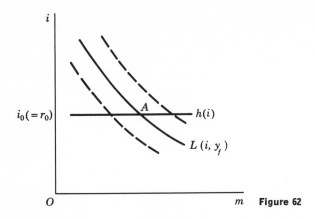

Figure 62

is illustrated in Figure 62. Whenever the demand curve for money shifts, for example, to the higher or lower dashed line, the monetary authority supplies any desired quantity of money at the equilibrium rate of interest in the real sectors. This is represented by the curve $h(i)$, horizontal at i_0. Whenever there is a disturbance in the banking sector, the monetary authority holds both the rate of interest and the quantity of money constant at the point A, on the unchanged demand curve for real cash balances.

The apparent simplicity of this policy is misleading, however. When there is no expectation of inflation, the money rate of interest and the real rate are equal. However, not only can inflation sometimes be expected, creating a discrepancy between the money rate and the real rate of interest, but mistakes of the monetary authorities can cause it. For example, if the monetary authorities err by setting the rate of interest too low and they create as much money as the public demands at that rate of interest, the price level will start rising. With the rate of interest too low, an excess of desired expenditures over full-employment output will keep driving prices up, and the authorities will have to keep increasing the money supply to keep the rate of interest down.

In such a case, the public will begin to expect further rises in the price level. When they do expect them, the demand for money will expand without limit even if the money rate of interest rises up to and above the real rate, as long as it remains less than the sum of the real rate and the expected rate of inflation. Our discussion in Chapter 4 showed that equilibrium over time is possible when the monetary authority creates just enough money to bear out the public's expectation of further inflation. Moreover, a runaway inflation will develop if the monetary authority stubbornly holds down the rate of interest and creates money at an increasing rate.

This analysis also implies that deflation, either steady or accelerating, would result if the monetary authority set the market rate of interest above the equilibrium real rate and then destroyed money so as to keep it there. If the fall in the price level were delayed by slow adjustment for any reason, the process would also involve unemployment and loss of output.

Thus the policy of responding to all changes in the demand function for money and to disturbances in the banking sector by creating or destroying enough money to hold constant the rate of interest has great dangers. If the monetary authority misjudges the equilibrium rate of interest, this policy will itself cause disturbances. However, failing to respond to monetary disturbances would transmit these disturbances into the real sectors, causing fluctuations in output and employment.

To stabilize the economy, the authorities must cope with three sources of disturbance: the real sectors, the private monetary sector, and mistakes of the authorities themselves. However, it is possible to state a full set of criteria for a stabilizing policy. If there is an upward shift in expenditures, there will be a tendency for the rate of interest, output, employment, and the price level to rise, and the banks will seek rediscounts to obtain more reserves. If the monetary authority holds the rate of interest below the equilibrium level, they will see the same symptoms, except where they prevent the rate of interest from rising. In both cases, the appropriate countermeasure, monetary restriction, pushes the rate of interest up to its equilibrium level; then the symptoms will disappear, regardless of their original source.

When a disturbance originates in the private monetary sector, there is no direct effect on real variables other than the rate of interest. For example, if the demand curve for real cash balances autonomously shifts downward, the quantity of money and the rate of interest will decline, and the banks will reduce rediscounts and reserves. The appropriate countermeasure is a restrictive policy that pushes the rate of interest back up to its old level. In this case, the quantity of money and the rate of interest decline while output is steady (or increasing because of the decline in the rate of interest). In contrast, in the other two cases the quantity of money, output, and, if permitted, the rate of interest are all rising. These differences in symptoms permit the choice of appropriate policy, even if the exact nature of the original disturbance is unknown. If output is steady or increasing while the rate of interest and the quantity of money are declining, the authorities should shift the supply curve of money to the left; if output, the rate of interest, and the quantity of money are all declining, they should shift it to the right.

The outward appearance of this set of policies would differ from a policy of steady growth of the money supply (as proposed by Friedman) in that the stock of money would grow faster than the long-run trend growth when the equilibrium interest rate is unusually low and would grow slower than the long-run trend growth when the equilibrium interest rate is unusually high. An "unusually low" equilibrium interest rate corresponds to a leftward shift of the expenditure sector curve, due to poor business expectations; an "unusually high" interest rate corresponds to the opposite shift of the expenditure sector curve. The policy would prevent purely monetary disturbances from having any effect on the growth rate of the money supply, if these originate in the banking system; if these were the only disturbances, the policy would agree with Friedman's. (Nevertheless, it would adjust the growth of the money supply to accommodate shifts in the demand curve for money at full-employment real income. This last source is of no practical importance compared to the others, however.)

5 THE POLICIES OF THE FEDERAL RESERVE BANKING SYSTEM OF THE UNITED STATES

In summary, the quantity of money should move opposite to any short-run movements in output and employment and should not be influenced by disturbances in the banking system. Suppose that long-run policy allows the money supply to grow in step with long-run growth in total output. Then, to stabilize output and employment, the growth in the money supply should be more rapid in periods of recession and less rapid in periods of boom.

The actual history of the money supply during recessions in output in the United States since the establishment of the Federal Reserve System is shown in Figure 63 (omitting the two World Wars). It can be seen at once that policy has consistently differed from that outlined here. In every recession since the establishment of the System, the growth of the money supply has slowed down or reversed during the declining phase of the recession; in the recovery phase the growth of the money supply has been more rapid than average. However, in the later stages of recovery, when economic activity frequently reaches boom proportions, the growth of the money supply has typically been slowed down.

The experience of peacetime, taken alone, suggests that the monetary authorities in this country have been willing to follow a stabilizing monetary policy in the late stages of recovery and in booms, but not in recessions. When output and employment are below full-employment levels, both during the declining phase and during the early recovery phase, the rate of growth of the money supply has been permitted to move in the same direction as output. Our analysis suggests that such a policy increases, rather than reduces, the instability of the economy.

The lower half of Figure 63 shows the movement of the rate of interest on United States Treasury bills over the same period. It can be seen that in general this rate, a volatile one that is highly correlated with interest rates generally, also tends to move up and down with activity. In particular, it tends to decline in the declining phase of a recession, though sometimes only after a delay, and to rise in the recovery phase. This combination of movements of output, the money supply, and the rate of interest in the declining and early recovery phases can be interpreted as the result of a rising supply curve of money, as described in Chapter 2. As output declines and therefore the demand schedule for money shifts downward to the left, the authorities allow the quantity of money and the rate of interest to fall below what they otherwise would

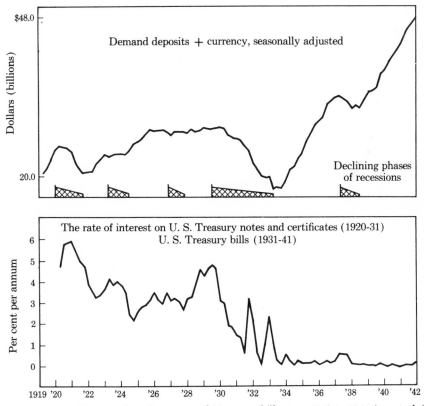

Figure 63(a)   The quantity of money and Treasury bill rates, 1919 to 1941 (quarterly)

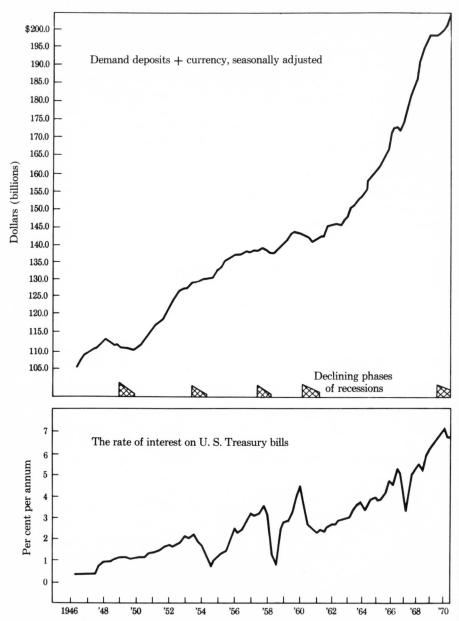

Figure 63(*b***)** The quantity of money and Treasury bill rates, 1946 to 1970 (quarterly)

have been. Thus the supply of money under these conditions has a positive elasticity as indicated by the upward sloping curve $h(i)$.

In the later stages of recovery, when the authorities become anxious about possible inflation, they appear to shift the curve $h(i)$ to the left, as shown in Figure 60. Such a shift is desirable if aggregate demand would otherwise become too great. The record of the monetary authorities in this country is therefore a mixed one. Part of the time their policy appears to contribute to stability, but too often it doesn't.

These attributes of monetary policy follow directly from the development of doctrine and practice in the Federal Reserve System, discussed in section 2 of this chapter. The System's leadership has learned that it must restrain the total quantity of Federal Reserve credit to prevent or restrain inflation in a boom, and it does. However, it has never assumed as a primary responsibility the prevention of monetary contraction in a recession. Its statutory responsibility to serve the needs and convenience of legitimate commerce has been interpreted to mean that when commerce wants to borrow less, the System need not prevent the contraction that results. Possibly the doctrine and practices of the System are changing; the inflation of the 1960s suggests they might be. The 1970s will tell.

6 POLICY AGAINST CREEPING INFLATION

Our analysis of inflation, in Chapter 4, showed in effect that the way to avoid inflation is to provide just enough secular growth in the money supply to match the secular growth in real output. This simple prescription may be enough, but we have to consider the possibility that sometimes it will hurt. Once the price level has started to rise, reversing it takes time and is likely to bring on a recession.

If our basic model is sound and our assessment of actual Federal Reserve policies is correct, the reason we observe occasional bouts of creeping inflation is that the Federal Reserve System sometimes allows the money supply to increase too fast. They allow the money supply to decline or stop rising during an economic downswing; and after the economy recovers they usually restrain the rate of growth of the money supply to no more than the rate of growth of output. The one time they let the money supply grow more rapidly than that, as a rule, is the early stage of the upswing while the economy is recovering from recession. At this stage, businessmen are increasing investment, are hiring back previously laid-off workers, and are increasing output. When optimism is everywhere, it is easy for households and firms to make commitments that will bring future increases in prices. The lags in the price level, which we examine more closely in the next chapter, mean that the rapid expansion of the money supply at this stage will have its price effects spread out over a period of months, or longer.

Now when the System has allowed the money supply to fall at the onset of recession, it would be painful and perhaps unwise to keep it from recovering during the early recovery stage. However, the picture would be different if the System were to expand the money supply sharply at the onset of recession, when households and businesses are pessimistic. In that case, the money supply would be more than ample to support recovery and could be firmly held back at that stage. If the timing is right, and the average growth of the money supply is also right, creeping inflation need never start.

However, it would be unwise to suppose that the timing will always be right, or that the System will always find it practical to keep a firm check on the secular growth of the money supply. The United States has never enjoyed periods of price stability of more than a few years, and even a well-conceived monetary policy might fail to maintain such stability. What should the System do if it faces a creeping inflation that has already started?

One possibility is to adjust the secular growth of the money supply to allow inflation to continue at a fixed rate and hold firmly to that line. The economy will adapt to it, and if it is only a matter of a few percent per year, the disruption and inconvenience it causes is slight enough to disregard. Another possibility is to permit the inflation to continue for a time, but to reduce the secular rate of growth of the money supply a little each year until the inflation has ended. To avoid bringing on a recession in this process, the System should allow for continued inflation for a while after the new policy is started because of lags in movement of the price level.

7 OPTIMAL POLICIES FOR GOVERNMENT EXPENDITURES

We noted in section 2 that some economists believe that government expenditures should be the main policy instrument for economic stability. The idea is straightforward. In Chapter 9 it was shown that shifts in government expenditure, especially in government investment, cause shifts in total expenditures. Hence if fluctuations in private investment cause shifts in the expenditure sector curve, as shown in Figure 59, these could be fully offset by shifts in government expenditures. The expenditure sector curve would then have no net shift but would remain at its initial position e_0e_0. The equilibrium rate of interest would remain unchanged, so that the quantity of money could stay on its long-run growth curve, and the price level would remain steady. Therefore, output and employment would remain stable without any need for a stabilizing monetary policy. Thus, we have two alternative methods of accomplishing substantially the same result, differing primarily in the path over time of the equilibrium rate of interest. We face an apparent dilemma as to which method of stabilization is superior.

A solution to this dilemma can be obtained by considering the elementary assumption that goods are scarce. Given that people would prefer to have more goods rather than less, efficiency requires using resources where they have the highest productivity. This rule applies equally to both the government and private sectors of the economy. In particular, it applies to the choice of how much to spend, that is, of how many resources to employ, on particular lines of government activity. Resources should be used in government activity until the services rendered by the last, or marginal, units of the resources are just as valuable as they would have been in private employment.[1] Given that either monetary or fiscal policy, or some combination of the two, can hold the economy at the full-employment level of output, government spending should always satisfy this rule as applied with resources fully employed. This rule provides a criterion for how much fiscal policy should be used in a deliberately stabilizing overall economic policy.

Consider first what it implies, in any given equilibrium situation, for different types of government expenditure. The key variable to consider is government investment activity. The rule that resources employed here should be as productive as in any alternative employment implies, among other things, that the prospective marginal productivity of government investment should equal the gross rate of interest. (The gross rate here refers to the rate before income taxes, property taxes, and any other taxes tending to reduce the rate of return to owners of wealth below the true marginal productivity of investment.) Government investments, like other investments, can be represented by a schedule that slopes downward, following a ranking by their productivity.

---

[1] We ignore the controversial issue of the treatment of risk, which does not affect the present argument. Although the practice is far from general, considerable progress has been made on the evaluation of the productivity of government investment, particularly in the area of public works and water resources. The practice is spreading, and standards of accuracy and validity of such evaluation are improving. There is little doubt the bulk of investment expenditures by government can be so evaluated with reasonable accuracy. For a detailed discussion of this general problem, see Roland N. McKean, *Efficiency in Government through Systems Analysis* (New York, John Wiley & Sons, Inc., 1958).

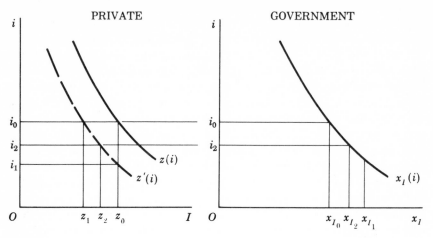

Figure 64

Suppose that with a given monetary and fiscal policy the equilibrium rate of interest is i_0. The rule for efficient government investment means that both government investment and private investment should have a marginal productivity of i_0. In Figure 64, the private and government components of aggregate investment are shown as two separate schedules, private on the left and government on the right. If the equilibrium gross rate of interest is i_0, the private sector will invest at the rate of z_0 and the government should invest at the rate x_{I_0}.

Now if the private investment schedule shifts downward from $z(i)$ to the new position $z'(i)$, and if the chosen policy were to hold all government expenditures constant and to stabilize the economy solely by the exercise of monetary policy, the interest rate would have to fall to i_1 in order to bring aggregate investment back up to its full-employment level. (This discussion ignores the effect of interest-rate changes on consumption; such an effect does not materially affect the present argument.) Both private and government investment would remain at their previous amounts, but the productivity of private investment would fall to i_1 while that of government investment remained at i_0. This outcome violates the rule of equating the marginal productivity of government investment to that of private investment. Similarly, if the chosen policy were to rely solely on government expenditure policy for stabilization, holding the rate of interest constant, the rule would again be violated. Private investment would fall to z_1, and government investment would be increased by the amount of that fall, to x_{I_1}; this would hold the sum of the two, $z_1 + x_{I_1}$, constant. In this case, the marginal productivity of government investment would fall to the lower level corresponding to x_{I_1}, while that of private investment would remain at i_0.

The policy that maximizes the overall productivity of the economy is an intermediate policy that holds the marginal productivity of the government investment always equal to that of private investment. In Figure 64, the equilibrium interest rate at which total investment is the same as before the downward shift of the private investment schedule, with both types of investment having a marginal productivity equal to that rate, is i_2. The optimal combination of investment activities would be z_2 for private investment and x_{I_2} for government investment. Private investment will be lower, compared with its level in the initial equilibrium, and government investment higher.

Efficient investment behavior by the government can be made automatic by the appropriate instructions to government agencies. At present in the United States, they use the interest rate on government bonds—sometimes the rate ruling currently or in the recent past, sometimes a rate ruling at some more distant time in the past. The stabilization aspect of the present argument would imply using the *current* rate, that ruling at the time the government investment is undertaken. The relation of this rule to economic stabilization can be thought of as secondary, if the monetary authority keeps the market rate of interest at its equilibrium level. Alternatively, this rule is an example of formula flexibility.

8 OPTIMAL MONETARY POLICY AND STABILIZING DEFICITS

Since there was no reference to the numerical value of the equilibrium real rate of interest in the preceding sections, their arguments apply in full to the case in which the equilibrium real rate falls nearly to zero. Those arguments are incomplete for this case, however, since nothing was said about cases in which the real rate of interest falls to such low values that massive increases in the quantity of money would be required to achieve overall equilibrium. Ordinary monetary policy within its traditional limits would not be sufficient in this case.

In Chapter 9, we found that equilibrium is attainable in a system in which the real rate of interest would otherwise be too low, through a tax cut combined with financing part or all of the government budget by money creation. This is the only practical method by which equilibrium can in this case be achieved with stable prices and with efficient resource allocation; when it is followed, the equilibrium rate of interest is positive, though small. Households will accept a flow of additions to their cash balances as income and will increase their consumption expenditures correspondingly. Then some size of tax cut financed by newly created money will shift the expenditure sector curve far enough to the right to make equilibrium possible at the minimum real rate of interest at which the acceptable instruments of monetary policy would be exhausted. People are no worse off holding more cash balances than if they held more physical wealth, both at low rates of return. A smaller physical addition to wealth combined with larger additions to cash balances, all with a low rate of return, is superior to a larger physical investment at a still lower rate of return. Thus the optimal policy, when the equilibrium rate of interest would otherwise be too low for monetary policy, would cut tax revenues and create enough money to maintain full employment at a workable rate of interest and a stable price level.

There is a bound beyond which monetary policy cannot go; if monetary expansion up to this bound fails to assure equilibrium the extra cash required must be supplied through a government deficit. The bound on effective stabilizing monetary policy in recession and depression can be stated in terms of the equilibrium rate of interest. The lowest rate that the monetary authorities can achieve by monetary policy alone will prevail when they have acquired all outstanding government securities and all other assets they consider eligible for purchase, and when they have set bank reserve requirements at the minimum permissible levels. This minimum achievable rate itself will depend on expectations in the monetary sector; the reserves that banks wish to hold at given interest rates depend on their assessment of the risk of a liquidity crisis, and the cash balances that households and firms wish to hold at given interest rates depend on their expectations as to the price level of assets, among other things. Thus, for example, the bound on the effectiveness of monetary policy in depressed conditions will be at a lower interest rate before a liquidity or banking crisis has threatened than after one has begun.

BIBLIOGRAPHY

Ando, Albert, E. Cary Brown, and Ann F. Friedlaender: *Studies in Economic Stabilization* (Wash., D.C., The Brookings Institution, 1968).
Annual Report of the Board of Governors of the Federal Reserve System for the year 1950, pp. 4–5; 98–101.
Arrow, Kenneth J.: "Criteria for Social Investment," *Water Resources Research*, vol. 1 (1965), pp. 1–8.
Baumol, W. J.: "On the Social Rate of Discount," *American Economic Review*, vol. 58 (1968), pp. 788–802.
Carson, Deane (ed.): *Banking and Monetary Studies* (Homewood, Ill., Richard D. Irwin, Inc., 1963).
Chandler, L. V.: "Federal Reserve Policy and the Federal Debt," in American Eco-

nomic Association, *Readings in Monetary Theory* (New York, McGraw-Hill Book Company, 1951), chap. 18.

Chapman, Charles C.: *The Development of American Business and Banking Thought 1913–1936* (London, Longmans, Green and Co., Ltd., 1936).

Clark, J. M.: "An Appraisal of the Workability of Compensatory Devices," in American Economic Association: *Readings in Business Cycle Theory* (New York, McGraw-Hill Book Company, 1944), chap. 14.

Culbertson, J. M.: "Friedman on the Lag in Effect of Monetary Policy," *Journal of Political Economy*, vol. 68 (December, 1960), pp. 617–621.

Culbertson, J. M.: "The Lag in Effect of Monetary Policy: Reply," *Journal of Political Economy*, vol. 69 (October, 1961), pp. 467–477.

Depres, Emile, Albert G. Hart, Milton Friedman, Paul A. Samuelson, and Donald H. Wallace: "The Problem of Economic Instability," *The American Economic Review*, vol. 40 (1950), pp. 505–538.

Economic Report of the President (Wash., D.C., U.S. Government Printing Office, 1963), pp. 70–77.

Friedman, Milton: "The Role of Monetary Policy," *American Economic Review*, vol. 58 (1968), pp. 1–17.

Friedman, Milton: "A Monetary and Fiscal Framework for Economic Stability," in American Economic Association: *Readings in Monetary Theory* (New York, McGraw-Hill Book Company, 1951), chap. 17.

Friedman, Milton: "The Effects of a Full Employment Policy on Economic Stability: A Formal Analysis," in *Essays in Positive Economics* (Chicago, The University of Chicago Press, 1953).

Friedman, Milton: "The Lag in Effect of Monetary Policy," *Journal of Political Economy*, vol. 69 (October, 1961), pp. 447–466.

Friedman, Milton: "The Supply of Money and Changes in Prices and Output," in United States Congress, Joint Economic Committee: *The Relationship of Prices to Economic Stability and Growth: Compendium* (March 31, 1958), pp. 241–256.

Gurley, John G.: "Fiscal Policies for Full Employment: A Diagrammatic Analysis," *Journal of Political Economy*, vol. 60 (1952), pp. 525–533.

Haber, William, and Merrill G. Murray: *Unemployment Insurance in the American Economy* (Homewood, Ill., Richard D. Irwin, Inc., 1966).

Hansen, Alvin H.: *Economic Policy and Full Employment* (New York, McGraw-Hill Book Company, 1947).

Hansen, Alvin H.: *Fiscal Policy and Business Cycles* (New York, W. W. Norton and Company, Inc., 1941).

Harberger, Arnold C.: "The Social Opportunity Cost of Capital: A New Approach," presented at Annual Meeting of the Water Resources Research Committee, Western Agricultural Research Council (Denver, Colorado, December 11, 1968).

Harris, Seymour E., L. V. Chandler, Milton Friedman, Alvin H. Hansen, Abba Lerner, and James Tobin: "Controversial Issues in Recent Monetary Policy: A Symposium," *Review of Economics and Statistics*, vol. 42 (August, 1960), pp. 245–282.

Harris, Seymour E. (ed.): *Postwar Economic Problems* (New York, McGraw-Hill Book Company, 1943), Part I.

Hart, Albert: "The 'Chicago Plan' of Banking Reform," in American Economic Association: *Readings in Monetary Theory* (New York, McGraw-Hill Book Company, 1951).

Hirshleifer, Jack: "Efficient Allocation of Capital in an Uncertain World," *American Economic Review*, vol. 54 (1964), pp. 77–85.

Hirshleifer, Jack: "Investment Decisions Under Uncertainty: Applications of the State-Preference Approach," *Quarterly Journal of Economics*, vol. 80 (1966), pp. 252–277.

Israel, Fred L. (ed.): *The State of the Union Messages of the Presidents 1790–1966* (New York, Chelsea House, Robert Hector Publishers, 1966).

Johnson, Harry G.: "Monetary Theory and Policy," *The American Economic Review*, vol. 52 (June, 1962), pp. 335–384.

Lewis, Wilfred, Jr.: *Federal Fiscal Policy in the Postwar Recessions* (Wash., D.C., The Brookings Institution, 1962).

Marglin, Stephen A.: "The Social Rate of Discount and the Optimal Rate of Investment," *Quarterly Journal of Economics*, vol. 77 (1963), pp. 95–112.

Marglin, Stephen A.: *Public Investment Criteria* (Cambridge, Mass., The M.I.T. Press, 1968).

Mayer, Thomas: "The Inflexibility of Monetary Policy," *Review of Economics and Statistics*, vol. 40 (1958), p. 358.

McKean, Roland N.: *Efficiency in Government Through Systems Analysis* (New York, John Wiley & Sons, Inc., 1958).

Mishan, E. J.: "Criteria for Public Investment: Some Simplifying Suggestions," *The Journal of Political Economy*, vol. 75 (1967), pp. 139–146.

Musgrave, Richard: "Credit Controls, Interest Rates, and the Management of the Public Debt," in L. Metzler et al.: *Income, Employment and Public Policy* (New York, W. W. Norton & Company, Inc., 1948).

Musgrave, Richard A.: *The Theory of Public Finance: A Study in Public Economy* (New York, McGraw-Hill Book Company, 1959).

Phelps, Edmund S.: *Fiscal Neutrality toward Economic Growth* (New York, McGraw-Hill Book Company, 1965).

Riefler, Winfield: *Money Rates and Money Markets in the United States* (New York, Harper and Row, Publishers, Incorporated, 1930).

Robertson, D. H.: "A Survey of Modern Monetary Controversy," in American Economic Association: *Readings in Business Cycle Theory* (New York, McGraw-Hill Book Company, 1944), chap. 13.

Rolph, Earl R., and George F. Break: *Public Finance* (New York, The Ronald Press Company, 1961).

Rosa, Robert V.: *Federal Reserve Operations in the Money and Government Securities Markets* (Federal Reserve Bank of New York, 1956).

Schlesinger, James R.: "Monetary Policy and Its Critics," *Journal of Political Economy*, vol. 68 (December, 1960), pp. 601–616.

Sen, A. K.: "On Optimizing the Rate of Saving," *Economic Journal*, vol. 71 (1961), pp. 479–496.

Simons, H. C.: "Rules versus Authorities in Monetary Policy," in American Economic Association: *Readings in Monetary Theory* (New York, McGraw-Hill Book Company, 1951), chap. 16.

Stein, Herbert: *The Fiscal Revolution in America* (Chicago, University of Chicago Press, 1969).

The Report of the Commission on Money and Credit: *Money and Credit* (Englewood Cliffs, N.J., Prentice-Hall, Inc., 1961).

Tobin, James: "Monetary Policy and the Management of the Public Debt: The Patman Inquiry," *Review of Economics and Statistics*, vol. 35 (1953), p. 118.

Tobin, James: "The Monetary Interpretation of History," *The American Economic Review*, vol. 55 (June, 1965), pp. 464–485.

Treasury Department: *Annual Report of the Treasury on the State of the Finances* (Wash., D.C., U.S. Government Printing Office, 1952), pp. 270–273.

Tullock, Gordon: "The Social Rate of Discount and the Optimal Rate of Investment: Comment," *Quarterly Journal of Economics*, vol. 78 (1964), pp. 331–336.

U.S. Federal Reserve Board: *The Federal Reserve System* (Wash., D.C., U.S. Government Printing Office, 1954).

U.S. Federal Reserve Board: *Digest of Rulings of the Federal Reserve Board—1914–1927, Inclusive* (Wash., D.C., U.S. Government Printing Office, 1928).

Vickrey, William: "Principles of Efficiency: Discussion," *American Economic Review*, supplement, vol. 54 (1964), pp. 88–92.

Warburton, C.: "The Misplaced Emphasis in Contemporary Business Fluctuation Theory," in American Economic Association: *Readings in Monetary Theory* (New York, McGraw-Hill Book Company, 1951), chap. 14.

White, William H.: "The Flexibility of Anticyclical Monetary Policy," *Review of Economics and Statistics*, vol. 43 (May, 1961), pp. 142–147.

Wicker, Elmus R.: *Federal Reserve Monetary Policy 1917–1933* (New York, Random House, Inc., 1966).

11

EXPECTATIONS
AND DYNAMIC
ADJUSTMENT

1 INTRODUCTION

The nature and causes of persisting swings in economic activity has remained one of the major unsolved riddles of economic analysis, although it has long been clear that fluctuations in investment are a central feature of general economic fluctuations. Why investment should fluctuate the way it does has remained an elusive question and has been a main focal point of speculative theorizing since the turn of this century. Most attempts to explain it have tried to pinpoint a single source of instability, such as monetary policy or the accelerator. Few of these attempts have been convincing enough to have much impact on subsequent economic thought. However, the Keynesian approach to macroeconomics, presented through the models in Chapters 2 and 3 of this book, has come to dominate analysis of this question. The growth models discussed in Chapter 5, for example, generally use a Keynesian style and format, even when they avoid specifically Keynesian assumptions. Some models pay special attention to expectations, and we shall do so also.

2 FACTORS UNDERLYING DYNAMIC ECONOMIC MOVEMENTS

The analysis of economic equilibrium in Chapters 2 and 3, always conducted in terms of some given set of economic behavior equations, can be thought of as being a very short-run analysis, a very long-run analysis, or anything in between. Which it is depends on the time period or degree of permanency for which the behavior equations themselves are specified. In either case, the analysis is static because the equations are taken as given, and because the only concern in connection with a shift in one of the equations is with its effect on the equilibrium values of the variables. Dynamic analysis goes further to consider the path from one equilibrium to another. It may include the short run, the long run, or both.

Broadly speaking, there are three reasons why economic equilibrium changes. First, the external influences on the economy change, such as the weather, politics, population, and technology. These changes will shift economic behavior equations, such as the production function, the consumption and investment functions, the supply of labor, and so on. Second, the behavior functions themselves shift for other reasons, because of economic factors that are not considered in the static models. The relationship of consumption to current income, for instance, will shift when expected income changes. Third, the behavior functions can be specified in terms of some longer run than the very short run; if so, behavior conforms to these functions after the passage of a certain period of time, or on the average over a certain period of time, but not at every moment. A supply curve, for example, may be drawn to show the amounts of supply eventually available at each price, were that price expected to remain constant; if the price changes, the immediate supply response will usually be less than that indicated by the curve, both because of doubts about the permanency of the new price and because the supplying firms will take some time to adjust output to new levels. All three types of shifts occur in actual experience, and all three contribute to dynamic analysis. Without external disturbances, the economy would in due course settle down to a long-run equilibrium position and stay there, having no reason for further shifts of the second two kinds. Without delays in the adjustment of expectations and in the response of supply to changed conditions, each external disturbance would lead at once to the consequent (long-run) equilibrium position; the time path of the economy would then be a series of static positions between the jumps connected with disturbances, and dynamic analysis would be trivial.

For the most part, dynamic analysis concerns itself with the responses of the economic system to arbitrary disturbances. External influences offer little hope for systematic analysis and must largely be taken as given. External influences are not absolutely unpredictable, however, and whatever continuity they have affects the consequent movement of the economic system. Even where disturbances are wholly random or unpredictable, moreover, it is possible for the economic system to respond to them with relatively continuous, fluent movement.

For example, suppose a technological advance will lead to a lowering of the equilibrium price of a commodity. The change in equilibrium price comes only after knowledge of the new technique has become dispersed among the firms supplying the commodity, and they have invested in new capital using the new technique. At the instant of discovery of the new technique, there may be little or no change in price; after a long enough delay, however, the price and quantity will have moved to their new long-run equilibrium values. In the intervening period, various intermediate prices and quantities will occur, as the supply curve shifts from its old to its new position with the spread of knowledge and the introduction of new capital. This is illustrated in Figure 65, in which the

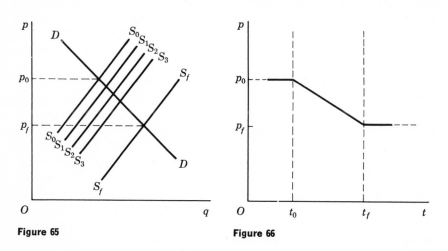

Figure 65

Figure 66

demand curve for the commodity is DD and the old supply curve is S_0S_0. The technological advance then implies an ultimate shift in the supply curve to S_fS_f; but for a period of time after the advance occurs the supply curve will shift through a series of positions S_1S_1, S_2S_2, S_3S_3, and so on. One possible time pattern of movement for these shifts of supply would be a constant rate of shift until the final position is reached; if so, the movement of the price, when demand is linear as shown, would be a steady fall from p_0 to the new equilibrium p_f. This is illustrated in Figure 66, in which the time of the technological discovery is shown as t_0 and the time at which final equilibrium is reached is shown as t_f. The price falls linearly through time between these two dates.

Three nonlinear possibilities for the manner of approach to the new equilibrium are shown in Figures 67 to 69. The pattern in Figure 67 illustrates the case in which the adaptation of supply moves slowly at first and then proceeds to the new equilibrium at an ever-increasing rate. The pattern in Figure 68 is roughly that of a logistic curve, showing an increasing rate of movement up to a point and a decreasing rate thereafter; this would occur if the pattern of Figure 67 obtained for a time, after

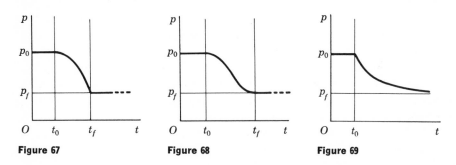

Figure 67   **Figure 68**   **Figure 69**

which various impediments to the universal adoption of the new technique, such as a failure of the knowledge of it to spread at equal speed everywhere, delayed the approach to final equilibrium. Another reason for delay could be that the main gains to be had from the use of the technique can be realized relatively easily and quickly, while the rest of the gains come in gradually at a decreasing rate as a result of further investment and adaptation. If these final delays are important while the initial delays from the dissemination of knowledge and other factors are negligible, the time pattern of Figure 69 would occur. Here the price approaches equilibrium slower and slower as the price nears equilibrium. A pattern of this last type might also occur if existing stocks of the commodity at t_0 were partly sold off at reduced prices in anticipation of the effects of the new technology.

If the pattern shown in Figure 69 involves asymptotic approach to equilibrium at a rate directly proportional to the remaining distance, its analysis becomes particularly simple; in that case only the remaining distance, and not the initial distance, determines the rate of price change. We can write for the change in price from one period to the next

$$p_{t+1} - p_t = \delta(p_f - p_t)$$

where δ is a constant. The dynamics that follows from this assumption has been relatively fully developed by various writers. For example, working with a pure-exchange general equilibrium model, Samuelson assumed that the rate of change of the price of each good is proportional to the excess of the demand for it over its supply.

$$\frac{dp_j}{dt} = a_j(x_j^d - x_j^s)$$

$$= a_j[F_j^d(p_1, p_2, \ldots, p_n) - F_j^s(p_1, p_2, \ldots, p_n)]$$

$$j = 1, 2, \ldots, n$$

where a_j is a positive constant for the jth good. Thus he obtained a set of n linear differential equations in the n prices; for these he found a set of conditions for convergence to a stable equilibrium that were closely related to the conditions satisfied by the solution of the underlying static model.[1] The demand and supply curves are of course the long-run ones; for this approach to make sense it must tacitly or explicitly be assumed that during the transition period the sequence of positions of the system results from instantaneous demand and supply functions that shift in such a way as to cause these dynamic equations to be satisfied.

An accelerating drop like that of Figure 67, based on cumulative reactions, is likely to lead to an overshoot like that of Figure 70, with converging cyclical swings around the new equilibrium. Profitable new technology often attracts new firms, whose output added to that of the old firms can carry the price to unprofitable low levels. Old firms may also

[1] P. A. Samuelson, *Foundations of Economic Analysis* (Cambridge, Mass., Harvard University Press, 1947), part II.

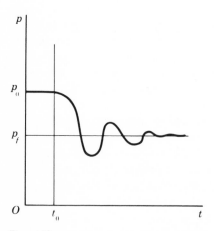

Figure 70

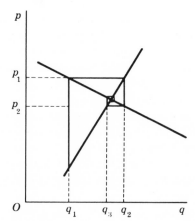

Figure 71

overreact to profitable opportunities. This phenomenon appears in many older theories of the trade cycle, and in a sense appears in the accelerator model, set out in Chapter 8. The best-known overshoot model is the cobweb model, usually applied to agricultural production. This model has a one-period lag between market price and consequent supply as given by the supply curve; market price is set by the demand-price for the available supply in the current period. Thus, in Figure 71, we start with less-than-equilibrium supply q_1, say because bad weather caused a poor crop. The market sets price p_1 for this quantity. Then, in the next period, farmers produce q_2 because they expect p_1 to continue. However, they are disappointed to receive only p_2. As a result, they reduce production in the third period to q_3, . . . , and so on. Price jumps above and below equilibrium, overshooting every time.

In the cobweb model, price always adjusts immediately to clear the market, while the supply adjusts only gradually to this price. In contrast, Samuelson's dynamics assumes that buyers or sellers remain unsatisfied (without specifying which), and that the price adjusts only gradually. While it adjusts, both intended supply and demand adjust instantaneously to the current price. The cobweb model makes sense for commodities sold in auction markets, like agricultural commodities, provided suppliers always expect the price to remain where it is. The Samuelson model makes sense for commodities for which potential buyers queue up without bidding up the price enough to clear the market, or suppliers accumulate stocks without lowering prices enough to clear them, as the case may be. The distinction is important, because the dynamics of the two kinds of markets differ. The cobweb model in Figure 71 is dynamically stable because the demand curve's slope is smaller in absolute value than the supply curve's slope. With an alternative dynamics, in which the quantity supplied at each price is always on the supply curve and in which the next period's supply equals this period's quantity demanded, this model would produce explosive price and output cycles. With this latter dynamics, the model would converge only if the demand curve's slope were *larger* in absolute value than the supply curve's slope. Likewise, a general equilibrium model has entirely different stability conditions if the rate of change of the quantity supplied is a function of the difference between supply price and demand price.

Real economies have both kinds of markets and in addition have capital accumulation and growth. A dynamic model with an equation for every market would have to include both kinds of markets and growth to have much hope of detailed applicability. However, to interpret economic fluctuations, we aggregate markets and simplify just as we did in the comparative statics of Chapters 2 and 3. If the results are less clear-cut, that reflects not on the method of aggregation but on our poor knowledge of what drives business expectations in the critical decision area of investment.

3 "STICKINESS" IN PRICE DYNAMICS

We noted in Chapter 4, on inflation, that presumed monopoly is a false and misleading explanation for changes in the price level. Neither a given extent of monopoly nor an increase in its extent can rationally account for an increase in the general price level, however superficially tempting this explanation may be. And inasmuch as rational economic analysis has succeeded in interpreting most sets of aggregate behavioral data, such as consumption, investment, the demand for money, as well as a rich variety of separate industry demand and supply functions, it would be foolish to abandon rational analysis when discussing the price level. Moreover inertia and momentum in the price level can be explained in rational ways.

Besides the effects of queuing, mentioned in the preceding section, prices have lags due to a variety of standard business practices. For example, the rents of houses, apartments, and business properties are generally quoted for leases of a year or longer, and rents actually paid are fixed for the remaining terms of leases outstanding. The sale prices of many items appear in catalogues that are published every six months or so, and as a general rule are not raised in between. (Moreover, not every catalogue price or "list" price is the price actually charged, and the discounts may be overlooked by a price surveyor.)

To see the effect of prices that remain fixed for a time because of contracts or standard practices, consider the case of rentals on one-year lease. Suppose that rents have been at an index level of 100 for over a year, and then rise to 112 on all new and renewed leases. One-twelfth of all leases come up for renewal each month, so that the average rent on all leases, new and old, would rise one point each month. After six months, the average would be 106. Suppose that the rental on new leases and renewals drops at the six-month point to 106, the going average. But even though the new level equaled the average, the average rent would still rise, because the old leases ending and coming up for renewal would still all be at 100, and would rise to 106. With this rise, the average rent would rise at one-half point per month, until after six more months it would reach 109. At this point, after a total of twelve months, old leases at 112 would start ending and coming up for renewal, so that if the new rent level remained at 106 the average would start falling. It would drop back to 106 in six months. In this example, the movement of the average lags behind that of new rentals by six months, which will be the typical lag; in special instances the lag could be as great as a year. Thus we get a "sticky" price series from an atomistic market.

Other markets operate on what appear to be tacit or implied contracts, where a set of customer firms buy steadily from large suppliers at prices that differ systematically from those set in competitive markets. For example, in nonferrous metals, especially copper, large firms operate alongside smaller primary suppliers and a competitive market in reclaimed scrap. Although large supplies are always available at competitive quotations from these alternatives sources, many customers buy from the large suppliers at their prices. The large firms hold their prices above the competitive price in a slack market and below it in a tight market, so that their prices swing less widely than does the competitive price. On the average, their customers do no worse than they would buying in the competitive market. Perhaps both parties to such transactions prefer the apparent risk reduction in the more stable price. Whatever the explanation, the successful stickiness of the large firms' prices can be rationalized only in terms of implied long-term contracts with their customers.

Our discussion of contracts and other influences that help make prices sticky, in competitive as well as monopolistic product lines, leads to further conclusions when we consider expectations. In a rising market, prospective tenants will try to delay leasing properties if they think that rents will soon fall back, but will hurry to rent if they think that rents will keep rising. Landlords will react the opposite ways. These reactions reflect the long-term nature of lease transactions. If rental property becomes scarce and rents start rising, in the typical case one might suppose that both tenants and landlords will be uncertain whether the scarcity represents a trend or is random, unless some strong new influence is known to have caused it. If they are uncertain, and it's really a trend, rents will move up more slowly than they would if all parties recognized the trend. Thus the uncertainty of expectations adds stickiness to *new* rentals, which is then further compounded by the averaging process. It is possible, though hard to verify or prove false, that expectations explain why the price level sometimes rises in the face of heavy (or moderate) unemployment. In any case, the combination of expectations and express or implied long-term contracts provides a major explanation for price level stickiness.

4 THE PHILLIPS CURVE AND MONOPOLY DYNAMICS

Several historical studies, notably one by A. W. Phillips, indicate that in the United Kingdom and the United States unemployment is lower when prices and wages are rising than when they are falling. The curve in Figure 72 shows the shape of the relationship as observed on the

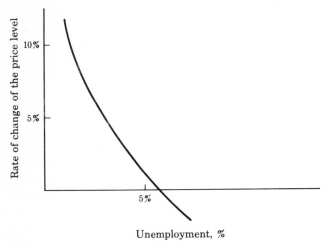

Figure 72 The Phillips curve, general form

average for the United States. In a rough way, our analysis in earlier chapters leads us to expect this relationship. If aggregate demand, indicated by the intersection of the monetary sector curve and the expenditure sector curve, exceeds full-employment real income, prices rise and unemployment falls below its normal level. If aggregate demand falls short of full-employment real income, unemployment rises and the price level falls. In a model that includes expected inflation or deflation, these statements apply to deviations from an initial inflationary or deflationary equilibrium.

In this connection, we have to consider a normal, sustainable level of unemployment, analogous to a normal vacancy percentage in rental apartments. When vacancies rise above a certain level, the ratio of apartment rents to the price level starts to fall; when they fall below that level, this ratio rises. Because of frictional unemployment and "structural" unemployment, there is an analogous percentage of unemployment that marks the tendency of real wages to rise or fall above or below their long-run trend value set by technology and population growth. This percentage of unemployment can be permanently sustained without forcing a change in expectations; in the case of a stable actual and expected price level, this percentage can be sustained without a shift to either inflation or deflation.

That the Phillips curve should appear this way tells us something about labor and product markets and their dynamics. As suggested by our earlier discussions of transitions between equilibria, the price level moves first and money wages second, so that a rising price and wage level implies a lag of real wages behind their equilibrium level. That in turn implies a fall in unemployment, giving the negative slope of the curve in Figure 72. If there were any substance to the idea that cost-push generated by labor monopoly was a force in inflation, the Phillips curve would have a positive slope instead. Union wages would rise *before* the price level, driving up real wages and causing increased unemployment. Thus the Phillips curve relationship contradicts the cost-push idea, and supports our analysis.

One of the details of the relationship requires further discussion, however. The observed curve typically has a higher position in the early upswing of a business cycle than in the final stage of the upswing and in the downswing. That is, it is higher when unemployment is falling than when it is rising. This shift of position appears in Figure 73. One

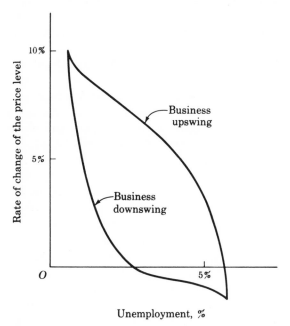

Figure 73 Typical Phillips curves as observed

explanation is that rising aggregate demand is more unevenly distributed than is falling aggregate demand, and so generates a smaller employment effect.

A second explanation reflects the dynamics of hiring. In the early upswing, some workers on part-time and others on low-priority duties like extra maintenance go full time on current production. Firms that can adjust this way keep down their hiring, while increasing output and prices, until they are confident that the upswing will continue. (If this happens only in some industries, while others hire actively, this explanation merges into the first.) Then when the boom tops out and unemployment moves back toward normal levels, even those firms that suffer a decline in output are reluctant to lay off labor until their expectations adjust downward. This type of hiring dynamics reflects a tacit long-term contract with each worker analogous to the lease of rental property. Workers experienced at a particular firm are worth more than workers hired there for the first time, so the firm tries to keep them on part-time or low-priority work when output falls. After a period of low output, however, the firm has to lay off more and more workers. These lags could explain the double form observed for the Phillips curve.

The cost-push explanation differs from the others in that it predicts that union wages will tend to lead an inflationary upswing rather than trail behind it. That makes it possible to disprove, and the facts are otherwise. The consistent experience in the United States has been that union wages rise *less* rapidly than nonunion wages in inflationary periods. The second explanation, possibly combined with the first, therefore stands.

The failure of union wages to keep up with inflation is sometimes matched by the behavior of prices set by large firms that seem to dominate an industry. We noted already that large firms selling copper and other nonferrous metals behave this way. In the inflation of the late 1940s following World War II, automobile and steel firms sold their products far below competitive market prices and had long waiting lines of unsatisfied customers. Gray markets sprang up in both commodities, which showed what their market-clearing prices were. Fear that unions would raise wages and take away the extra profits was a reported explanation for this behavior, where these firms correctly expected prices would later fall and would embarrass them if the wage level went too high in the meanwhile. (Like everyone else at that time, they apparently feared a possible relapse into the prewar depression.) Whatever the explanation, and whether or not these firms had monopolies in their respective markets, the evidence does suggest that unions and large firms adjust their prices less often and by smaller amounts *both upward and downward* than one would expect under perfect competition. If monopoly is a factor, the reason might be that the monopolist faces uncertainty about future elasticities of demand, as well as about the amount he can sell at a given price; because of this compound uncertainty, he may delay longer before adjusting his expectations than does a competitive firm. Such evidence as we have suggests that this does happen, and that prices charged by large firms lag behind other prices in a general movement.

5 EXPECTATIONS AND ADAPTATION

The assumption that the rate of change of price or quantity is proportional to the distance remaining to equilibrium has been used widely in practical applications to reflect lags in price and quantity adjustment, and as a general rule has worked well. An analogous assumption about expectations has also worked well in practice. In the latter case, there are sound theoretical reasons why this should be true. Accordingly, we shall expand on this general approach, even though for some types of lags it is a rough approximation.

We shall begin with an elementary expectations model. For simplicity, assume that the expectation of a given variable can be expressed as a single expected value, even though in some applications the variance and other properties of the expectation might also be important. We also disregard a variety of external influences on expectations. Consider an observed variable x_t, of which the household or firm forms an expectation x_{t+1}^* of the value it will have in the period $t + 1$. Generally speaking the household or firm has based past decisions on past expectations of the variable. Typically it has found that the variable is only partly predictable. As a general rule also, each new value as it occurs provides some new information about where the variable will be in the future, adding to the knowledge about the variable gained from the past. One possible way of representing these facts is to say that past experience is summarized in the expectation that prevailed just before the latest value was observed, that is, in x_t^*, and that the new expectation will be some combination of this previous expectation and of the observed current value x_t. In particular, consider a weighted average of the two:

$$x_{t+1}^* = \beta x_t + (1 - \beta)x_t^* \tag{90}$$

where β is a constant weight. Ordinarily we would assume that β is a fraction, $0 < \beta < 1$. If so, the new expectation will fall between the old expectation and the realized value x_t.

Another way of looking at this hypothesis concerning expectations can be seen by rewriting (90) into an expression in the old forecast and the error of forecast:

$$x_{t+1}^* = x_{.t}^* + \beta(x_t - x_t^*) \tag{91}$$

The expression $x_t - x_t^*$, the difference between the actual value and what was forecast, is the error of forecast. This way of putting it says that the new forecast is a revision of the old one, the revision being the fraction β of the error of forecast. The household or firm finds it erred but doubts that the new value will be maintained; it expects the variable to lapse part way back toward what it had previously expected. The fraction of the error by which it revises its forecast, that is, β, is the coefficient of expectations.

To apply this model of expectations to behavioral data requires an assumption about the earliest expectation. Equation (90) or (91) enables us to find the new expectation only if we have the old one. One solution to this problem comes from repeated application of the formula (90) to older and older values of the expectation, until the choice of an initial value no longer affects the calculation. In place of x_t^* in (90), we substitute

$$x_t^* = \beta x_{t-1} + (1 - \beta)x_{t-1}^*$$

which is (90) applied one period earlier. This gives

$$\begin{aligned} x_{t+1}^* &= \beta x_t + (1 - \beta)[\beta x_{t-1} + (1 - \beta)x_{t-1}^*] \\ &= \beta x_t + \beta(1 - \beta)x_{t-1} + (1 - \beta)^2 x_{t-1}^* \end{aligned} \tag{92}$$

Similarly, we can substitute for x_{t-1}^* in (92), and then for x_{t-2}^* in the result, and so on indefinitely. After m repetitions of this procedure, the result is

$$\begin{aligned} x_{t+1}^* &= \beta x_t + \beta(1 - \beta)x_{t-1} + \beta(1 - \beta)^2 x_{t-2} + \cdots + \beta(1 - \beta)^m x_{t-m} \\ &\qquad + (1 - \beta)^{m+1} x_{t-m}^* \end{aligned}$$

$$= \beta \sum_{j=0}^{m} (1 - \beta)^j x_{t-j} + (1 - \beta)^{m+1} x_{t-m}^* \tag{93}$$

The coefficient of x_{t-m}^* in this expression is a fraction raised to the power $m + 1$; by making m large we can make this term as small as we please, if past expectations are bounded. That is, if we go back far enough in time (make m large), the error introduced by using an erroneous initial value of x^* becomes negligible. Therefore a reasonable way to proceed is to use a large number of terms in (93) and then to assume that x_{t-m}^* was equal to x_{t-m}. The expression (93) for x_t^* then becomes a weighted average of past values of x_t.

A similar theory results for the adjustment of households and firms to changed economic circumstances, where we assume that the household or firm moves a fraction of the remaining distance in each period toward its ultimate desired position. This assumption is inaccurate for variables like rents, discussed in the preceding section, but even so it is a fair approximation. Suppose the behavior equation of the household or firm, showing its desired long-run value of z_t^*, given y_t, is

$$z_t^* = a + by_t \tag{94}$$

where a and b are constants. Suppose also that the household or firm begins the period with an actual value z_t. Then if its fraction of adjustment is a constant δ, it will move during the current period to an actual value

$$
\begin{aligned}
z_{t+1} &= z_t + \delta(z_t^* - z_t) \\
&= (1 - \delta)z_t + \delta z_t^* \tag{95}
\end{aligned}
$$

$$z_{t+1} = (1 - \delta)z_t + \delta a + \delta b y_t \tag{96}$$

Equation (96) is obtained by substituting (94) into (95). For some purposes, (96) can be applied directly; but within the present context we wish to eliminate z_t. To do so, we proceed exactly as we did in the preceding paragraph to obtain

$$
\begin{aligned}
z_{t+1} = \delta a \sum_{j=0}^{m} (1 - \delta)^j + \delta b \sum_{j=0}^{m} (1 - \delta)^j y_{t-j} \\
+ (1 - \delta)^{m+1} (a + by_{t-m}) + \text{small error term} \tag{97}
\end{aligned}
$$

In this case, z_{t+1} is a linear function of a moving average of past values of y_t.

In both the expectations case and the adjustment case, the moving average applies the highest weight to the most recent observed value of the variable being averaged and applies declining weights to earlier and earlier values. The decline in weights is exponential, driven by rising powers of $1 - \beta$ or $1 - \delta$. In cases where the coefficient of expectations β or the coefficient of adjustment δ is close to 1 (expectations respond very sensitively to errors of forecast, or adjustment is rapid), the fraction in the expression (93) or (97) that rises to increasing powers is nearly zero, and the decline in weights is rapid. In this case, the latest actual value has a large weight in the average, and the prior values have a small total weight. That is, when expectations respond quickly to experience or when adjustment is rapid, behavior will be closely tied to the most recently observed values of the relevant variable and will depend relatively little on prior values. When expectations respond only sluggishly to experience or when adjustment is slow (β or δ is close to zero), behavior will depend less on the latest values and more on prior ones.

Values of β and δ greater than 1 can also be considered. For such values, expectations and adjustments overshoot the past movements of the series on which they are based; with the passage of time they overshoot by larger and larger amounts and move outward on an explosive path. It might sometimes happen that expectations and adjustments really are explosive. A point of more general relevance, however, is that many time series fluctuate around a normal percentage growth line, which means that such time series are themselves "explosive"—they tend to grow at a certain average percentage per year, moving upward without limit. Where this is true, it is possible for the optimal β for adjustment to be greater than 1. This result will not imply any greater explosiveness than is already present in the basic series, and so is reasonable.

In applications of these models, the coefficients β and δ are estimated from the data, as are the other coefficients of such relationships as (97). It has in fact been applied with apparent success to a remarkable variety of problems involving either expectations or adjustment, including the following:

1.   Expected rate of inflation as a variable in the demand for money in eight hyperinflations in Europe and one chronic inflation in South America

2.   Inventory decisions of business firms

3.   Expected price as a variable in the planting decisions for individual agricultural crops, and delayed adjustment of plantings

4.   Interest-rate structure, that is, long-term rates, short-term rates, and expected future short-term rates

5.   Expected (permanent) income as a variable in the consumption function

6.   Adjustment of stocks of housing and durable goods to desired levels

A significant omission from the above list is expected sales or prices, as variables determining plant and equipment investment expenditures by business firms. Such expenditures may or may not partly involve an expectations model of the type discussed here; the evidence is inconclusive.

The success of this model for such varied problems of expectations and adjustment suggests that it represents fairly well an important element in the overall behavior of the economic system, and that it can be relied upon as a major idea in the analysis of economic fluctuations.

6   THE THEORY OF OPTIMAL FORECASTING

By contrast with the model for adjustment to change, the theory of expectations outlined in the preceding section not only succeeds in applications, but it also has a solid theoretical foundation. For an important class of time series, the linear function of past values of the series that minimizes the error variance of forecast (if past values are all that help predict) is a set of exponentially declining weighted averages of the type (93). That is, if error variance is the criterion, there is no better linear function of past values of a series for making forecasts of it than this one. The class of time series for which this is true includes any time series v_t that can be represented as a linear function of some of its own past values subject to disturbances and that is observed with some degree of error; if the true value v_t is observed with an error ϵ_t, such a series is represented by the two equations

$$w_t = v_t + \epsilon_t \tag{98}$$

and

$$v_t = a_1 v_{t-1} + a_2 v_{t-2} + \cdots + a_n v_{t-n} + \xi_t \tag{99}$$

where n is the number of its own past values of which v_t is a function and where ξ_t is a random disturbance. A series of the type (99), though subject to continuous new disturbances, tends to have a degree of persistency of its values from period to period, of its trend, of the rate of change of its trend, and so on, depending on the coefficients a_j and on how many of them there are. The proof of the optimal character of this method of forecasting is given for a simple case in Appendix B to this chapter.

The disturbances ξ_t become part of the true values v_t and so influence the later values of the series as these appear in the autoregressive function (99); thus these disturbances may be referred to as "permanent." The errors of observation ϵ_t, by contrast, are not a part of the true values v_t and so do not affect its subsequent values; if the errors are random over time, they do not affect subsequent w_t, either, and so may be referred to as "transitory." Both kinds of random element, however, interfere with accurate forecasting of the w_t; even if the past values of the v_t were perfectly known we could not forecast their future values perfectly when the future disturbances are unknown.

The minimum error variance forecast of a series of the type w_t will involve not merely a single exponentially declining weighted average of its past values but as many such averages as there are past-value terms in (99), that is, n of them. The weight coefficients [analogous to $1 - \beta$ in equation (93)] for the averages used may all be different, and will depend on the coefficients of (99) and on the variances and covariance of the error and disturbance terms. Thus the expectations model set out in the preceding section gives its user efficient forecasts of the variable in which he is interested only when that variable's true or permanent value depends on only one past value. In practice, however, forecasts using only one weighted average tend to have an error variance only a little larger than that for the most efficient forecast; the one best average does most of the work done by an optimal combination of several. Therefore the theoretical support for the simple expectations model is quite strong, provided the situations to which it is applied involve variables to be forecast that have the properties of equations (98) and (99).

Further, if the behavior of one industry or segment of the economy produces a variable that a second industry or segment needs to forecast, and if the first bases its behavior on an expectations or adjustment model of the type discussed here, then it is nearly optimal for the second to do so. The equation for the formation of expectations (90) and the adjustment equation (95) are themselves autoregressive equations analogous to (99) with the current observations x_t and z_t entering in the role of the disturbance term. Generally the observers of the resultant behavior will observe it with some degree of error, and the behavior itself will contain random elements. Although x_t and z_t are scarcely random in such a case, the presumption is strong that the second group will obtain optimal or nearly optimal forecasts by using the expectations model set out here. Then, other groups making forecasts of variables produced by the second group will obtain nearly optimal forecasts in the same way, and so on. Once someone starts it a chain relationship follows, spreading this kind of forecasting throughout the system.

Now we must show that there is some reason for someone to start this behavior in the first place. One way is through the adjustment model; because of delays in the dispersion of knowledge, in embodying it in new capital, and other similar delays associated with costs of rapid adjustment, it pays some industries to adjust slowly. There are probably many industries to which this model applies. If so, it justifies widespread use of the expectations model and then a cumulative spread of its use in widening circles of interaction. A second way is through the behavior of exogenous variables—the variables that affect economic behavior without themselves being a dependent part of the interacting economic system. Many such variables have evident tendencies to persistency of a kind represented by the autoregressive function (99). If a war starts in 1939, the probability that there will be a war going on in 1940, and even in 1941, is greater than it otherwise would have been; and if it starts getting worse it is a good guess that it will keep on getting worse for a while. When military expenditure or some other such magnitude starts rising or falling, it is likely at least to stay at its new level and even to keep on rising or falling for a time. As another example, the weather with its influence on crops is known to have a similar year-to-year tendency. (See Figures 74 and 75, below.) Such exogenous variables have an unpredictable disturbance element, sometimes a large one, and generally also have errors of observation and other transitory elements. Thus they have in a rough way the characteristics of an autoregressive variable observed with error, like w_t of equation (98). These arguments point toward pervasive exponentially declining weighted averages of the type (93). They are sometimes good forecasting tools for the exogenous forces that impinge on the economic

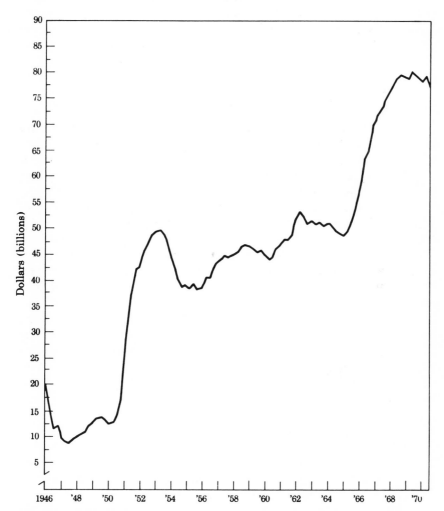

Figure 74 National defense component—government purchases, quarterly, 1946-I through 1970-II (seasonally adjusted, annual rates). (*From Survey of Current Business*)

system and are also good forecasting tools for the economically determined variables within the system.

A more detailed discussion of the properties of exponential moving averages appears in Appendix A to this chapter, with examples in Appendixes B through D. It shows that these averages smooth their input data; that is, a household or firm predicting and acting upon a comparatively random, nonperiodic series behaves in a smoother, more periodic way. The tendency toward periodicity increases with cumulative applications of the process, and with it the tendency increases to overshoot in the reaction to a disturbance. These tendencies help to explain the apparent partial periodicity in fluctuations in the economy.

7 SOME GENERAL OBSERVATIONS

There remain two major gaps in our analysis of economic fluctuations. One is the absence of any detailed analysis of the exogenous forces impinging on the economy; the second is the cursory discussion of individual sectors, particularly of the variable most central to economic fluctuations, investment.

That exogenous forces can be represented by disturbed autoregressive series observed with error, viz., equations of the type set out in (98) and (99), can only be postulated, not proved. By and large such variables—weather, political and military decisions, new discoveries, and so on—are hard to predict. To the extent that we know something of what to expect from them, it is most typically the case that we base our judgment primarily on the experience of the recent past, and to a lesser extent on the experience of the more distant past. If so, the representation given by the equations of disturbed autoregressive series may be appropriate, if indeed any mathematical representation is. Its plausibility is supported by Figures 74 and 75, showing United States national defense expenditures (quarterly, 1946 to 1970) and wheat yields (annually, 1920 to 1966), respectively, two of the major exogenous variables in our economy; both are similar in movement to parts of the disturbed autoregressive series shown in Figures A-4 to A-9 in Appendix A. However, what matters is not whether the disturbed autoregressive representation is in fact accurate, but whether households and firms act as if it were. While it cannot be said positively that they do, the evidence from successful applications of our expectations and adjustment models suggests that they do.

However, the big variable that must still be considered as in part exogenous is business expectations. Part of the variation in investment, e.g., most of that of residential housing construction, can be explained in

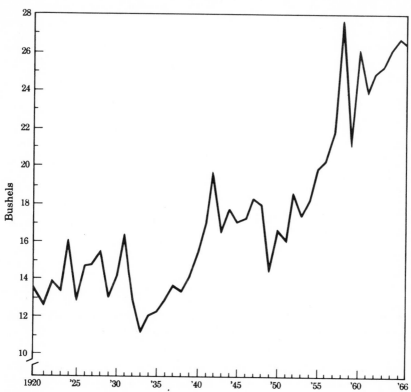

Figure 75 Wheat yield per harvested acre annually, 1920 through 1966. (*U.S. Department of Agriculture, Agricultural Statistics*)

terms of gradual or fractional adjustments of stocks of capital to desired levels, the latter being determined in part by expected income. Both the adjustment process and expected income come under the analysis of this chapter. It is also true that investment in the aggregate moves in a manner broadly similar to that of other economic series; the figures for gross private domestic investment, quarterly, 1946 to 1970, shown in Figure 76, have a semiperiodic fluctuating appearance like that of the series we have been considering. However, the major fluctuations over time of business expectations and investment, apart from those brought on by obvious external influences such as wars, remain a mysterious and challenging phenomenon.

We may conjecture that many swings of investment come from a strong accelerator mechanism, interacting with the multiplier to produce the cumulative collapse and recovery described in the last section of

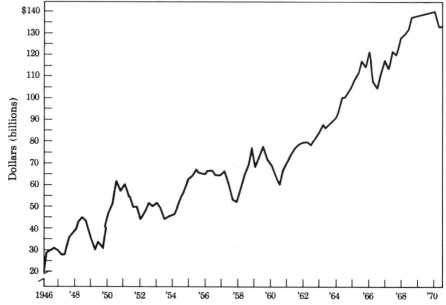

Figure 76 Gross private domestic investment, quarterly, 1946-I through 1970-II (seasonally adjusted annual rates). (*From Survey of Current Business*)

Chapter 5. But this mechanism mingles with other, unpredictable influences on business expectations, and is itself so unpredictable that it is of little help in interpreting economic fluctuations. We do as well to assume that the random impulses are large and that the economy responds to them with damped, though possibly cyclical, reactions.

BIBLIOGRAPHY

Archibald, G. C.: "The Phillips Curve and the Distribution of Unemployment," *The American Economic Review, Papers and Proceedings*, vol. 59 (1969), pp. 124–134.

Attiyeh, Yossef: "Wage-Price Spiral versus Demand Inflation: United States, 1949–1957" (unpublished Ph.D. dissertation, Chicago, 1959).

Bailey, Martin J.: "Prediction of an Autoregressive Variable Subject Both to Disturbances and to Errors of Observation," *Journal of the American Statistical Association*, vol. 60 (1965), pp. 164–181.

Baumol, William J.: *Economic Dynamics* (New York, The Macmillan Company, 1951).

Burns, Arthur F.: "Hicks and the Real Cycle," *Journal of Political Economy*, vol. 60 (1952), p. 1.

Christenson, C. L.: "Variations in the Inflationary Force of Bargaining," *American Economic Review Supplement*, vol. 44 (1954), p. 347.

Deaver, John: "The Chilean Inflation and the Demand for Money" (unpublished Ph.D. dissertation, Chicago, 1960).

Eckstein, O., and T. Wilson: "Determination of Money Wages in American Industry," *Quarterly Journal Economy*, vol. 76 (1962), pp. 379–414.

Frisch, Ragnar: "Propagation Problems and Impulse Problems in Dynamic Economics," in *Economic Essays in Honor of Gustav Cassel* (London, George Allen & Unwin, Ltd., 1933).

Griliches, Z.: "Distributed Lags: A Survey," *Econometrica*, vol. 35 (1967), pp. 16–49.

Haberler, Gottfried: *Prosperity and Depression*, 3d ed. (Geneva, League of Nations, 1941), part I.

Hicks, J. R.: *A Contribution to the Theory of the Trade Cycle* (New York, Clarendon Press, 1950), chaps. 2–8.

Johnson, Harry G.: "The Neo-Classical One Sector Growth Model," *Economica*, vol. 33 (August, 1966), pp. 265–287.

Jorgenson, D. W.: "Rational Distributed Lag Functions," *Econometrica*, vol. 34 (1966), pp. 135–149.

Kendall, M. G.: *The Advanced Theory of Statistics*, vol. 2 (London, Charles Griffin & Company, Ltd., 1948), chap. 29.

Klein, Lawrence: "The Use of Econometric Models as a Guide to Policy," *Econometrica*, vol. 15 (1947), part III.

Lewis, H. G.: *Unionism and Relative Wages in the United States* (Chicago, The University of Chicago Press, 1963).

Lipsey, Richard G.: "The Relation between Unemployment and the Rate of Change of Money Wage Rates in the United Kingdom, 1862–1957: A Further Analysis," *Economica*, vol. 27 (1960), pp. 1–31.

Lucas, Robert E.: "Adjustment Costs and the Theory of Supply," *Journal of Political Economy*, vol. 75 (1967), p. 321.

Lucas, Robert E., and Leonard A. Rapping: "Price Expectations and the Phillips Curve," *The American Economic Review*, vol. 59 (1969), p. 342.

Masters, Stanley H.: "The Behavior of Output per Man during Recessions: An Empirical Study of Underemployment," *The Southern Economic Journal*, vol. 30 (1967), pp. 388–394.

McGuire, T. W., and L. A. Rapping: "The Role of Market Variables and Key Bargains in the Manufacturing Wage Determination Process," *Journal of Political Economy*, vol. 78 (1968), pp. 1015–1036.

Meade, J. E.: "The Adjustment of Saving and Investment in a Growing Economy," *The Review of Economic Studies*, vol. 30 (July, 1963), pp. 151–166.

Meiselman, David: *The Term Structure of Interest Rates* (Englewood Cliffs, N.J., Prentice-Hall, Inc., 1962).

Metzler, Lloyd: "The Nature and Stability of Inventory Cycles," *Review of Economic Statistics*, vol. 23 (1949), p. 113.

Metzler, Lloyd: "Three Lags in the Circular Flow of Income," in *Income, Employment and Public Policy* (New York, W. W. Norton & Company, Inc., 1948).

Mitchell, W. C.: "Business Cycles," in American Economic Association: *Readings in Business Cycle Theory* (New York, McGraw-Hill Book Company, 1944).

Moore, Geoffrey H.: *Statistical Indicators of Cyclical Revivals and Recessions*, Occasional Paper 31 (New York, National Bureau of Economic Research).

Muth, J. F.: "Optical Properties of Exponentially Weighted Forecasts of Time Series with Permanent and Transitory Components," *Journal of American Statistical Association*, vol. 55 (1960).

Muth, J. F.: "Rational Expectations and the Theory of Price Movements," *Econometrica*, vol. 29 (1961), pp. 315–335.

Nelson, Charles: "Forecasting Sums of Discrete Linear Processes," Forthcoming.

Nerlove, Marc: *Distributed Lags and Demand Analysis for Agricultural and Other Commodities* (U.S. Department of Agriculture, Agricultural Handbook 141, 1958).

Nerlove, Marc: "Estimates of the Elasticities of Supply of Selected Agricultural Commodities," *Journal of Farm Economics*, vol. 38 (1956), p. 496.

Nerlove, Marc: *The Dynamics of Supply: Estimation of Farmers' Response to Price* (Baltimore, Maryland, The Johns Hopkins Press, 1958).

Phelps, E. S. (ed.): *Microeconomic Foundations of Employment and Inflation Theory* (New York, W. W. Norton & Company, Inc., 1969).

Phelps, E. S.: "Money Wage Dynamics and Labor Market Equilibrium," *Journal of Political Economy*, vol. 76 (1968), pp. 687–711, part II.

Phelps, E. S.: "The New Microeconomics in Inflation and Employment Theory," *The American Economic Review, Paper and Proceedings*, vol. 59 (1969), pp. 147–159.

Phillips, A. W.: "The Relation Between Unemployment and the Rate of Change of Money Wage Rates in the United Kingdom, 1861–1957," *Economica* (1958).

Rees, Albert: "Discussion," *American Economic Review Supplement*, vol. 44 (1954), p. 363.

Rees, Albert: "Patterns of Wages, Prices, and Productivity," in C. Myers (ed.): *Wages, Prices, Profits and Productivity* (New York, National Bureau of Economic Research, 1959).

Rees, Albert: "Postwar Wage Determination in the Basic Steel Industry," *American Economic Review*, vol. 41 (1951), p. 389.

Rees, Albert: "Wage Determination and Involuntary Unemployment," *Journal of Political Economy*, vol. 59 (1951), p. 143.

Samuelson, Paul A.: *Foundations of Economic Analysis* (Cambridge, Mass., Harvard University Press, 1947), part II.

Samuelson, Paul A.: "Interactions between the Multiplier Analysis and the Principle of Acceleration," in American Economic Association: *Readings in Business Cycle Theory* (New York, McGraw-Hill Book Company, 1944), chap. 12.

Samuelson, Paul A., and Robert M. Solow: "Analytical Aspects of Anti-Inflation Policy," *American Economic Review Supplement*, vol. 50 (1960), pp. 177–194.

Schultze, Charles L.: "Recent Inflation in the United States," Study #1 (Joint Economic Committee, September, 1959).

Slichter, Summer H.: "Do the Wage-fixing Arrangements in the American Labor Market Have an Inflationary Bias?" *American Economic Review Supplement*, vol. 44 (1954), p. 322.

Slutzky, Eugen: "The Summation of Random Causes as the Source of Cyclic Processes," *Econometrica*, vol. 5 (1937), p. 105.

Suits, Daniel B.: "Forecasting and Analysis with an Econometric Model," *The American Economic Review*, vol. 52 (March, 1962), pp. 104–132.

Tobin, James: "A Dynamic Aggregative Model," *Journal of Political Economy*, vol. 63 (1955), p. 103.

Wold, H.: *A Study in the Analysis of Stationary Time Series*, 2d ed. (Uppsala, Sweden, Almquist and Wiksells, 1954).

Yule, G. U.: "On a Method of Investigating Periodicities in Disturbed Series with Special Reference to Wolfer's Sunspot Numbers," *Philosophical Transactions of the Royal Society*, section A (1927), p. 267.

A APPENDIX
EXPECTATIONS
AS SMOOTHING
FUNCTIONS

1 THE CYCLICAL TENDENCY OF MOVING AVERAGES

The computation of any moving average, even from random numbers, introduces "cycles," that is, a degree of periodicity, into the resulting averaged data. This phenomenon has misled many an analyst in search of cyclical tendencies in time series: he has "discovered" periodicities in moving average data that were merely the periodicities that the averaging process itself had introduced. In the present context, this periodic character of moving averages is a real phenomenon, not a construct. Many economic series come from a specific kind of averaging process and therefore have genuine periodicities.

As a convenience, we will use polar coordinates. We can think of a regular cycle as one revolution along the circumference of a circle and can measure parts of a cycle in radial units, or fractions of a complete circle. A circle of unit radius has a circumference of 2π units; a complete circle, 360°, represents 2π radians of radial measure. If we let these 2π radians represent one complete cycle in a periodic time series with a cycle length of P time periods, then in radial measure the angle θ covered in one time period is given by

$$\theta = \frac{2\pi}{P} \tag{A-1}$$

That is, θ is the angular measure of the fraction of a cycle $1/P$ that is completed in one time period.

Consider any time series x_t, and a moving average y_t formed from it by the formula

$$y_t = \sum_{j=-k_1}^{k_2} a_j x_{t-j} \tag{A-2}$$

where k_1 and k_2 are constants, with $k_1 > 0$. (If $k_1 = k_2$, that is, if the average is made up of an equal number of terms preceding and following the date assigned to y_t, the average is "centered." This is the typical case; it is not a necessary characteristic of all moving averages, however, and obviously is not of the exponentially weighted ones we have considered here. It is also typical of computed moving averages that the a_j are equal for all the values of j within the span of the average; again, this is not true of the exponential averages we consider here.) Consider further, for illustrative purposes, the special case in which the series x_t is simply a random sequence of numbers drawn independently from a normal distribution with zero mean. In this case the series y_t, given by (A-2), will have an average total period of fluctuation (measured by the average length of time between crossing from negative to positive values of y_t) whose corresponding angle θ has the cosine[1]

$$\cos \theta = \frac{\displaystyle\sum_{j=-k_1}^{k_2-1} a_j a_{j+1}}{\displaystyle\sum_{j=-k_1}^{k_2} a_j^2} \tag{A-3}$$

For example, if the a_j are all equal, say to the inverse of the number of terms in the average, and if $k_1 = k_2 = k$, so that the number of terms is $2k + 1$, we have

$$a = a_j = \frac{1}{2k + 1} \quad j = -k, -k+1, \ldots, -1, 0, 1, \ldots, k-1, k$$

---

[1] See M. G. Kendall, *The Advanced Theory of Statistics*, vol. 2 (London, Charles Griffin and Company, Ltd., 1948), pp. 378–387.

Since $a_j a_{j+1} = a_j{}^2 = a^2$, the only difference between the numerator and the denominator of (A-3) in this case is the number of terms.

$$\cos \theta = \frac{2ka^2}{(2k+1)a^2} = \frac{2k}{2k+1} \tag{A-4}$$

Thus for a five-term moving average ($k = 2$) we would have

$$\cos \theta = \frac{4}{5} \qquad \theta = 0.645 = \frac{2\pi}{P_5}$$

where P_5 is the length of cycle introduced by the five-term moving average. Then

$$P_5 = \frac{2\pi}{0.645} = 9.76$$

That is, taking this moving average introduces a cycle some $9\frac{3}{4}$ periods long (e.g., $9\frac{3}{4}$ years long if the basic data are annual) into the resulting averaged data.

The term "cycle" in this context is used loosely, to mean the average length of time between equivalent stages of fluctuations with some degree of smoothness or nonrandomness. The smoother and more regular these fluctuations are, the closer they will come to being cycles in the strict sense of a perfectly periodic function such as a sine curve. How smooth and regular the nonrandom fluctuations are that are introduced into a random series by taking a moving average depends on the character of the average. We shall see some examples of this below in section 4.

2 PERIODICITIES OF CUMULATED EXPONENTIAL AVERAGES

In sections 5 and 6 of Chapter 11, we saw that efficient forecasts of economic time series are exponentially weighted moving averages of past values of the series being forecast. We have just noted that any moving average introduces into random data periodicities that can readily be calculated. Now consider the periodicities of economic behavior based on forecasts of the kind indicated. Suppose that some economic sector bases its behavior on an observed exogenous variable w_t, an imperfect measure of v_t, whose movements follow the autoregressive scheme

$$v_t = g v_{t-1} + \xi_t \tag{A-5}$$

where g is a constant fraction and ξ_t is random. The optimal forecast of

w_{t+1} is approximately

$$w^*_{t+1} = \alpha_0 \sum_{j=0}^{t} \alpha_1{}^j w_{t-j} \tag{A-6}$$

for some α_1 and α_0, if w_0 was the first observed value of the series. Suppose further that this sector then chooses a desired value of a variable z^*_{t+1} by the equation

$$z^*_{t+1} = b_0 + b_1 w^*_{t+1} + u_{t+1} \tag{A-7}$$

where u_{t+1} here denotes all other influences on z^*_{t+1}, both systematic and random; and suppose finally that during the coming period the sector adjusts only part way toward the desired level from the actual level z_t:

$$z_{t+1} = z_t + \delta(z^*_{t+1} - z_t)$$

Proceeding as in the derivation of (93) and (97), we obtain

$$z_{t+1} = \delta b_0 \sum_{i=0}^{t+1} (1 - \delta)^i + \delta b_1 \sum_{i=0}^{t+1} (1 - \delta)^i w^*_{t+1-i}$$
$$+ \delta \sum_{i=0}^{t+1} (1 - \delta)^i u_{t+1-i} \tag{A-8}$$

Now since $w_t = v_t + \epsilon_t$, equation (A-6) can be written

$$w^*_{t+1} = \alpha_0 \sum_{j=0}^{t} \alpha_1{}^j v_{t-j} + \alpha_0 \sum_{j=0}^{t} \alpha_1{}^j \epsilon_{t-j} \tag{A-9}$$

When this is substituted for every w^*_{t+1-i} in (A-8), with appropriate modifications of subscripts, we obtain

$$z_{t+1} = \delta b_0 \sum_{i=0}^{t+1} (1 - \delta)^i + \delta b_1 \alpha_0 \sum_{i=0}^{t+1} \sum_{j=0}^{t-i} (1 - \delta)^i \alpha_1{}^j v_{t-i-j}$$
$$+ \delta b_1 \alpha_0 \sum_{i=0}^{t+1} \sum_{j=0}^{t-i} (1 - \delta)^i \alpha_1{}^j \epsilon_{t-i-j} + \delta \sum_{i=0}^{t+1} (1 - \delta)^i u_{t+1-i} \tag{A-10}$$

Thus z_{t+1} contains double exponentially declining weighted averages of v_{t-i-j} and ϵ_{t-i-j}. Further, after applying to (A-5) the derivation of (90) to (93), to obtain

$$v_t = \sum_{k=0}^{t} g^k \xi_{t-k} \tag{A-11}$$

we can substitute this for every v_{t-i-j} in (A-10), to obtain

$$z_{t+1} = \delta b_1 \alpha_0 \sum_{i=0}^{t+1} \sum_{j=0}^{t-i} \sum_{k=0}^{t-i-j} (1 - \delta)^i \alpha_1{}^j g^k \xi_{t-i-j-k} + \cdots \tag{A-12}$$

plus other terms of double and single summation in ϵ and u. Thus the behavior of the economic sector under consideration determines an economic variable z_{t+1} partly as a triple exponentially declining weighted average of the random series ξ_t, plus double and single exponentially declining weighted averages of ϵ_t and u_t, respectively. In general, u_t, the unmeasured and perhaps unobservable other influences on the sector's desired value z_t^*, will not be random; as a general rule (in the light of what was said in section 4) it will be some kind of disturbed autoregressive series also. If so, it fortifies the present line of argument and so can be disregarded.

Consider the cyclical properties of series of different-order exponential averages considered here, e.g., v_t, w_t^*, and z_t, which are first, second, and third order, respectively. Equation (A-3), in section 1, enables us to determine the average period per fluctuation of these averages. In the case of v_t, whose moving-average formula is given by (A-11), the numerator of (A-3) becomes

$$\sum_{j=0}^{t} a_j a_{j+1} = \sum_{j=0}^{t} g^j g^{j+1} = \sum_{j=0}^{t} g^{2j+1}$$

the denominator becomes

$$\sum_{j=0}^{t} a_j{}^2 = \sum_{j=0}^{t} g^{2j}$$

and their ratio is g:

$$\cos \theta_v = \frac{\displaystyle\sum_0^t g^{2j+1}}{\displaystyle\sum_0^t g^{2j}} = \frac{g \displaystyle\sum_0^t g^{2j}}{\displaystyle\sum_0^t g^{2j}} = g \qquad\qquad \text{(A-13)}$$

Hence the period of fluctuation of v_t is

$$P_v = \frac{2\pi}{\cos^{-1} g} \qquad\qquad \text{(A-14)}$$

If, for example, $g = \frac{1}{2}$,

$$P_v = \frac{2\pi}{\cos^{-1} 0.5} = \frac{2\pi}{1.05} \approx 6$$

v_t has a period of fluctuation of about 6 units of time.

For a second-order case such as the first part of w_{t+1}^* shown in (A-9) [taking due account of (A-11)], it is shown in Appendix C to this chapter that approximately

$$\cos \theta_{w^*, v} = \frac{\alpha_1 + g}{1 + \alpha_1 g} \tag{A-15}$$

for large values of t, where α_1 and g are the weight coefficients indicated in (A-6) and (A-11). If, as before, $g = \frac{1}{2}$, and if $\alpha_1 = \frac{1}{4}$ (as generally speaking the optimal α_1 will be less than g),

$$\cos \theta_{w^*, v} = \frac{.25 + .5}{1 + (.25)(.5)} = .667$$

Then

$$P_{w^*, v} = \frac{2\pi}{\cos^{-1} .667} = 7.47$$

In addition w^* has another period, 4.77 units, from the second term of (A-9). It will be seen below that the fluctuations of w_t^*, a composite having one period shorter than that of v_t and one slightly longer, are smoother than the fluctuations of v_t. Similarly, the third-order series z_t based on the same coefficients α_1 and g and also on $1 - \delta$ has at least one longer period than the longest of w^*, and a smoother fluctuation.

Thus the procedure of making optimal forecasts of or fractional adjustments to already autoregressive time series, cumulated at one stage after another, tends to lengthen the longest period of fluctuation from among the various components and to smooth the movement more and more at each stage. These tendencies are general when the distributed lag coefficients are real positive constants; this is remarked upon further below.

An example of the sequence of variables v_t, w_t, w_{t+1}^*, and z_{t+1} might be military expenditures and the consequent investment in the affected industries. Let v_t of equation (A-5) represent actual current military outlays of the federal government, apart from pure transitories, errors of measurement, etc., and let w_t represent the amounts of these expenditures observed by the affected firms. These firms will then make forecasts w_{t+1}^* in order to determine their desired stocks of plant and equipment z_{t+1}^* [equation (A-7)]. If they adjust only fractionally in the current period to the desired stock, their actual total stock at the beginning of the coming period will be z_{t+1}, as expressed in equations (A-8), (A-10), and (A-12). Net investment by these firms is $z_{t+1} - z_t$; should we perform this subtraction using (A-8) we would obtain an elaborate expression representing in effect the income term in the accelerator model, discussed in Chapter 8. Carrying the sequence further, we note that this net investment is income to the productive services employed by the firms in question; the series of net investment over time will by the same logic be incorporated in distributed lag moving averages for the expected, or permanent, income of these productive services. Their consumption, determined partly as a function of this, is part of the current income of the productive services employed in consumption goods industries, which determine their consumption in a similar manner and so on. (Thus a sequence of distributed lag functions goes with the sequence in the multiplier process.)

If we could be sure that other investment depended on this same type of mechanism, the whole of income would be a sum of all such components plus the income dependent upon them through multiplier sequences. Every part of national income would consist of distributed lag functions of current and past random disturbances and errors of observation. The reasonableness of this view receives some support from the discussion and examples presented below in sections 4 and 5.

3 COMPLEX WEIGHT COEFFICIENTS IN THE EXPONENTIAL AVERAGES

We have limited our attention to real positive fractions as the weight coefficients in moving-average variables. There is no need to do this, however; it is both feasible and relevant to consider also complex numbers. (As we are still mainly interested in stable systems, we shall limit our attention to complex numbers of modulus less than 1.) Observed phenomena are measured only with real numbers, but complex numbers can aid in some of the related calculations. If we form two moving averages x_t^* and x_t^{**} from the same series x_t using a pair of complex conjugate numbers as the two weight coefficients, that is,

$$x_{t+1}^* = \sum_{j=0}^{t} (c_1 + c_2 i)^j x_{t-j}$$

and   (A-16)

$$x_{t+1}^{**} = \sum_{j=0}^{t} (c_1 - c_2 i)^j x_{t-j}$$

(where i denotes the imaginary number $\sqrt{-1}$), and if we then multiply each of the results by one of another pair of complex conjugates and sum them,

$$(c_3 + c_4 i)x_{t+1}^* + (c_3 - c_4 i)x_{t+1}^{**} = x_{t+1}'$$ (A-17)

the result x_{t+1}' is a real number, where c_1, c_2, c_3, and c_4 are any real numbers.

The series x_t' obtained by (A-16) and (A-17) can also be calculated using the same real coefficients in the formula

$$x_{t+1}' - 2c_1 x_t' + (c_1^2 + c_2^2)x_{t-1}' = 2c_3 x_t - 2(c_1 c_3 + c_2 c_4)x_{t-1}$$ (A-18)

starting with appropriate initial values x_0' and x_1'. [To obtain the formula when the distributed lag weight coefficients and combining coefficients of (A-16) and (A-17) are all real, set c_2 and c_4 equal to zero.]

If an exogenous variable v_t follows the two-stage autoregressive scheme

$$v_t = g_1 v_{t-1} + g_2 v_{t-2} + \xi_t \tag{A-19}$$

it can also be represented, as the v_t of (A-5) and (A-11) was, in terms of all the values of $\xi_{t-j}, j = 0, 1, \ldots, t$. More than one such representation is possible. One of them uses g_1 and g_2 directly; another, more pertinent here, uses the roots λ_1, λ_2 of the equation

$$\lambda^2 - g_1 \lambda - g_2 = 0$$

to form exponentially weighted averages of the ξ_{t-j}. Whatever these roots are, such averages (and their sums) have average periods given by the formula (A-3) and more specifically by (A-15), with λ_1 and λ_2 taking the places of α_1 and g in the latter. The cyclical character of the series v_t is of a wholly different kind, however, according as λ_1 and λ_2 are real or complex. If they are complex the equation (A-19) represents in discrete time a disturbed sine curve. If $\xi_t = 0$ for all $t > 1$, all points of v_t will fall on a sine curve (damped if $\lambda_1 \lambda_2 < 1$) exactly. Even when disturbed, v_t has a regular appearance if the modulus of the roots is near 1, as can be seen in the graph of such a series in Figure A-1. This stands in contrast to the behavior of a series generated with real values of λ_1 and λ_2; see Figure A-2. The series in Figure A-2 has fairly smooth fluctuations, but not the regular periodicity of Figure A-1. The distinction is less clear when the moduli of the roots are substantially less than 1, but is still valid.

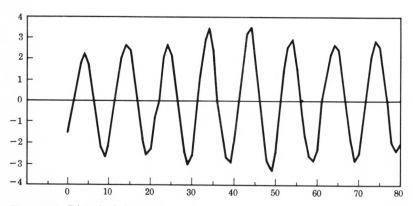

Figure A-1 Disturbed sine curve

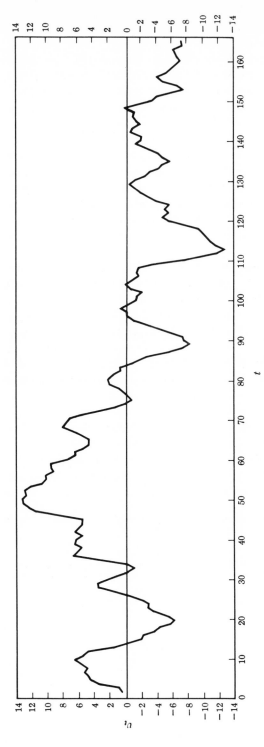

Figure A-2 Disturbed autoregressive series satisfying the equation $v_t = 1.529 v_{t-1} - .566 v_{t-2} + \epsilon_t$

Thus complex weight coefficients in moving averages contribute to movements with a periodic appearance. This point is closely related to the conclusions in a classic article by Slutzky.[1] He found that a cumulative sequence of moving averages, each computed as a moving average of the previous one starting from purely random numbers, will in certain cases converge on a pure sine curve. One essential condition is that the weights used in the successive averages, when expressed as combined weights on the original random numbers, should tend in the limit to produce a finite average period of fluctuation as given by (A-3). The second condition is that the weights should tend in the limit to produce the curvature of a sine curve, as measured by the correlation between the level of the series in question and its centered second difference; for a sine curve, this correlation is -1.

Slutzky showed that a cumulative moving-average sequence built up using only positive weights will fail to satisfy his first condition. Such a sequence will produce a series that drifts off in one direction without returning. This would be the result of cumulative application of the forecasting models discussed here, if real positive weights were used at every stage, provided the weights used at each stage remain above some minimum positive value. (Otherwise the result may tend, even in the limit, to retain a partly random, partly smoothed character.) Another possibility is that the sequence will tend toward a definite cyclic process combining cycles of different periods.

A type of moving average that tends toward a simple sine curve is obtained by repeating the two-term average with weights $(1,1)$ n times and then the "average" (first difference) process of weights $(1,-1)$ any smaller number $k < n$ times. The weights of the moving average of the basic series of random numbers that this combination implies are shown

[1] Eugen Slutzky, "The Summation of Random Causes as the Source of Cyclic Processes," *Econometrica*, vol. 5 (1937), p. 105.

Table A-1   Weights implied by the Slutzky moving-average process

Values of k	Values of n			
	2	3	4	5
(0)	(1,2,1)	(1,3,3,1)	(1,4,6,4,1)	(1,5,10,10,5,1)
1	$1, 1, -1, -1$	$1, 2, 0, -2, -1$	$1, 3, 2, -2, -3, -1$	$1, 4, 5, 0, -5, -4, -1$
2		$1, 1, -2, -2, 1, 1$	$1, 2, -1, -4, -1, 2, 1$	$1, 3, 1, -5, -5, 1, 3, 1$
3			$1, 1, -3, -3, 3, 3, -1, -1$	$1, 2, -2, -6, 0, 6, 2, -2, -1$
4				$1, 1, -4, -4, 6, 6, -4, -4, 1, 1$

in Table A-1 for a few small values of k and n. For example, if the average $(1,1)$ is applied five times starting with the random sequence ϵ_t, we have

$$x_t^{(1)} = \epsilon_t + \epsilon_{t-1}$$
$$x_t^{(2)} = x_t^{(1)} + x_{t-1}^{(1)} = \epsilon_t + 2\epsilon_{t-1} + \epsilon_{t-2}$$
$$\cdot \ \cdot \ \cdot \ \cdot \ \cdot \ \cdot \ \cdot \ \cdot \ \cdot \ \cdot \ \cdot \ \cdot \ \cdot \ \cdot \ \cdot \ \cdot \ \cdot$$
$$x_t^{(5)} = x_t^{(4)} + x_{t-1}^{(4)} = \epsilon_t + 5\epsilon_{t-1} + 10\epsilon_{t-2} + 10\epsilon_{t-3} + 5\epsilon_{t-4} + \epsilon_{t-5}$$

If it is then differenced three times, we have

$$y_t^{(1)} = x_{t+1}^{(5)} - x_t^{(5)}$$
$$y_t^{(2)} = y_{t+1}^{(1)} - y_t^{(1)}$$
$$y_t^{(3)} = y_{t+1}^{(2)} - y_t^{(2)} = \ \cdot \ \cdot \ \cdot \ = x_{t+3}^{(5)} - 3x_{t+2}^{(5)} + 3x_{t+1}^{(5)} - x_t^{(5)}$$
$$= \epsilon_{t+3} + 2\epsilon_{t+2} - 2\epsilon_{t+1} - 6\epsilon_t + 6\epsilon_{t-2} + 2\epsilon_{t-3} - 2\epsilon_{t-4} - \epsilon_{t-5}$$

That is, we have a moving average of the ϵ_t with the weights $(1,2,-2,-6, 0,6,2,-2,-1)$, which are shown for $k = 3$, $n = 5$ in Table A-1. If a moving average of the series $y_t^{(3)}$ uses these last weights, and the resulting series is averaged again with the same weights, and so on indefinitely, the resulting series will tend toward a pure sine curve, regardless of the particular random sequence with which one starts.

The repetition of distributed lag moving averages with given complex weights will produce weight distributions that approximate those of the process just illustrated. For example, the weight distribution for the pair of weight coefficients $(2/5)(1 \pm i\sqrt{3})$ alone, and then that which results after four successive averages with these coefficients, is shown in Figure A-3, along with that of 24 repetitions of $(1,1)$ combined with 8 repetitions of $(1,-1)$.

These examples are purely illustrative, showing the tendency of the repetition of distributed lag averages with complex weight coefficients to approach symmetric weight distributions similar to those of Slutzky's example.

In general, it is not known what the conditions are for the introduction and repetition of complex-weight coefficients in optimal forecasting processes. Appendix D shows that under stated conditions the optimal weight coefficients will be complex for forecasting a second-order autoregressive series built up only with real positive weight coefficients and observed with error. Comparable conditions for higher-order series, even if obtained, form little basis for generalization. At present, it can merely be said that convergence toward a sine curve or toward a cycle made up of many sine curves are just two of several possible outcomes of cumulative application of optimal forecasting methods when the exogenous forces on the economy can be represented by an autoregressive equation of the type (99).

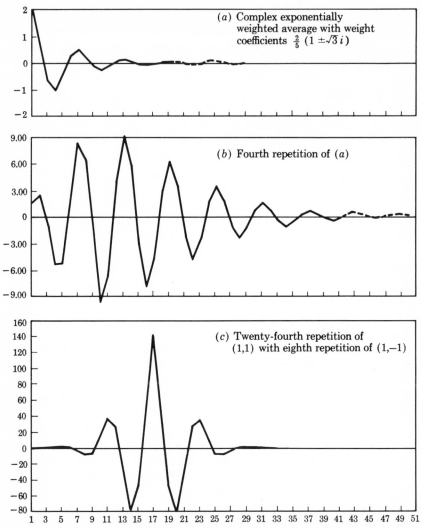

Figure A-3 Weights for moving averages of random numbers implied by repetition of Slutzky process and of complex exponentially weighted average

4 SOME ILLUSTRATIVE HYPOTHETICAL AND PRACTICAL EXAMPLES

In Figure A-1 we saw an illustrative example of a series based on complex coefficients of unit modulus, showing a persistent, regular cycle. Consider other examples using both real and complex coefficients, to illustrate the range of possibilities. Suppose we construct from random

normal numbers an exogenous autoregressive series v_t using equation
(A-5), with $g = \frac{1}{2}$. Figure A-4 shows the resulting series. If households
and firms basing decisions on this series observe it with error, and if the
combined variance of this and other transitories is the same as the variance
of the disturbance series ξ_t that generates v_t, the optimal weight coefficient
α_1 for computing the forecast w^*_{t+1} [equation (A-6)] is .234, that is, just
under $\frac{1}{4}$. The second-order term in the resulting series of forecasts is the
series graphed in Figure A-5.

Now suppose that w^*_{t+1} determines a behavioral variable z^*_{t+1}, as
in equation (A-7), and suppose that adjustment is complete in each
period (viz., $\delta = 1$, so that $z_{t+1} = z^*_{t+1}$). Suppose further that the series
of this behavioral variable is observed with error (and possibly that u_{t+1}
contains transitory as well as permanent additions to the series) by other
economic sectors, and must be forecast by them as a basis for their
behavior. For a wide range of values of the variances of the error and
disturbance terms, the optimal forecast weights will be a complex conjugate pair; as an example, the pair

$$\alpha_2,\ \bar\alpha_2 = .171 \pm .149i$$

have been used, which have a comparatively low modulus, so that the
cyclical tendency they impart to the resulting series is heavily damped.
The resulting forecasts, say z'_{t+2}, consist of a sum of fourth-, third-,
and second-order distributed lag moving averages, as was shown above
in section 2. The fourth-order part is shown in Figure A-6 for comparison
with Figures A-4 and A-5, to illustrate the effect of compounding α_2 and
$\bar\alpha_2$ (complex) with the real coefficients previously employed. (The series in
Figure A-6 is a complex exponentially weighted moving average of the
series in Figure A-5.) The series in Figure A-6 has a more pronounced
cyclical appearance than that in Figure A-5, even though the modulus of
α_2 and $\bar\alpha_2$ is low and damping is rapid.

When real and complex numbers with higher absolute values, that is,
with less rapid damping and hence greater smoothing power, are used
the corresponding comparisons yield even more pronounced results. In
Figures A-7 to A-9 we have the series v_t, the second-order term of w^*_{t+1},
and the fourth-order term of z'_{t+2} that are obtained when we set $g = .9$,
$\alpha_1 = .629$, and $\alpha_2,\ \bar\alpha_2 = .309 \pm .273i$ (as before, α_1 and $\alpha_2,\ \bar\alpha_2$ are optimal
forecasting values under certain assumptions). Here the change when
additional weight coefficients are compounded is especially pronounced.

In general, it is evident that greater smoothness and regularity
result both when the absolute values of the weight coefficients are higher
and when the order of the exponentials system used is higher. The latter

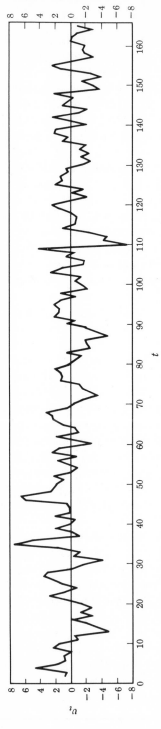

Figure A-4 Exponentially weighted moving average of 165 random normal numbers with weight coefficient .5

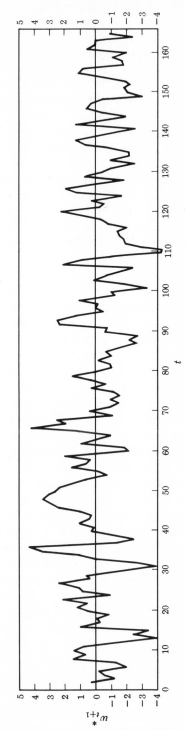

Figure A-5 Double exponentially weighted moving average of 165 random normal numbers with weight coefficients .5 and .234

effect, as we have noted, is pronounced even when the absolute values are comparatively low.

The general sweep of movement of some of the illustrative series we have just considered, in Figures A-4 to A-9, resembles that in many economic time series, except for trend. In a rough way, the general appearance of economic fluctuations tends to confirm the applicability of the present line of analysis; this is in addition to the detailed evidence from individual sector studies mentioned in section 5 of Chapter 11.

Another test of this analysis comes from actual attempts to forecast economic variables. One of the ways of testing a sophisticated economic model has been to compare its ability to forecast a given variable, say w_{t+1}, with the forecast given simply by the value of the latest observation available; that is, the forecast w_{t+1}^* is

$$w_{t+1}^* = w_t \qquad \text{(A-20)}$$

Crudely this is a form of the autoregressive forecasting discussed here; indeed, as the weight coefficient for the single exponential average approaches zero (as it optimally does if the errors of observation and other transitories become negligible), the optimal forecast becomes

$$w_{t+1}^* = gw_t \qquad \text{(A-21)}$$

if g is the autoregressive parameter for an underlying true series such as that of (A-5). The use of (A-21) would subject the sophisticated model to a more severe test than does (A-20), and where transitories are present a still more severe test would be offered by the right exponential average. In fact, however, the vast majority of the more elaborate forecasting models with simultaneous equations and the like have failed to equal even the forecasting ability of (A-20). More elaborate models, using economic analysis like that of the earlier chapters of this book and using also forecasting analysis like that here, should in principle produce more successful forecasts than those given by the autoregressive technique alone.[1] This is further evidence of the soundness of this approach as a part of the analysis of economic fluctuations.

Two examples of economic time series for which this technique gives good forecasts are shown in Figures A-10 and A-11. Figure A-11 shows the United States Index of Wholesale Prices (nonfarm, nonfood component) P_t monthly for the thirty-three-year period 1927 to 1959, inclusive,

---

[1] See Charles Nelson, "Forecasting Sums of Discrete Linear Processes," forthcoming. Of course, forecasting is not the only goal of economic analysis. An important practical application of national income models is the evaluation of the consequences of policy changes and of other externally caused shifts in equations of the models. The techniques of this chapter are of only secondary relevance to such applications.

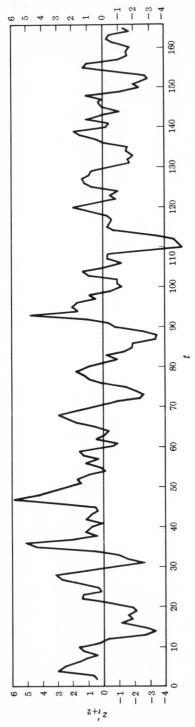

Figure A-6 Quadruple exponentially weighted moving average of 165 random normal numbers with weight coefficients .5, .234, and .171 ± .149i

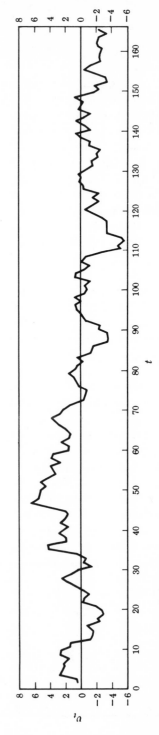

Figure A-7 Weight coefficient .9

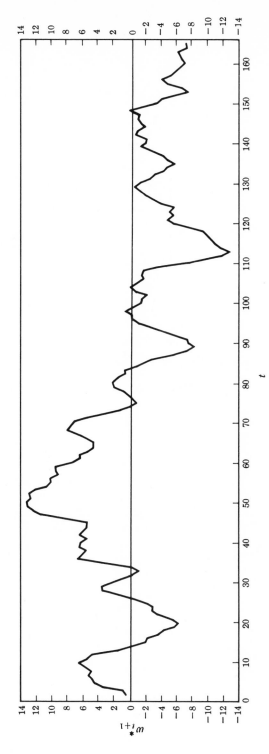

Figure A-8 Weight coefficients .9 and .629

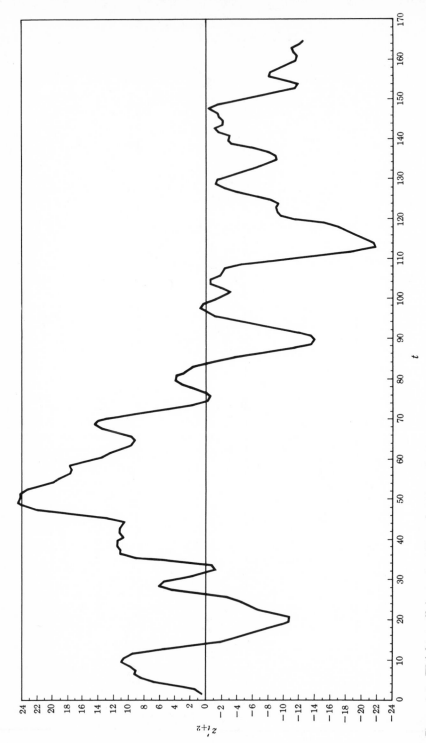

Figure A-9 Weight coefficients .9, .629, and .309 ± .273i

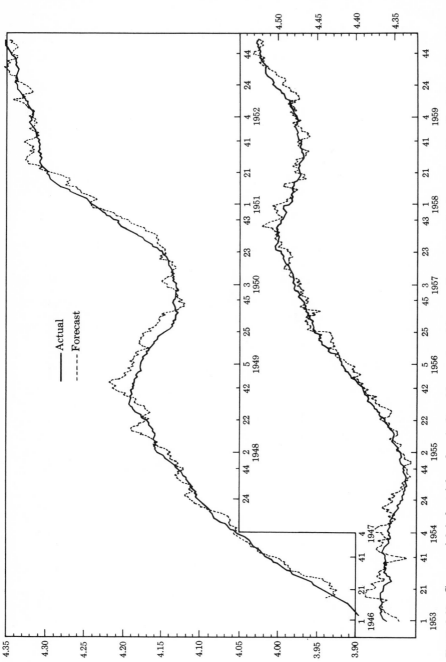

Figure A-10 Commercial, industrial, and agricultural loans of weekly reporting member banks, seasonally adjusted, weekly, 1946 to 1959, actual and thirteen-week-advance forecasts: $R^2 = .9947$

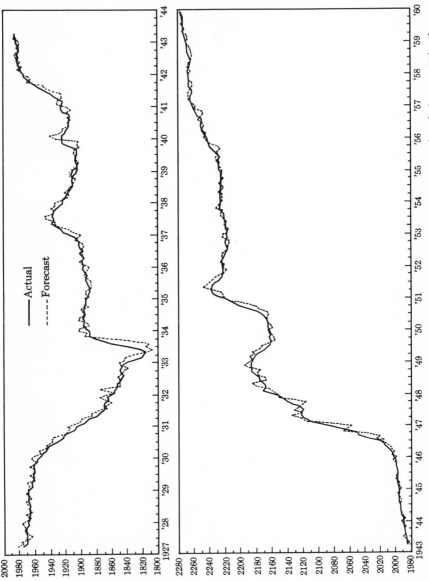

Figure A-11 Nonfarm, nonfood wholesale price index, monthly, 1927 to 1959, actual and three-month-advance forecasts: $R^2 = .9974$

plotted with the values forecast three months ahead using the equation

$$P_{t+3} = (-.003 \pm 22.8i) \sum_{j=0}^{t} (.0142 \mp .0486i)^j P_{t-j}$$

$$+ (1.23 \pm 47.0) \sum_{j=0}^{t} (.091 \mp .0133i)^j P_{t-j} + .83 \sum_{j=0}^{t} (.130)^j P_{t-j}$$

$$+ .59 \sum_{j=0}^{t} (.000006)^j P_{t-j} \quad \text{(A-22)}$$

Figure A-10 shows the seasonally adjusted commercial, industrial, and agricultural loans, weekly, of those large member banks that report weekly to the Federal Reserve Board, plotted with the values forecast thirteen weeks ahead using the equation

$$L_{t+13} = 5.44 + (1.33 \pm 1.43i) \sum_{j=0}^{t} (.45 \pm .15i)^j L_{t-j}$$

$$+ (.078 \pm 35.6i) \sum_{j=0}^{t} (.55 \mp .02i)^j L_{t-j} + 1.34 \sum_{j=0}^{t} (.05)^j L_{t-j} \quad \text{(A-23)}$$

In both cases, the forecast equation was selected by experimentation so as to get approximately the best forecasts. Forecasts are shown for three months beyond the latest date used in the exponential averages; in each case the forecast series is compared with the actual series, and the coefficients of determination (R^2) are given. It can be seen that these R^2 are very high; forecasts superior to these that do not rely on any information about past values of the series itself will be very hard indeed to attain.[1]

---

[1] The corresponding R^2 for one-month-advance forecasts of the wholesale index used was .9997; for one-week-advance forecasts of commercial, industrial, and agricultural loans it was .9999.

B APPENDIX

OPTIMAL FORECASTS
OF A SECOND-ORDER
AUTOREGRESSIVE VARIABLE

Consider an autoregressive variable v_t defined by

$$v_t = a_1 v_{t-1} + a_2 v_{t-2} + \xi_t \qquad \text{(B-1)}$$

where a_1 and a_2 are constants and ξ_t is a random variable with zero mean. If v_t is observed with error or contains any other purely transitory component [not shown in (B-1)], the variable w_t actually observed is

$$w_t = v_t + \epsilon_t \qquad \text{(B-2)}$$

Let ϵ_t be a random variable with zero mean. By successive substitutions, using (B-1) for all values of $j = 1, 2, 3, \ldots$, to eliminate all v_{t-j}, (B-1) is transformed to

$$v_t = \sum_{j=0}^{\infty} d_j \xi_{t-j} \qquad \text{(B-3)}$$

where $d_0 = 1$, $d_1 = a_1$, $d_2 = a_1^2 + a_2$, $\ldots$, and where

$$d_j = a_1 d_{j-1} + a_2 d_{j-2} \qquad \text{for every } j \geq 2 \qquad \text{(B-4)}$$

Then

$$w_t = \sum_{j=0}^{\infty} d_j \xi_{t-j} + \epsilon_t \tag{B-5}$$

Now consider the forecast variable w_{t+1}^*, constructed as any linear combination of past values of w_t, using weights b_i:

$$w_{t+1}^* = \sum_{i=0}^{\infty} b_i w_{t-i} = \sum_{i=0}^{\infty} \sum_{j=0}^{\infty} b_i d_j \xi_{t-i-j} + \sum_{j=0}^{\infty} b_i \epsilon_{t-i} \tag{B-6}$$

The error variance of forecast will be

$$V = \mathbf{E}(w_{t+1} - w_{t+1}^*)^2$$

$$= \mathbf{E} \left(\sum_{j=0}^{\infty} \sum_{i=0}^{\infty} b_i d_j \xi_{t-i-j} + \sum_{j=0}^{\infty} b_i \epsilon_{t-i} - \sum_{j=0}^{\infty} d_j \xi_{t-j+1} - \epsilon_{t+1} \right)^2 \tag{B-7}$$

Since both ξ_t and ϵ_t are random, we can obtain an expression for (B-7) in terms of their variances by expanding the square in (B-7). All the cross-product terms between ξ_{t-k} and ξ_{t-m}, for all $k \neq m$ and all m, have zero expected values, as do the corresponding ones for the series ϵ_t and all cross products between the two series ξ_t and ϵ_t.

It is convenient to write the double sum inside the parentheses in (B-7) in the equivalent form

$$\sum_{i=0}^{\infty} \sum_{j=0}^{i} b_{i-j} d_j \xi_{t-i} = \sum_{i=0}^{\infty} \sum_{j=0}^{\infty} b_i d_j \xi_{t-i-j}$$

Then

$$V = \left[\sum_{i=0}^{\infty} \left(\sum_{j=0}^{i} b_i d_{i-j} \right)^2 + \sum_{j=0}^{\infty} d_j^2 - \sum_{i=0}^{\infty} \sum_{j=0}^{i} b_j d_{i-j} d_{i+1} \right] \sigma_\xi^2$$

$$+ \left(1 + \sum_{i=0}^{\infty} b_i^2 \right) \sigma_\epsilon^2 \tag{B-8}$$

Our problem is to find the set of values of the b_i that minimizes V.

Taking partial derivatives of (B-8) with respect to all the b_i, we have, for every $k = 0, 1, 2, \ldots$,

$$\frac{\partial V}{\partial b_k} = 2\sigma_\xi^2 \left(\sum_{i=k}^{\infty} \sum_{j=0}^{i} b_j d_{i-j} d_{i-k} - \sum_{i=k}^{\infty} d_{i-k} d_{i+1} \right) + 2\sigma_\epsilon^2 b_k \tag{B-9}$$

At a minimum of V all these derivatives are zero, and so are linear combinations of them. To eliminate the infinite sums in (B-9), we first form the expression

$$W_k = \frac{\partial V}{\partial b_{k-2}} - a_1 \frac{\partial V}{\partial b_{k-1}} - a_2 \frac{\partial V}{\partial b_k} = 0 \qquad \text{(B-10)}$$

and then

$$Y_k = W_k - a_1 W_{k-1} - a_2 W_{k-2} = 0 \qquad \text{(B-11)}$$

The expression (B-11), after substitution from (B-10) and (B-9) and after elimination of terms using (B-4), becomes

$$
Y_k = a_2 \sigma_\epsilon{}^2 b_{k+2} - a_1(a_2 - 1)\sigma_\epsilon{}^2 b_{k+1} - (\sigma_\xi{}^2 + \sigma_\epsilon{}^2 + a_1{}^2 \sigma_\epsilon{}^2 \\
+ a_2{}^2 \sigma_\epsilon{}^2) b_k - a_1(a_2 - 1)\sigma_\epsilon{}^2 b_{k-1} + a_2 \sigma_\epsilon{}^2 b_{k-2} = 0 \\
\text{for } k \geq 2 \quad \text{(B-12)}
$$

This expression is an exact fourth-order difference equation in the b_k having the solution $b_k = c_1 \lambda_1{}^k + c_2 \lambda_2{}^k + c_3 \lambda_3{}^k + c_4 \lambda_4{}^k$, where c_1, c_2, c_3, and c_4 are constants and the λ_j are the four roots of the polynomial

$$
a_2 \sigma_\epsilon{}^2 \lambda^4 - a_1(a_2 - 1)\sigma_\epsilon{}^2 \lambda^3 - (\sigma_\xi{}^2 + \sigma_\epsilon{}^2 + a_1{}^2 \sigma_\epsilon{}^2 + a_2{}^2 \sigma_\epsilon{}^2)\lambda^2 \\
- a_1(a_2 - 1)\sigma_\epsilon{}^2 \lambda + a_2 \sigma_\epsilon{}^2 = 0 \quad \text{(B-13)}
$$

By virtue of the symmetry of this polynomial, two of the roots are the inverses of the other two; without loss of generality, we can put

$$\lambda_3 = \frac{1}{\lambda_1} \qquad \lambda_4 = \frac{1}{\lambda_2}$$

so that

$$b_k = c_1 \lambda_1{}^k + c_2 \lambda_2{}^k + c_3 \left(\frac{1}{\lambda_1}\right)^k + c_4 \left(\frac{1}{\lambda_2}\right)^k$$

It can be shown that none of the roots is of unit absolute value; without loss of generality, we can number the roots in such an order that $|\lambda_1| < 1$ and $|\lambda_2| < 1$. Since we are concerned only with stable systems, that is, autoregressive equations (B-1) that converge on zero as $t \to \infty$ if $\xi_t = 0$ for all $t > 0$, we can dismiss the roots of (B-13) of greater than unit absolute value; that is,

$$c_3 = c_4 = 0$$

and

$$b_k = c_1 \lambda_1{}^k + c_2 \lambda_2{}^k \qquad \text{(B-14)}$$

The minimum error variance values of c_1 and c_2 are obtained by evaluating (B-11) for $k = 0, 1$, substituting (B-14) into the resulting two equations, and solving them for c_1 and c_2. Then we have the minimum error variance (linear) forecast of w_{t+1} as

$$
\begin{aligned}
w_{t+1}^* &= \sum_{k=0}^{\infty} (c_1 \lambda_1{}^k + c_2 \lambda_2{}^k) w_{t-k} \\
&= c_1 \sum_{k=0}^{\infty} \lambda_1{}^k w_{t-k} + c_2 \sum_{k=0}^{\infty} \lambda_2{}^k w_{t-k}
\end{aligned}
\tag{B-15}
$$

a weighted sum of two exponentially weighted averages of past values of w_t. This proves the assertions on optimal forecasting in section 4, for the second-order case defined at the beginning of this appendix. The corresponding proof for more general assumptions is given in item 3 and for another special case in the 1960 article by J. F. Muth, both in the bibliographical references for Chapter 11.

C APPENDIX
THE PERIOD OF A SECOND-ORDER SYSTEM

Appendix A includes the assertion that the moving average

$$\sum_{j=0}^{t} \alpha_1{}^j v_{t-j} = \sum_{j=0}^{t} \sum_{k=0}^{t-j} \alpha_1{}^j g^k \xi_{t-j-k} \tag{C-1}$$

that is, the first of the two terms making up w_{t+1}^* in (A-9), has a period approximately defined by

$$\cos \theta_{w^*,v} = \frac{\alpha_1 + g}{1 + \alpha_1 g}$$

for large values of t. In this appendix it is shown that

$$\lim_{t \to \infty} \cos \theta_{w^*,v} = \frac{\alpha_1 + g}{1 + \alpha_1 g}$$

First we note that the double sum (C-1) can also be written

$$\sum_{j=0}^{t} \sum_{k=0}^{j} \alpha_1{}^{j-k} g^k \xi_{t-j} \tag{C-2}$$

so that the total weight a_j assigned to a given past value ξ_{t-j} is

$$a_j = \sum_{k=0}^{j} \alpha_1^{j-k} g^k \tag{C-3}$$

Now since these weights consist of rising powers of the fractions α_1 and g, so that $|\alpha_1| < |g|$ implies $|a_j| < |jg^j|$, it is known that sums of the type

$$\sum^{t} a_j a_{j+1} \quad \text{and} \quad \sum^{t} a_j^2$$

necessarily converge for increasing t. Thus the limit notation can be dropped; we seek to evaluate

$$\cos \theta_{w^*, v} = \frac{\displaystyle\sum_{j=0}^{\infty} a_j a_{j+1}}{\displaystyle\sum_{j=0}^{\infty} a_j^2} = \frac{\displaystyle\sum_{j=0}^{\infty} \sum_{k=0}^{j} \sum_{h=0}^{j+1} \alpha_1^{2j+1-h-k} g^{h+k}}{\displaystyle\sum_{j=0}^{\infty} \sum_{k=0}^{j} \sum_{h=0}^{j} \alpha_1^{2j-h-k} g^{h+k}} \tag{C-4}$$

It is readily verified that

$$a_j = \sum_{k=0}^{j} \alpha_1^{j-k} g^k = \frac{\alpha_1^{j+1} - g^{j+1}}{\alpha_1 - g} \tag{C-5}$$

Hence

$$\sum_{j=0}^{\infty} a_j^2 = \sum_{j=0}^{\infty} \left(\frac{\alpha_1^{j+1} - g^{j+1}}{\alpha_1 - g} \right)^2$$

$$= \frac{\displaystyle\sum_{j=0}^{\infty} \alpha_1^{2j+2} - 2 \sum_{j=0}^{\infty} (\alpha_1 g)^{j+1} + \sum_{j=0}^{\infty} g^{2j+2}}{(\alpha_1 - g)^2}$$

$$= \frac{1}{(\alpha_1 - g)^2} \left(\frac{\alpha_1^2}{1 - \alpha_1^2} - \frac{2\alpha_1 g}{1 - \alpha_1 g} + \frac{g^2}{1 - g^2} \right) \tag{C-6}$$

This expression simplifies into

$$\sum_{j=0}^{\infty} a_j^2 = \frac{1 + \alpha_1 g}{(1 - \alpha_1^2)(1 - \alpha_1 g)(1 - g^2)} \tag{C-7}$$

This is the denominator of (C-4).

To obtain the numerator of (C-4), we note that

$$a_{j+1} = g a_j + \alpha_1^{j+1}$$

and hence that

$$\sum_{j=0}^{\infty} a_j a_{j+1} = g \sum_{j=0}^{\infty} a_j^2 + \alpha_1 \sum_{j=0}^{\infty} a_j \alpha_1^j \tag{C-8}$$

Substituting from (C-5) and (C-7) into (C-8), we obtain an expression that simplifies into

$$\sum_{j=0}^{\infty} a_j a_{j+1} = \frac{\alpha_1 + g}{(1 - \alpha_1^2)(1 - \alpha_1 g)(1 - g^2)} \tag{C-9}$$

The ratio of (C-8) to (C-7) is the desired formula,

$$\cos \theta_{w^*, v} = \frac{\alpha_1 + g}{1 + \alpha_1 g}$$

D APPENDIX

COMPLEX FORECASTING WEIGHTS IN THE SECOND-ORDER CASE

Because of its symmetry, (B-13) must either have four real roots or four complex ones. (In the latter case, λ_1 and λ_2 are a complex conjugate pair.) The purpose of this appendix is to show the conditions that imply complex roots. By virtue of its symmetry, (B-13) can be written

$$a_2 \sigma_\epsilon{}^2 \left(\lambda^2 + \frac{1}{\lambda^2} \right) - a_1(a_2 - 1)\sigma_\epsilon{}^2 \left(\lambda + \frac{1}{\lambda} \right)$$
$$- (\sigma_\xi{}^2 + \sigma_\epsilon{}^2 + a_1{}^2\sigma_\epsilon{}^2 + a_2{}^2\sigma_\epsilon{}^2) = 0 \quad \text{(D-1)}$$

If we make the substitution

$$\eta = \lambda + \frac{1}{\lambda}$$

we have

$$a_2 \sigma_\epsilon{}^2 \eta^2 - a_1(a_2 - 1)\sigma_\epsilon{}^2 \eta$$
$$- (\sigma_\xi{}^2 + \sigma_\epsilon{}^2 + a_1{}^2\sigma_\epsilon{}^2 + a_2{}^2\sigma_\epsilon{}^2 + 2a_2\sigma_\epsilon{}^2) = 0 \quad \text{(D-2)}$$

Since none of the roots has unit modulus, the inverse of λ cannot be its conjugate; hence the roots of (D-2) will be complex if and only if those of (B-13) are. We need only consider the discriminant of (D-2), therefore.

The discriminant of the quadratic (D-2), that is, the expression that is negative if and only if the roots of (D-2) are a complex conjugate pair, is

$$D = \sigma_\epsilon^4 a_1^2 (a_2 - 1)^2$$
$$+ 4a_2\sigma_\epsilon^2(\sigma_\epsilon^2 + \sigma_\xi^2 + a_1^2\sigma_\epsilon^2 + a_2^2\sigma_\epsilon^2 + 2a_2\sigma_\epsilon^2) \quad \text{(D-3)}$$

A necessary condition for $D < 0$ is evidently $a_2 < 0$, since a_1 and a_2 are real numbers. Further, $D < 0$ simplifies into

$$\sigma_\epsilon^2(a_1^2 + 4a_2)(a_2 + 1)^2 < -4a_2\sigma_\xi^2 \quad \text{(D-4)}$$

where the term on the right is positive since $a_2 < 0$. It can be seen that a sufficient condition for (D-4) to hold is

$$a_1^2 + 4a_2 < 0 \quad \text{(D-5)}$$

This means that the roots x_1, x_2 of the equation

$$x^2 - a_1 x - a_2 = 0 \quad \text{(D-6)}$$

are complex; hence if the second-order autoregressive scheme (D-1) has coefficients a_1, a_2 that imply complex roots for its complementary equation (D-6), the optimal forecast variable w_{t+1}^* of (B-6) and (B-15) necessarily has complex weight coefficients λ_1, λ_2. When (D-5) is satisfied, v_t of (B-3) is a complex exponentially weighted average of past values of ξ_t since the d_j satisfy (B-4); that is, v_t is a damped, disturbed sine curve.

However, (D-4) can be satisfied even when (D-6) has real roots, viz., when

$$0 \leq \sigma_\epsilon^2(a_1^2 + 4a_2)(a_2 + 1)^2 < -4a_2\sigma_\xi^2$$

This condition is very easily satisfied, with plausible roots for (D-5) and a wide range of ratios $\sigma_\xi^2/\sigma_\epsilon^2$.

This is the proposition referred to in section 3 of Appendix A.

12
THE CONCEPT
OF
INCOME

1 INTRODUCTION

Government tries to measure individual incomes to enforce the tax laws and to permit invidious comparisons, for example to define poverty or to justify subsidies to farmers. It measures aggregate income to measure business fluctuations and growth, to compare one region with another in economic potential or welfare, and to measure national potential. All these reasons for measuring income have some connection with material welfare, and derive naturally from the household's view of its income as a measure of its own material welfare. Material welfare can differ markedly from cash income or taxable income, however, so that neither concept is fully acceptable for national income accounting.

These discrepancies create problems for the national income statistician and for the analyst. What we count in material welfare is partly a matter of convenience and habit. Everyone counts in welfare his opportunities to enjoy intangible services, such as symphony concerts and views of the great outdoors, if he has to pay for them directly; but if payment is indirect and the intangibles appear to be free, one is unsure whether the good or service is scarce and desirable. If it is, it enters into the household utility (indifference) function, and therefore into behavior functions such as the consumption function. Unfortunately, however, if we go beyond cash-flow income to impute income equivalents for benefits received in kind, there is no end to the subtlety and difficulty of the process.

A redeeming feature of these problems is that for aggregate analysis like that in this book, most of the subtleties of national income analysis have little effect on its application. Although perfect imputation would no doubt permit better fits for estimated consumption functions, the improvement would be slight and the analysis of economic fluctuations but little improved. Most of these imputed quantities vary only gradually, complicating analysis of long-term growth but having little effect on short-term economic movements. Some of them can be important for cross-sectional comparisons but have little effect on national totals. Those that do vary nationally over short-term fluctuations, such as the value of leisure to an unemployed head of household, are so highly correlated with the conventional totals that they can safely be left out, as they now are. However, improving our analysis of aggregate consumption will require getting many of these concepts right.

To study consumer choice, we do not strictly need a definition of income; what we need is information about opportunities to enjoy material welfare in the present and future. If a household consumes little currently and adds to its wealth, it can consume more in the future than it otherwise could. The constraint on the household is its total set of opportunities to consume in present and future, which include a variety of high and low opportunities for current consumption. However, we like to simplify this enormously varied set of opportunities, both in our private reckoning and in economic analysis. Therefore we define income as a guideline to measure these opportunities with a single variable.

If a household consumes too lavishly in the current period, it will start running into trouble paying its bills and will eventually be forced to cut back. If a household consumes very little, it builds up its opportunities to consume more in the future. Therefore, a natural definition of income in this context is the largest amount the household could consume without ever having to cut back: the highest constant consumption stream it could maintain indefinitely.

In a world of perfect certainty, and especially in an unchanging world, we could measure this highest possible constant consumption stream easily. However, the world's uncertainties prevent us from knowing exactly how much it is. Therefore we resort to various expedients to approximate it. One way is to assume that the future will always be like the present and to estimate how much we could consume while leaving our physical resources constant. If all our resources, including physical capital and nature, remain truly constant, we should have the same potential welfare in the future as at present. To maintain it, we have to provide for resources used up currently, such as the depreciation of physical plant and equipment.

Business firms estimate the depreciation of their physical plant and equipment, but the tax laws and accounting conventions require that these estimates be based on what these items had cost when they were new. When the price level changes, what it costs to keep plant and equipment at the same physical quantities and qualities changes also; but conventional allowances disregard these changes. Thus even the convention of using maintenance of capital as the criterion for measuring income (that is, of deducting depreciation allowances from gross product to obtain net product and income) presents problems. Moreover, this convention disregards changes in future welfare potential, some of which are partly predictable.

In addition to these problems, there is no clear line between goods in the process of production and final goods enjoyed by consumers or added to wealth. While this distinction is straightforward in principle, it has to be partly arbitrary in practice. In some cases, such as some expense account items of business representatives, goods and services which are clearly consumption goods and services on any reasonable interpretation are classed as productive and are therefore omitted from the measured incomes of the persons enjoying them. In other cases, such as the costs of commuting to and from work, goods and services that almost certainly are productive, adding nothing to the satisfaction enjoyed by the persons receiving them, are classed as consumption and are therefore included in the incomes of these persons.

Moreover, there is no clear line between those aspects of life imputable to economic welfare and those not imputable. A drive past a garbage dump to take a sick child to a hospital receives the same credit in the national income accounts as does a Sunday drive in a beautiful countryside. A visit to the dentist's office receives the same credit as attendance at a symphony concert, if both cost the same. Time spent in school preparing to earn a future income, which could have been spent earning an immediate income instead, receives no credit at all. In contrast, time spent putting out fires by professional firemen keeping down fire losses to existing resources, counts as part of national product. Some of these anomalies can be cleared up by straightforward imputation and by special studies, but some are beyond reach.

2 NET PRODUCTION AND CURRENT INCOME

For many purposes material wealth serves as a measure of long-run income potential. This idea supports the use of wealth *maintenance* as the criterion for determining net production and income in any given period.

It further enables us to concentrate on measurable, tangible goods and services to a much greater extent than is otherwise possible. Out of the gross quantities of goods and services supplied in a given period some are clearly productive, contributing directly or indirectly to the maintenance of capital. In the simplest case imaginable, the capital stock at the end of a period would be identical in every detail with the capital stock at the beginning, with consumption during the period equal to net production. If so, the productive goods and services devoted to maintaining capital exactly do so, and business firms see fit to replace or maintain every element of capital in exactly its previous form and quantity. All other goods and services, other than those devoted to maintaining capital, contribute to the satisfactions of consumers.

In practice, the world is never this simple, even in those rare instances where consumption is exactly equal to net production. Some elements of capital are not kept unchanged or replaced over a period, and some are increased. It is still proper to say that capital is maintained if the value of the increased elements is in total equal to the value of the decreased ones, where both are valued at prevailing prices, since in that case their contribution to long-run income potential is the same.

Furthermore, the amount of productive goods and services will not be exactly equal to the amount required for the maintenance of capital at its previous total value; most years it is greater, and capital increases. Consumption is accordingly less than net production. In a few years, capital decreases, and consumption is greater than net production.

Whatever the amount of net production in a given period of time, it belongs to someone. The claims to ownership of the goods and services representing net production are net current income to the persons possessing these claims. In the view of each person, his net income is the total of his receipts minus the nonconsumption payments required to maintain his wealth, other than cash, constant. (Such payments include costs incurred in the process of earning the income.) Usually his receipts will be cash, which represents generalized claims to ownership on goods and services becoming available for consumption or addition to wealth. Initially, however, his income is the share of net production which he owns because of the contribution of his productive services to its creation; subsequently he exchanges this for other forms of net production which he prefers, usually by the medium of cash.

The natural tendency of people to pay more attention to receipts rather than accruals tends to obscure the fact that current income and net production are two aspects of the same thing, and that for most purposes the two concepts are interchangeable. Their equality is as inevitable as the equality of the two sides of a balance sheet, and arises for the same reason. The equality of income and production is an equality of *flows* of goods and services to the claims to them, while the balance sheet equality is an equality of stocks of goods in existence at a point in time to the claims to them. The left-hand side of a balance sheet shows net assets, items of wealth; the right-hand side shows net claims to ownership of those items of wealth. The net assets add up to the net claims to their ownership. Similarly, total net production must be the same amount as the total claims to its ownership, after due allowance for the maintenance of physical capital.

Nevertheless, from a certain point of view production and income can be thought of as widely separated and conceptually distinct. Most finished production flows to consumption, which is drawn directly from the capital stock, for the most part; that is, relatively little labor, land, and other productive services are directly involved in the act of consumption itself. Productive services are for the most part engaged in creating capital, including inventories, mostly to replace what is consumed. Accordingly, the accruing claims of the owners of productive services are in the first instance mostly claims to newly created capital and only indirectly through many intermediaries are claims to final net production of consumer goods and services.

The intermediary firms through which owners of productive services have indirect claims to final product engage in offsetting transactions on capital account. In particular, the final intermediaries providing consumer goods and services are mainly releasing capital, from their point of view, which must be replaced and which to that extent is netted out of their income account. Thus the bookkeeping identity of net product and net income tends to be obscured, especially if one pays primary attention to transactions, such as ultimate sale for consumption. Similarly, in the actual process of gathering and tabulating national income and product statistics the figures on income payments and accruals mostly come from a different set of firms from those reporting for the product accounts; and accordingly, because of differing errors and omissions on the two sides, the two accounts will fail to be exactly equal.

The identity between income and product was first remarked upon extensively at the beginning of the nineteenth century by the French economist J. B. Say, who expressed it by saying that supply creates its own demand. He noted that the community as a whole can always afford to purchase its own total net product, because its total net income is necessarily equal to it.[1] He argued this in protest to the then common usage derived from the point of view of the business intermediaries and final sellers, speaking of "overproduction" of all goods and services. Since we have not reached that state of bliss in which no one wants more consumption goods or further additions to wealth, he remarked, and since income is always exactly sufficient to buy the whole product, it is nonsense to speak of general overproduction. Overproduction can only be partial, not general. As a pertinent example of his point there might be over-production of all *consumer* goods, while people were attempting to add to wealth at a faster rate than business firms had expected or intended to do. Accordingly there would be underproduction of investment goods (other than previously unexpected inventory gains) exactly equal to the over-production of consumer goods and of inventories. These statements are clear enough, but they often spell trouble in the form of a later loss of output, as we know from experience.

3   COMPONENTS OF NET PRODUCTION

Economically speaking, net production has two components, con-sumption and addition to wealth. The measurement and accounting of net production are made more complicated, however, by the problems associated with the accounts of the various levels of government and with transactions with other countries.

Expenditures, and the use of resources, by government consist of three types of things: consumption (things that give satisfaction to individual households), net addition to wealth, and intermediate goods and services (necessary for the maintenance and replacement of existing wealth). The third type, intermediate goods and services, which includes both some goods and services supplied to the private sector of the economy and also the maintenance of such government-owned capital as highways and post offices, is not a part of net product, properly measured. However, no meaningful separation of government accounts into the three types has been made, either by government statisticians or by outsiders. Accordingly, government is reported as a separate category, in addition to consumption and addition to wealth (in the private sector), and the total

[1] These remarks give one of several possible interpretations of Say's point of view, about which there is still some debate. It appears that he himself failed to distinguish between a purely definitional proposition, such as that given here, and a factual one concerning the possibility of economic depression.

of net product is overstated by the amount of the intermediate services supplied by the various levels of government.

An example of the intermediate services supplied by government is police protection. This service is not carried on because of any direct satisfaction or utility it gives to households, but rather is carried on to minimize the various illegal intrusions on our private lives that would prevent us from enjoying the things that we have. Police protection is one of the regrettable costs of having the consumption and addition to wealth that are already counted separately in national product; to include it as an additional part of product is double counting. This point may be seen more clearly if we consider the effect on our welfare, and on the national accounts, if a change of circumstances (such as a serious crime wave) makes it necessary to increase the amount of police protection. The additional taxes we have to pay to finance this, and the corresponding reduction in private consumption and addition to wealth, represent a loss of welfare to the households of the community. As the accounts are now kept, this is not shown, because the reduction in the private sector is off-set by the increase in the government sector, keeping the total unchanged.

Protective services of all kinds, including national defense, represent the biggest single element of double counting in the national accounts. Together they absorbed 42 percent of the goods and services purchased by government in the United States in 1968, and over 10 percent of the net national product. A few other government expenditures involve similar double counting but are relatively small.

As we have noted, the rest of the government accounts are not separated into consumption and addition to wealth. For many purposes such a separation would be desirable; it awaits the necessary data.

The total addition to wealth in the private sector is reported in two parts: private domestic investment and net foreign investment. The latter is simply the net balance on current (goods and services) account of transactions with other countries, primarily exports minus imports. Any excess of receipts from exports over payments for imports is an addition to the wealth of nationals of this country.

The reported aggregates of private consumption and investment both include imported goods and services. In effect, the convention is followed that these are "produced" by the domestic economy by virtue of its having produced the exports to pay for them. In particular, an addition to wealth is treated as domestic investment if the physical capital involved is put in place domestically, though it may have been imported. Net foreign investment includes net additions to claims on physical capital put in place abroad (which may have been exported from this country) and net additions to monetary claims on other countries.

4 COMPONENTS OF NET INCOME

In practice, there are several ways to divide income into components, depending on the problem at hand. One long-honored convention is to divide it according to the type of productive service whose owners receive it, where the "types" are defined in terms of certain distinguishing economic characteristics of the services. First, we may distinguish between human and nonhuman productive services. Outright permanent ownership rights to nonhuman productive services can usually be sold, whereas these rights to human productive services cannot usually be sold. This distinction between human and nonhuman is not an economic distinction per se, and the characteristics of outright salability as against the ability to hire, contract, or lease is of limited economic importance. This distinction is therefore more a conventional than an economic one.

Productive services may also be distinguished according to whether their supply is directly determined by economic choices or is affected only in incidental and indirect ways by economic choices. Thus physical wealth can be divided into capital and "land." The supply of capital is the direct result of economic decisions to reproduce and maintain it, whereas the supply of land, correctly interpreted, is incapable of being altered by direct individual action. The land component of a piece of property is its intrinsic superiority, in its best economic use, over alternative pieces of property; it is the value associated with a location or site as such. Mineral deposits and original soil qualities, which can be exhausted and not precisely reproduced, but whose rate of exhaustion and semireproduction are the direct results of economic decisions, represent an awkward intermediate category between land and capital. These distinctions help address some problems, but they have little to do with the analysis of income. In connection with income analysis, the distinction between land and capital is more a conventional than an economic one.

It is also conventional to divide human productive services into labor and entrepreneurship. The latter is responsible decision making governing the organization and conduct of productive processes, for the account and risk (with respect to income received) of the entrepreneur; labor is any physical or mental productive service not involving ultimate responsibility for the organization and conduct of productive processes. This distinction has in recent years been losing its conventional sanction, partly because of the difficulty of applying it to business organizations having salaried management. In any case, it is of little importance for income analysis.

Certain other ways of classifying income are of more interest and importance for income analysis. From the practical standpoint of data collection, it happens to be convenient to classify incomes according to whether they are received as contractual payments or as residual "profits," and in part according to other criteria partly related to some of the ones previously discussed. Contractual payments, express and implied, appear entirely in the three categories of wages and salaries, rents, and interest incomes. The first of these is mainly income of labor; the second, of hired or leased properties (including both land and capital); and the third, of money loaned out. Residual, noncontractual incomes are divided into the profits of corporations and the net incomes of unincorporated enterprises, a distinction of very limited economic interest.

5 THE MEASUREMENT OF NET INCOME

In practice, national income is estimated by summing up the total incomes in various convenient accounting categories. Data on the compensation of employees, that is, wages, salaries, and supplements such as payroll taxes, exist for most contractual wage payments because they are reported to the Social Security Administration in connection with social security taxes. Wages and salaries not covered by these taxes have to be estimated. Rental and interest income of persons, with intermediate transactions between business firms canceled out, are estimated partly from the amounts of these on income tax returns and partly by indirect methods. The same is true of the incomes of unincorporated enterprises, which include most farms and independent professionals, such as doctors and lawyers. Corporate profits are estimated from income tax returns.

Enterprise income in general is estimated net of the cost of maintaining capital (wealth) intact. As customary accounting practices, and the tax laws, require each business to do this on its own, ready-made accounting data provide us with national data on net income after provision for the maintenance of wealth. Neither accounting practice nor the tax laws require that these estimates be economically meaningful or accurate, however. A true estimate of depreciation would be what it costs at current prices to maintain total wealth intact. In practice, what is estimated by and large is what it costs to maintain the money value of total wealth, using the original cost of the wealth, not the current replacement cost. Further, for this purpose the fraction of the original value of a piece of property that is lost each year through use and the passage of time is estimated in an arbitrary way having little relation to its true loss of economic value. Occasionally private researchers try to obtain more meaningful estimates of the amount required to maintain wealth constant, but no systematic information on this is available from any source.

The estimates of enterprise income are inconsistent with these general rules, and with the maintenance of wealth approach, in one major respect: all capital gains on resale of property are excluded from income. If a machine is bought at low prices and is later used until it wears out producing scarce products that make it more valuable than its original cost, the resulting gain appears in the ordinary profit figures and in national income. In contrast, if the machine is sold at a profit before it wears out the capital gain will be excluded from national income. The purchaser, by taking higher depreciation allowances based on the price he paid for the machine, will reduce the national income estimates below what they would have been had the original owner retained the machine and used it in the same way to generate the same true income. Since most capital equipment is kept by its original purchaser until all or most of its economic value is exhausted, the main damage is in arbitrary and misleading depreciation figures.

On any capital other than long-term (depreciable) capital, official income estimates exclude from profits any element of capital gain. This exclusion is the inventory valuation adjustment. The data on inventories come from sample surveys, and the estimates of capital gains derive from price indexes matched as closely as possible to the types of goods involved. The procedures and results differ according to each firm's inventory accounting procedures.

Of all the parts of the national income accounts, those dealing with inventories, that is, the change in inventories (product side) and the inventory valuation adjustment (both the product and income sides), are the most volatile and the most unreliable. They change sharply from one period to the next in fact; and the estimates are often drastically revised in the transition from preliminary to final values.

It would appear that a similar adjustment for long-term capital would be entirely consistent with the maintenance of wealth approach to income estimation. This is only approximately correct because of certain other problems.

First, capital values and their depreciation should ideally be adjusted not only for changes in the price level but also for variations in maintenance expenditures. Maintenance costs appear as current expenses and in effect are assumed to be exactly equal to the amounts required to keep capital equipment depreciating at the rates stated in the depreciation accounts. If a firm chooses to alter its maintenance expenditures, however, this will alter the true economic rate of depreciation of the firm's equipment. An important example of this phenomenon occurred during the Second World War. Because of the scarcity of all types of capital equipment for replacement, most capital equipment was more assiduously maintained than during peacetime. There was therefore a sharp rise in maintenance expenditures but no corresponding drop in the figures reported for depreciation. On the contrary, wartime tax regulations permitted increased allowances for depreciation, to stimulate investment. Also, many purchases of new producers' durable goods were paid for by the government, or were written off as current expenses, and so were not counted as private additions to wealth. For these reasons, additions to wealth during the Second World War were grossly underestimated. Then, they were probably overestimated just after the war, because of a reduction of maintenance to levels below normal. Second, as already indicated, there are no systematic estimates of true economic depreciation. Third, the notion of the maintenance of wealth, valued at current prices, is subject to the paradox of apparent self-contradiction. If the notion is consistently applied in every period, after several periods the total of wealth can have changed in spite of the apparent maintenance of wealth at a constant level in each period. This phenomenon is closely analogous to that of "drift" in a price index which is made up of linked index relatives with different weights in each period. It will be discussed further in section 8.

6 THE MEASUREMENT OF NET PRODUCT

The principal sources of information on production of consumer goods are censuses of business, manufacturing, and agriculture, available only for certain years. Movements outside these years are estimated from other data, such as sample surveys of retail sales. In general, it is necessary to estimate the fraction of total production and sales that go to ultimate consumers as against the fraction going to other business firms to be absorbed in current production, and to government. Wherever the estimates come from a manufacturing or wholesale source, it is also necessary to estimate final prices to consumers. Data from trade associations, sample surveys, and many miscellaneous sources are also employed.

Methods of estimation of private domestic additions to wealth are basically similar to those for consumption. Machinery, equipment, and other obvious long-term investment goods are estimated from production figures obtained from censuses and surveys of manufacturers, with adjustments and subtractions similar to those for consumer goods. Inventory changes are estimated from sample survey data. Construction estimates come from a wide variety of sources of differing completeness and reliability.

Data on government purchases of goods and services are derived from government budget accounts by removing transfer payments and grants-in-aid, and by various other adjustments, all derived from the government accounts themselves. Net foreign investment is estimated from the official balance-of-payments data and from other official sources.

Figure 77 displays some of the main flows in the national income accounts, without doing full justice to their complexity. Capital goods producers and firms at all stages of farming, mining, manufacturing, and distribution use factors of production from households, for which they pay wages, rent, interest, and profits. The government also pays wages and rent for productive services from households. (Households also pay wages and rent to other households for domestic services and for dwelling units. Thus every element of the economic system contributes to the income side of the national accounts.) Goods flow forward from the raw materials producer through the stages of production until they are ready for consumers and then normally flow through wholesale and retail distribution to them. At each stage, inventories may increase or decrease and so enter into the final product as investment. Each stage buys plant and equipment, from the capital goods producers, which enter into final product as investment. (To this extent, all elements also contribute directly to final product, inasmuch as household and government transactions that originate income also enter directly into the product accounts.)

Payments for factors of production are recorded mainly through payments and statements to social security and unemployment insurance and through income tax returns. In the case of government, they are reported in government budgets and accounting reports. Thus these payments are reported by almost all elements of the economic system that make them. In contrast, sales of final products to consumers are estimated from the reported sales of finished goods producers, with estimated transportation and distribution costs added on from other sources. As noted, the government total of all forms of final product is estimated from government budgetary accounts. Thus apart from inventory change the finished goods estimates come from relatively few sources: finished goods producers, capital goods producers, and government.

Service industries consolidate finished production for consumers with distribution, but otherwise agree with Figure 77. The product originating in households represents a consolidation of all stages of production in one, for accounting purposes, as it includes only sales of productive services from one household to another or to itself.

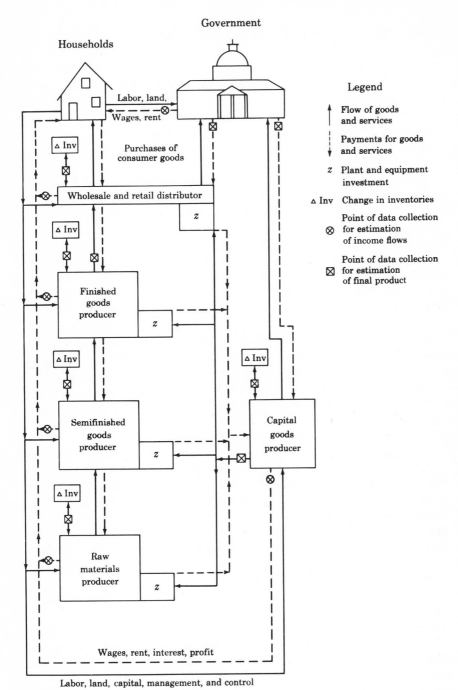

Figure 77 Schematic flows of national income and product. (Note: The figure omits tax payments to government and the flow of savings to investment.)

7 IMPUTED PRODUCTION AND MARKET TRANSACTIONS

Generally speaking, accounting data are relatively plentiful and valuation is relatively easy for those transactions that pass through a market exchange process. However, many flows of valuable goods and services are not exchanged through the market, and it is difficult to place a valuation on them that makes them comparable to goods and services that are exchanged. This difficulty has led official estimators of national income and product to lay down the rule that they would primarily concern themselves with market transactions, except where this leads to incongruously large omissions that are easily corrected.

The main imputations for nonmarket flows of goods and services are food produced and consumed on farms, the rental value of owner-occupied housing, and the services of commercial banks and other financial intermediaries. The first two of these items are goods and services consumed by the owners of the enterprises that produce them. The third item refers to services not sold directly for a price but bartered, in effect for an offsetting service.

A commercial bank in effect converts illiquid assets into liquid, readily transferable ones, and incurs costs. It covers these costs with the excess of its interest receipts over its interest payments; the bank pays little interest on its deposit liabilities. In exchange for its services in connection with deposits, and for their comparative liquidity, it receives these deposits at low interest compared with what the depositor could earn on alternative, less liquid assets. The bank may also have service charges, but in practice these are of minor importance.

Now ordinarily when an enterprise receives capital from the public and transfers it to other enterprises, neither product nor income from that capital would be thought of as originating in the firm that passed it on. Hence it is reasonable to follow the general rule that the income and product originating in a firm shall depend only on its *net* interest payments, that is, interest paid minus interest received. If this rule were applied to banks, however, their contribution to income and product would be negative because their interest income pays for purchases of supplies as well as factor payments.

In practice, the way this anomaly is handled is to assume that banks supply gross product, or "sales," equal to their service charges plus the difference between their interest receipts and their interest payments. The part of this imputed to consumers is counted in the consumer goods and services part of national product. A similar imputation might make sense for any firm that serves as an intermediary.

The question naturally arises, are there any other major omissions and anomalies, or departures from an ideal measure of income and product? Even without profound scrutiny and analysis of present income concepts, it can be seen that there are. The main anomalies can be considered under a single heading, that of the allocation of human and other resources between leisure and paid employment.

The direct enjoyment of one's leisure is similar in principle to using one's personal resources to produce goods not sold on the market (such as food produced and consumed on farms). That leisure is regarded by people as valuable is beyond question, since they sacrifice cash income (which they could obtain by moonlighting) to have it. Changes in the proportion of their time that is available for leisure therefore enter into economic welfare in the same way as do changes in cash income or in the quantities of material goods and services available.

There are several ways in which leisure may vary. The hours of the working week can be shortened; vacations and holidays can become longer and more frequent; retirement can occur earlier in life. All these changes have in fact been taking place with the passage of time in most countries, adding to leisure.

In addition, unpaid productive activity can change relative to paid employment. Housewives enter and leave the paid labor force, with offsetting variations in the amount of housework they do (we assume). Young people prolong their education, staying out of the paid labor force for a longer time. These changes will often not be regarded by the persons involved as changes in leisure but merely as worthwhile changes in their work.

In all these cases of changes in leisure and in unpaid productive activity, the resulting changes in money income misstate the resulting changes in economic welfare. If money income goes down because of a voluntary increase in leisure or in unpaid employment, the change must be advantageous or the persons involved would not voluntarily have done it. The logical corrective for this problem would be to impute value to leisure in the same way that value is now imputed to an owner-occupied house and to food produced and consumed on farms. An owner-occupied house is credited with the rent it would command in the rental market; food produced and consumed on farms is credited with the sale value it would have to the farmer. Similarly, leisure and unpaid employment of persons (and other resources) could be credited with the wages or other income they could earn if they entered paid employment.

Corresponding entries should be made in the product accounts. Leisure enjoyed for its own sake, and those forms of unpaid employment that yield products or services of direct utility, should be counted in consumer goods and services at the valuations just indicated. The income sacrificed by the student in school, and his direct school expenses, are primarily investment in future earning power, however; they should accordingly be counted in addition to wealth. The using up of existing human resources with the passage of time should be counted as depreciation, as a partial offset.

As all the suggested imputations could be made with an accuracy comparable to those now being made, by using prevailing wages for the services of the persons whose leisure is to be valued, it is surprising that little has been done about them. One possible reason is the difficulty in handling those year-to-year changes in "leisure" that are not comparable to the ones being discussed here, e.g., unemployment. If a worker is dismissed or laid off from his job in a recession, both the value to him of the spare time this gives him and the wage he could expect to earn if he persisted in seeking employment will be much less than otherwise. Similar problems exist in valuing the time of workers on strike. Equally difficult problems are in fact disposed of in one way or another in the current national income estimates, however, and presumably these could be also.

8 SOME COMPLEX PROBLEMS OF IMPUTATION

The problems of imputation that have been discussed so far have the comparatively simple solution of pricing a nonmarket good or service with an identical market one. Several other problems of imputation are less easily solved, usually because a direct market comparison is hard to find. The solution in principle to these problems is to make indirect or residual comparisons of the values of other goods in association with the things to be valued, or in some cases to estimate what the relevant market comparison would be if it existed. Examples of these problems are discussed in the next six subsections.

INSTRUMENTAL GOODS AND SERVICES MISLABELED AS CONSUMER GOODS AND SERVICES

Many goods and services counted as consumption in the national product estimates are instrumental goods and services yielding no utility. For example, time spent commuting to and from work is not the same thing as leisure time spent at home or spent on a Sunday drive, and the cash expenses of commuting contribute little to the consumer's welfare. Usually a person would accept a lower-paying job if it involved less commuting time and expense, other things equal. Direct evidence of this is the lower level of rents and residential land values in suburbs than close in to cities; the person closer in must sacrifice income, in effect, by paying a higher rent or a higher price for a house.

The difference in rents between the suburbs and the city will reflect not only differences in commuting costs but other factors as well. These other factors represent a second example of the distinction between instrumental goods and consumer goods, which arises because some goods can be bought only in bundles, not separately. Living in the city permits closer access to some goods than in the suburbs and the country but also requires paying higher transportation and distribution costs on goods produced outside the city. Thus some prices will be higher, and some lower, in the city than in the country. (Also, the environment in the city is intrinsically more pleasant than that in the country to some people, and just the reverse to others. See below.) Generally speaking, a peach or a tomato cannot be bought in the city without including some transportation and distribution that they do not possess on the farms where they are produced; but to see a Broadway show the country-dweller must pay the cost of transporting himself in.

These differences in cost do not produce differences in satisfaction from a given amount of the good consumed; they are simply part of the cost of living and working in one place rather than in the other. When a person moves from the country to the city, he generally earns a higher income; but this is in part offset by the higher cost, on balance, of a representative bundle of identical consumer goods in the city than in the country. This difference in cost ought properly to be reflected in estimated real income, at least for rural-urban comparisons.

CONSUMER GOODS IN CONDITIONS OF EMPLOYMENT

Just as some things labeled as consumer goods are instrumental goods without intrinsic utility, so also some instrumental goods yield direct utility. This is true whenever a job has incidental benefits for which the employed person would be willing to pay if he had to. The classic example of this is that of the Kaiser's lieutenant. It is said that when the Emperor of Austria went to the opera, he was accompanied by one or the other of two aides. One of them enjoyed opera very much; the other detested it. The first would gladly have paid for the occasions he was asked to accompany the Emperor to the opera; the second would have paid to avoid them.

Similarly, many jobs have particularly pleasant or unpleasant characteristics. A moderate amount of job-connected travel to worthwhile places would be considered by most people to be an advantage; continuous travel would not. Some jobs involve unusual danger or other unpleasantness, for which extra compensation must be paid to get people to do the job. Some jobs include very obvious elements of income in kind, such as restaurant meals and entertainment on an expense account.

INVESTMENT GOODS IN CONDITIONS OF EMPLOYMENT

Besides the possibility that a job offers pleasant amenities, it can include an investment in the person holding it. This will be true, for example, if the job he holds has excellent chances of promotion, or otherwise prepares him for an increase in income, and where he therefore accepts a lower current income than he could otherwise obtain. This circumstance is essentially the same as that of the addition to wealth involved in education and should be handled in the same way.

ENVIRONMENT AS A GOOD

Many aspects of the environment will make one place more attractive in which to live and work than another. A well-known example is difference in climate: in a mild climate it takes less fuel to heat homes and factories than in a cold climate, and people are more comfortable. Another example, mentioned earlier, is the relative attractiveness of living in the country or the city.

A tendency for people and for enterprises to crowd into the more attractive areas drives up site rents, which enter national income, as do higher rents in urban centers. To the extent that workers accept lower wages to work in the more attractive areas, this also will be reflected in higher site rents or "profits," as will differences in fuel costs. Comparisons of real incomes in different places can include corrections for these differences.

CAPITAL GAINS AND SPECULATION

Generally speaking, it is desirable to exclude from income any purely nominal changes in wealth due to changes in the price level. Capital gains from this source are not income arising from claims to current production. However, some capital gains *do* arise from productive activity, e.g., from speculation that transfers goods from consumption at a time when they are plentiful and cheap to consumption at a time when they are scarce and expensive.

The appendix to this chapter presents an example of successful speculation and relates it to the problem of measuring wealth and income. It shows that capital gains arising from changes in the general price level and the interest rate are properly left out of current income, but that there is a good case for including in income those capital gains that result from changes in relative prices. The present method of calculating inventory valuation adjustment, to exclude from income capital gains on business inventories, requires extensive manipulation of many price indexes. Our analysis suggests that instead the adjustment should use a single price index for the general price level, so as to leave all other capital gains on inventories in income. It also suggests adding to income the capital gains accrued on other real assets, net of gains due to a rise in general price level.

CONVENTIONAL GOODS, DIFFERENCES IN TASTES, AND INTERPERSONAL SUBJECTIVE EFFECTS OF CONSUMPTION

It may be said in anticipation of the next section that most problems of valuation and imputation are solved by taking values at the margin, given the quantities available. These values at the margin apply uniformly to all persons and enterprises engaging in transactions in the goods involved. Values attached to "intramarginal" or "extramarginal" units are not considered.

A possible exception to this rule concerns goods consumed by conventional necessity, where the consumer himself in some cases gets no satisfaction from them. A man may not particularly enjoy being clean-shaven, for example, but feels he has to be. In a society that was wholly indifferent about this, some men would take the trouble to remain clean-shaven and some would not; for the latter, the time and out-of-pocket costs absorbed by shaving are instrumental goods to other people's consumption rather than consumer goods, and should ideally be deducted from their estimated net incomes.

One might here argue the contrary view that the prevailing convention should rule as to whether a good is intrinsically desirable or not. If most people in the community feel definitely better off when nearly all the men are clean-shaven than when they are not, then it adds to consumer utility for a man to shave whether he himself likes it or not. Insofar as being clean-shaven is required for this job, it would be double counting to treat his shaving as a consumer good, just as it is double counting to count as consumption the cost of commuting to work. The handling of this case has been outlined at the beginning of this section.

Economically, there is little difference between cases where one person's consumption pattern attracts other people's approval or disapproval for the subjective reasons of custom and tastes, on the one hand, or for more objective and universally agreed reasons, on the other. For example, little or no economic basis can be found for distinguishing between most people's unfavorable reaction to the nuisance caused by jet-engine noise around an airport and some people's disapproval of jet air travel because they think it wicked and unnatural to travel so fast. Again, the ill feeling some people get in a crowded elevator if several men therein are smoking cigars is not economically distinct from the irritation some people feel when they see a woman smoking a cigarette while walking down the street.

In many cases, external economies and diseconomies of production and consumption are automatically reflected in the national income and product estimates. Jet noise around an airport or the smoke emitted from a factory tends to depress surrounding property values and rents; an attractive public park will tend to raise surrounding property values and rents. Here the changes in rents translate into measured income the external economies and diseconomies involved.

External economies and diseconomies of consumption connected with differences in tastes, social custom, and the like are not translated into measured income in many cases, however. The costs to an individual of grudging conformity, and the costs to others and himself when he does not conform, are generally not reflected in income because the community and its markets do not offer alternative places to live and work in sufficient variety for everyone to escape the costs or to translate them into higher and lower rents.

If some external economies and diseconomies are automatically translated into differences in income, a case can be made for imputing values to all of them and adjusting income accordingly. This is not a proposition based on ethics but one that follows from the desirability of consistency in the treatment of essentially similar things. But of course this process has a practical limit.

SUMMARY, FURTHER REMARKS, AND CONCLUSIONS ON IMPUTATIONS

A great many things, both tangible and intangible, have the characteristic that in their presence people either sacrifice income or they require additional income. In general, this provides a basis for placing a value on these things for measurement of true income from the point of view of economic welfare. If two jobs are similar in every relevant respect except the one aspect whose value is to be estimated (such as commuting time and cost), the difference in wages for the two jobs provides us with an estimate of the value of this aspect as an advantage or disadvantage of the job which has it. This is a residual method of estimation.

Direct estimation is possible only where the thing or aspect to be valued is sometimes bought and sold in its own right, as for example is the case with the rental value of owner-occupied homes and food produced and consumed on farms. (An arbitrary valuation that seems reasonable, but has no market basis, may also be made, as is the case with the imputation for financial intermediaries.) Residual estimation makes possible a whole range of imputations that could not otherwise be carried out, because the things to be valued are in the nature of the case tied as complements to other goods and services.

Direct estimation is possible for the valuation of transportation and distribution and some other cases of instrumental goods now counted in consumption, some cases of consumer goods that are part of the conditions of employment, and true economic depreciation. Residual imputation is required for most instrumental goods now counted in consumption and for most consumer and investment goods that are part of the conditions of employment.

More complex imputation procedures are required for the income element of capital gains. The steps in estimating the income element of capital gains, after adequate adjustments have been made for true economic depreciation would be (1) to deflate the proportionate change in the market value of previously existing wealth by the proportionate change in an appropriate index of the prices of consumer goods, and (2) to deduct from the remainder the total change in capital values that is the result of a change in the level of interest rates. The balance remaining after these adjustments is the true income and addition to wealth element in capital gains.

All the imputations mentioned up to this point in this section have the element in common that existing market prices are to be used as the basis for imputation. This is the rule generally followed in the national income and product accounts, and in other cases where the total of a product or class of products is to be valued. That is, every loaf of a given kind of bread sold under given conditions is valued at the same price (the price at which it is sold), even though, for example, if less bread were sold that smaller amount would command a higher price. In doing it this way, we ignore consumers' surplus and producers' surplus and value everything at the margin.

There is no pretense that this procedure measures the contribution to income and product of each good and service on an all-or-nothing basis; that is, the procedure followed tells us nothing about how much better off we are to have a given good or service than we would be if we did not have any of it at all. Indeed, trying to measure this latter all-or-nothing value would be pointless. Although we would be willing to allocate more of our incomes to any one product than we now do, if necessary, in order to avoid going without it altogether, we could not possibly simultaneously allocate a larger share of income to *everything* (including additions to wealth) *at once*. As income and product must add up to the same total, the only problem is how to allocate it among its component parts. The marginal rule, that is, valuation at market price, is far and away the simplest one to follow and is the only one worth considering in most cases.

A possible class of exceptions consists of those cases where an all-or-nothing situation does exist, that is, where the market does not afford everyone the opportunity to buy as much or as little of a good or service as he likes. In such a case, valuation at the price he pays is actually in conflict with the marginal rule, since the price he would be willing to pay for a little more (or would accept for giving up a little) of the good or service is significantly different from the average price paid for the amount bought. Here the argument in favor of the marginal rule is an argument against the use of market price; and consistency in the overall methodology calls for an adjustment for the discrepancy.

The most important example of this kind of thing arises in connection with external economies and diseconomies of consumption and with the unmeasured consumption element in different environments. These are identical problems from an economic point of view. We wish to place a value on a difference in climate, where the community and its markets do not afford the opportunity to make unlimited choice among the alternatives considered. It offers only a relatively small range of all-or-nothing bargains. Hypothetical controlled experimentation, which in practice means an arbitrary "reasonable" valuation, or possibly extrapolation of value differences from actually available alternatives, offers the only solution.

If all the imputations suggested here were made, national income and product would be reported as a larger figure than is now the case, primarily because of the imputed value of leisure. A way of keeping this within bounds, without significantly affecting the meaning of the results, would be to make the allowance for leisure by adjusting actual employment to a standard workweek, such as forty hours. For all persons with less than forty hours paid employment per week, such as most students and housewives, an imputation would be made for what they would have earned if they had been paid for forty hours work per week. For all persons working more than this, a deduction from income would be made for the imputed value of the leisure lost.

The overall result would be a national income and product total only moderately larger than the one calculated by present methods, say about 40 to 50 percent larger. This would have no very great significance by itself. It would merely make explicit the mental adjustments and qualifications we now make on ordinary income figures. It is the changes in income over time, especially the decade-to-decade changes, and the international and interregional comparisons that would be significantly affected. Comparisons of economic welfare of several different kinds would become more accurate and meaningful.

9 INCOME AND UNCERTAINTY

The problem of uncertainty is illustrated by the Biblical story about the seven good years and the seven bad years. A community with leaders gifted with foresight stored up grain during seven years of unusually good harvests and was thereby enabled to live reasonably well during seven subsequent years of crop failure. Current income and production were unusually high in the first seven years, unusually low in the second seven. Because of their foresight, however, the community's leaders were under no illusions about the level of living they could afford to enjoy while the harvests were good.

During the years when they were storing up grain, their tangible wealth was increasing; but their true wealth position was not improving because the coming crop failures were getting ever nearer as the supplies increased. From a long-run point of view, therefore, their production potential and the amount they could prudently consume were no higher during the seven good years, nor any worse during the seven bad years, than at other more normal times. It can be said that their true income and production potential, known with certainty, were constant over the whole period. It can also be said that their true wealth was constant.

Measuring true income is generally not so easy as in the example of the seven good years and seven bad years. Our foresight is not as good as was that of the community leaders in that ancient example; a considerable range of uncertainty surrounds our estimates, as individuals and as a community, of how much we can expect to earn and produce in the long run. To the extent that we base our consumption on our long-run prospects rather than on our current income, however, we are obliged to make the best estimates that we can. It appears from actual experience that people make these estimates and determine their consumption accordingly. If they do, it helps to explain actual consumption behavior if we can successfully estimate what they estimate their true incomes to be.

True income in this sense is the maximum rate of consumption that could be maintained permanently; and if one does not choose to consume at this maximum rate, choosing to add to wealth instead, this increases the true income of future periods.

Besides such deliberate, intentional changes in income, new and unexpected experience leads to revisions in long-run expectations. For example, a farmer will generally have a fairly accurate idea of the crop yields he can expect to get from his land on the average. He is able to recognize an unusually good or bad year for what it is and will in general let such a year be reflected much more in his additions to tangible wealth than in his consumption. A series of very good or very bad years, compared with his previous expectation, will probably result in a revision in his expectation, however. He is unlikely to be so sure that the climate never changes, and that his understanding of the climate is so perfect, that his expectation is completely unaffected by experience. Similar remarks apply to other people's estimates of their true incomes.

10 TRUE INCOME AS A PRACTICAL WORKING CONCEPT

The measurement of current income, discussed in previous sections, primarily presents problems of statistical method and imputation; the measurement of true income, however, primarily presents problems of inference. Although in principle we might imagine a direct measurement technique for true income, such as experimenting to find the incomes people would accept under long-term contract in exchange for their existing prospects, in practice it must be inferred from objective information about past and present values of current income and about consumption behavior. The past behavior of income, including the typical patterns it follows over a person's lifetime, is the best information a person himself generally has about his long-term prospects; it is also the best information the outside observer generally has. Since different people will conclude different things from the same information, their consumption behavior also provides evidence on what they consider their long-term income prospects to be.

Proceeding in this indirect way necessarily requires making arbitrary assumptions. In particular, some assumptions must be made about how to interpret observed variations in consumption. For example, one may choose to assume that all variations in consumption either are the result of variations in true income or are random. The arbitrariness of this procedure, and the uncertainty it implies concerning the evaluation of true income, can be narrowed down by studying a wide range of different evidence on income and consumption; but it cannot be eliminated entirely.

This discussion implies, among other things, that current income as ordinarily defined is an essential part of economic analysis, even where true income is the relevant variable. Accurate and conceptually sound measurement of current income and of its components is a prerequisite to even approximately accurate measurement of true income. True income is interesting not because it simplifies measurement, but because it aids the interpretation of economic behavior.

11 CONCLUDING NOTE: MONEY INCOME AND REAL INCOME

The preceding discussion has considered how to define and measure income so as to make differences in income correspond to real differences in economic welfare.

For completeness, this discussion must include some further mention of changes in the general price level over time. Even if the problems for depreciation accounting created by changes in the price level are appropriately disposed of, changes in income over time will in general represent the combined effects of changes in real economic welfare and nominal changes due to changes in the price level. For many purposes, it is useful and desirable to separate the two kinds of changes.

Accordingly, it is necessary to devise a measure of movements in the general price level, or to devise a direct measure of how income would change if the general price level did not change. Either of these procedures implies a decomposition of changes in income into the two component parts, the real changes and the nominal changes. A direct measure of one of the components implies the other as a residual, when the total change in current money income is known.

The procedure usually followed in this connection is to divide measured income by an index of the general price level. In the case of Real Gross National Product of the United States, this operation is performed separately on consumption, investment, and so on, and the resulting estimates are added to give the total. This is an intermediate procedure between the two just mentioned.

It should be borne in mind that for the most part when we talk about changes in income we mean changes in real economic welfare, not nominal changes resulting from changes in the price level. At times, however, the contrary is true, and it is important to specify what we mean. Usually the words "production" and "output" are taken for granted as referring to real magnitudes, but "income" can be taken in either sense. For clarity, one can refer consistently to real income, where that is what is meant, or assume at the start of discussion that the general price level remains constant, so that changes in money income are real changes.

BIBLIOGRAPHY

Ackley, Gardner: *Macroeconomic Theory* (New York, The Macmillan Company, 1962).

Bible, Genesis, chapter 41.

Kuznets, Simon: "Long Term Changes in the National Income of the U.S.A. since 1870," International Association for Research in Income and Wealth, *Income and Wealth*, series II.

Shoup, Carl S.: *Principles of National Income Analysis* (Boston, Mass., Houghton Mifflin Company, 1947).

U.S. Department of Commerce: *National Income,* 1954 edition (supplement to *Survey of Current Business*), part II.

U.S. Department of Commerce: *The National Income and Product Accounts of the United States, 1929–1965* (Wash., D.C., U.S. Government Printing Office, 1966).

A APPENDIX

APPENDIX TO CHAPTER 12

The point about capital gains in section 8 may be illustrated with an example using two commodities A and B. Suppose that the producers of these commodities own fixed inventories totaling 1,000 units of each commodity, regardless of prices and the volume of sales. When there are price fluctuations, the exclusion of capital gains implies that no entries will be left in the income account that arise from capital gains and losses on the inventories. Over a series of periods, it would not matter if they were, as long as inventories are held constant, and prices ultimately return to their original values. In this case, the total capital gain over the series of periods would be zero, so that the only effect it would have on income if capital gains were counted as net income would be that income would be redistributed among periods. Total wealth would be correctly stated as unchanged for the series of periods as a whole, in either case.

However, suppose that a successful speculator, Mr. J., forecasts the price changes of commodities A and B. In period 1, suppose that each commodity's price is 100, but Mr. J. foresees that in period 2 commodity A will sell at 133 and commodity B at 67. He therefore bids up slightly the price of A, reducing its consumption and obtaining some new inventories (additional to those owned by producers of A); and he arranges with producers of B to lease from them some of their owned inventories, at a fee compensating them for doing without their physical presence from period 1 to period 2, which he then sells at a slightly reduced price, inducing their consumption. If he does these things for 10 units of each commodity, total inventories are unchanged, but now are made up of 990 units of B and 1,010 units of A, both valued at (about) 100 per unit.

In period 2, Mr. J.'s price expectations are borne out. He then sells off his 10 units of A, slightly reducing the tightness of its supply and increasing its otherwise constricted consumption, at a profit (capital gain). Since the price of A is about double that of B, he can apply the total proceeds of sale to buying 20 units of B, curtailing its otherwise increased consumption; 10 units of these he uses to return to producers as per his "lease" and the other 10 are approximately his profit in this period. As he expects prices to return to their original levels in the third period, he now leases and sells 10 units of A, as he had done with B before, and he purchases 20 additional units of B, both changes producing changes of the same size in consumption. None of these actions in period 2 alters the total of inventories, *as valued in prices of period* 2; his total sales for consumption of 20 units of A are just equal in value to his purchases and addition to inventory of 40 units of B. As a result of his actions, 990 units of A and 1,030 units of B are carried as inventories into period 3, when prices return to 100 for both commodities.

At equal prices for A and B, Mr. J. can sell $20B$ to obtain $20A$ (altering total consumption by these amounts). After returning the 10 units of A that were "leased" to him by its producers, he owns 10 units of each commodity, which are his gross profit. Total wealth has been increased to 1,010 units of each commodity, and prices are the same as they were in period 1. However, when capital gains are excluded from income, each of his operations is deemed to have maintained wealth constant. The wealth of each period was held constant at the prices of that period; Mr. J.'s creation of new wealth occurred only by virtue of his having transferred some consumption of each commodity from a period in which it was relatively plentiful and cheap to a period in which it was relatively scarce and expensive. Such transfers result in capital gains.

Similarly, Mr. J. would have incurred capital losses had he bought dear and sold cheap; and there would be a corresponding destruction of wealth not recorded in the income (and product) accounts. The paradox would then occur that wealth was reckoned to have remained constant, in the calculation of net income, yet wealth would be less in the third period than in the first, valued in the common prices of the two periods.

To the extent that wealth is created or destroyed by the transfer of consumption from one period to the next (that is, by changes in inventories carried over) this is on a par with any other creation or destruction of wealth, and ignoring it ought not to be considered consistent with the maintenance-of-wealth criterion for defining income. However, apparent changes in wealth arising from price changes affecting *given* (fixed) inventories are not changes in wealth at a single set of prices, such as current prices. It has been shown, however, that these two statements are contradictory.

The problem posed by capital gains would seem to be the more complicated because in practice there is no way to distinguish between speculation and the holding of stocks to facilitate current production. Producing enterprises do in fact vary the quantities of stocks held, thinking of it not as speculation but as prudent management. In general, if their foresight is comparable to Mr. J.'s, they will vary stocks, and cause consumption to vary, in substantially the same way he does. Consequently capital gains from successful speculation will be associated with purely nominal capital gains and will be indistinguishable from them in any specific instance.

Finding a solution to this problem requires some reflection on the measurement of changes in wealth. Apart from a physical addition to wealth, a change in the total market value of existing wealth may occur (1) because of a change in the general price level of consumer goods, (2) because of a change in the rate of interest and in the marginal productivity of capital, (3) because of a change in the relative prices of consumer goods. A change in the market value of wealth due to a change in the general price level should be excluded from income and from addition to wealth in current prices. It is also clear that a change in the market value of wealth due to a change in the rate of interest, another form of price change, should be excluded from income. All that remains to be considered, therefore, is a change resulting from a change in the relative prices of consumer goods. Such a change is what was involved in the cases of commodities *A* and *B*, in which Mr. J. speculated. He had altered the composition of inventories toward a relative increase in the amount of that commodity whose relative price was about to rise, and a reduction in the amount of the one whose price was about to fall. The subsequent change in *relative* prices, operating on this change in inventories, increased the total market value of wealth.

In any such case, it is entirely reasonable to call the change in wealth genuine. If the community is fortunate enough to have relatively much capital tied up in the production of a commodity that has become more scarce and valuable, and relatively little tied up in the production of a commodity that has become more plentiful and cheap, then its total capital will in fact generate more income than before. There is no paradox in letting this change in wealth be counted in income and addition to wealth.

INDEX